We Humans

Our initial 100 days during the COVID-19 pandemic

BILL K KOUL

ISBN: 978-1-922409-50-8
Published by Vivid Publishing
A division of Fontaine Publishing Group
P.O. Box 948, Fremantle
Western Australia 6959
www.vividpublishing.com.au

A catalogue record for this
book is available from the
National Library of Australia

To preserve and uphold humanity, and in service to the human race, this book is dedicated to life and living

Contents

REALISATION

When I was about to merge, I became aware. When I became aware, I woke up. When I was about to realise, I fell asleep. When I slept, I dreamt. The illusion and reality had become like day and night, both in thought. The world was nothing more than a thought. Nothing was beyond thought. Thoughts were like bubbles, and so was I.

I wish that, at the end of the day, I close my eyes without guilt that I did not try enough and do my best. Nonetheless, due to my insignificance in the Higher Design, I am neither ashamed of anything I have done nor fearful of anything known or unknown.

Humans will not change much, as our numbers will keep increasing and, as such, our challenges too will keep increasing as they are much of our own making. In every age, however, the intrinsic goodness in humans will prevail over their dark side and the human race will keep surviving.

Life will go on …

MOTHER NATURE

Mother Nature can be both benevolent and cruel. While it nourishes and nurtures life, it can also be extremely destructive.

Humans too come in several shades of good, bad and ugly; some act as angels and some as demons. As such, there are no angels and demons in a form separate from humans. Some humans sacrifice themselves, altruistically, for the good of others while some humans sacrifice others, selfishly, for their personal benefit. Some humans take it upon themselves to unconditionally act as God's servants and serve others selflessly; and some humans empower themselves as God's chosen authority and enslave others. Surprisingly, there are many humans who keep shuffling between various shades of the good, the bad and the ugly.

All great and noble people of the past and the present are humans. All oppressors and tyrants of the past and the present too are humans. All those who work for life — to save human lives and make them comfortable — have been humans. Equally, all those who endeavour to destroy other lives and make other human lives miserable are also humans.

There is a great need to stitch this world back together, little by little, by carefully disseminating the information being fed to us on a daily basis from all directions, otherwise propaganda — — undertaken by powerful individuals with extreme thoughts who misuse and abuse social media and mass media — will rip this world apart and send us packing back several decades or even centuries.

Be careful in drawing conclusions and passing judgement on people, situations and incidents. Assess carefully the veracity of every bit of information received by you and the credibility of the source or the person who passes that information to you. Judiciously discard the information if the person is dodgy or untrustworthy. Accept the information only if you can trust the person with your life or the life of your children, and also if the person does not have any personal axe to grind.

ABOUT THE AUTHOR

Bill K. Koul is an engineering consultant by profession but a philosopher and writer by passion. He blogs on his website (https://billkkoul. com) on varied topics, such as education, politics, philosophy of life, gender inequality, and life and liveability. In addition, he writes for various Indian newspapers and magazines. Based in Perth, Western Australia, he also lectures on the history and issues of Kashmir.

Bill was born in the early sixties in Srinagar, Kashmir. In late December 1989, he bid farewell to Kashmir and lived as a refugee in India till the end of 1994. In early 1995, he moved to Malaysia and worked there as a consulting engineer for a few years. Finally, he migrated to Australia in 1997 after passing Engineers Australia's Test by Examination in late 1996.

Since 2016, when not working, Bill has spent his time travelling around the globe or writing. In addition to this book, he has authored the seven other nonfiction books: *22 Years — A Kashmir Story* (2017); *My Life Does Not Have to Be Unhappy* (2017); *Issues White-anting India* (2017); *Does India Need a Dictator — to Rescue a Sinking Nation?* (2018); *A Bouquet of Random Thoughts — Conversations with Myself* (2019); *The Exiled Pandits of Kashmir — Will They Ever Return Home?* (2020); and *The Charmed Triangle — Religion, Science & Spirituality – breaking out of belief* (2020).

In these books authored over a short time, the topics written about are varied — social engineering, politics, mental health and Kashmir — though all deal with humans. In all his books, Bill has used a philosophical approach to understand the issues and propose solutions.

Kashmir, to a lesser or greater extent, has featured in all his works, and does in this book too.

In addition to his full-time engineering work, Bill is working on a number of other book projects, including a book on 'the art of engineering', which attempts to portray his learning from the philosophies of both engineering and human life in general and how they follow similar natural laws, and a novel.

ACKNOWLEDGEMENTS

My thoughts emanate like bubbles from my mind. I try to capture them before they disappear and share them around. Their source may be the Central Station, invisible but all pervading. I have nothing that belongs to me, my body or my thoughts. My physical existence is due to my parents and Mother Earth. My spirit belongs to the Central Station.

On the basis of numerous lessons — some sweet but mostly bitter — learnt by me in this polarised world of ours, my general message to the readers is:

I acknowledge life for all its teachings. I acknowledge my mother, Rani (Mrs Jai Kishori Koul), for giving birth to my body and intellect; and my teacher, Bhaisahib (Mr Bansi Lal Hakhu), for nourishing my soul and expanding my intellect. I acknowledge my father, Mr Jawahar Lal Koul, for exposing me to many aspects of life, as an engineer, a citizen and a son.

I must acknowledge Rekha, the love of my life and the mother of our two beautiful children, for her support through my life and, especially, the current pandemic days. My family has helped me to learn, grow and expand. Therefore, I acknowledge my wife, Dr Rekha Bhan Koul, our son, Dr Kongposh Koul, and daughter, Deeksha Ladakhi Koul, for exposing me to the coalface of life as a married man and a father, without which life would never have been complete or completely understood. Also, I sincerely thank Shadi Shahgaldi for drawing a thoughtful illustration for the cover of this book and also the cover of my previous book, *The Charmed Triangle*.

Last, but not least, I acknowledge my publisher, Vivid Publishing, an imprint of Fontaine Press, and in doing so, I acknowledge Jason

Swiney, Publishing Director of Fontaine Publishing Group, for bringing this timely book to the world and my editor, Kelly Somers, for her excellent piece of editing work with this book within a relatively short period of time.

Bill K. Koul, Perth, 1 September 2020

INTRODUCTION

This book, *We Humans*, is for those humans who are not born yet. They must know how we humans acted and behaved even during the COVID-19 pandemic days. This book provides a report card for the human race during the pandemic.

This book neither calls for perfect or ideal humans nor for perfect or ideal societies. It calls for acceptance of humans and societies as they are and, thus, for acceptance of all shades of the good, the bad and the ugly in humans and societies as they naturally exist.

This book has nine chapters, each concluded with a poem. Aside from the first and last chapters, they cover the period between November 2019 and July 2020:

- Chapter 1 provides a general commentary about life on Earth and human evolution, and a philosophical comment about human nature generally and how humans have not changed much through their evolution.
- Chapter 2 discusses various shades of human nature, taking as its starting point the shocking death of George Floyd in the USA and how that country and the rest of the world reacted to it, including the cries of Australian Indigenous people and the Dalits of India.
- Chapter 3 tries to decipher mysterious human behaviour on both individual and collective levels – as common people and politicians – with several real-life vignettes and anecdotes. It also provides a commentary on gender inequality and a discussion on missing females.
- Chapter 4 discusses life in Kashmir during the COVID-19

pandemic lockdown and two painful case histories that illustrate the value of a human life in Kashmir.

- Chapter 5 discusses geopolitics during the COVID-19 pandemic and how the world is currently positioned precariously, all due to the ego and personal political ambitions of some powerful leaders.
- Chapter 6 gives a detailed account of the ongoing India–China conflict and its history. It emphasises why a military conflict between the world's two most populated countries, which contain about 36 percent of the total world population and have among the world's most powerful defence forces and economies, can be disastrous for the entire region and the rest of the world.
- Chapter 7 provides a philosophical commentary on the challenges the world faces at the moment.
- Chapter 8 provides a philosophical commentary on the timely opportunities provided to humankind by the COVID-19 pandemic.
- Chapter 9 features the author's reflections on life in short paragraphs.

Many shades of imperfection exist in each one of us, which we try to manage through our education and training. As such, none of us is absolutely 'good' or absolutely 'bad' or 'ugly'; each one of us is born with varying degrees of each of these characteristics. To expect perfect and ideal humans and, therefore, perfect and ideal societies is a recipe for frustration, unhappiness and discord. To demand perfection in other humans, without being perfect ourselves, or understanding the absolute meaning of 'perfection', is not only unwise, it is a sheer waste of time and resources. It is more prudent to accept humans with all their imperfections and then learn, — by education, — how to manage those imperfections — in oneself and others — for a more peaceful and meaningful coexistence on the planet.

Given that the terms 'perfection' and 'imperfection' are highly sub-jective, — both individually and collectively, — as are the terms 'good', 'bad' and 'ugly', no humans or societies can ever be universally or abso-lutely deemed perfect or ideal. The definition of what is perfect or ideal can be interpreted differently in different places and times, whether in capitalist economies or not, as well as be influenced by religious beliefs, ethnic cultures and traditions.

We learn to appear sophisticated but our sophistication gets invari-ably tested, from time to time, when we are confronted by people or situations, especially when our lives or material interests are compro-mised or at stake. We react in a manner not much different to that of our distant, hunter and gatherer ancestors. Our ways may have changed with time and become more complicated but, underneath, we haven't changed much.

Human behaviour cannot be divided strictly into the aforemen-tioned three parts of the human character. Most humans exhibit varying shades of all three primary behaviours — sometimes good, sometimes bad and sometimes ugly — which can change over the course of an hour, a day, a week, a month or a year. The same person can exhibit different responses to the same or a similar incident if the boundary conditions vary, such as the person's health, mood, circumstances and situation. As such, a person may act or appear to be an 'angel' at some point of time to some people and a 'demon' to others.

This book compels the reader to face themselves and accept their multifarious character, to feel humbled with humility and to develop respect for other humans, whose fallibility we generally hold in contempt, and who we scorn for not meeting our myopic expectations of idealistic behaviours. The book challenges readers to accept the 'good', the 'bad' and the 'ugly' in everyone and, in doing so, to be less judgemental and scornful of fellow humans.

Many aspects of life and living have no right or wrong answers. In most situations of everyday life, most humans, knowingly or unknowingly, judge others and cast aspersions on them, without realising that they themselves exhibit the same or similar behaviours. While the book describes various mysterious shades of human character in life, it also illustrates our general feelings, especially our fear, of death.

This book was conceived during the COVID-19 pandemic and, therefore, it provides a philosophical commentary on the opportunities available to humans by the pandemic and a glimpse of what life may look like after the pandemic. It captures the enigmatic side of humans through a compilation of some important world events that occurred during the pandemic, alongside interesting real-life vignettes and anecdotes that illustrate the multifarious human being.

The pandemic has clearly exposed humans. The world has seen the angels who are fighting round the clock to save human lives and, equally, the many powerful individuals who have tried to exploit the opportunities provided by the pandemic for their own political advantage. But, in all this, most humans have shown their vulnerability to disease, exploitation and helplessness due to their poverty. I suggest that these socio-economically and politically disadvantaged humans have only two options about God: (1) to entirely lose their faith in God; or (2) to put all their faith in God and none in humans.

It seems there is not ONE God; there can't be. Either there is no God or there are several Gods. The real question is: 'Which God should poor people, who make up the majority of humankind, turn to?'

How this book was conceived

'Where is your dog today?' shouted a regular morning walker from across the road, as we passed each other on The Esplanade, along Canning River in the Perth suburb of Mount Pleasant, around 6am on the morning of 13 April 2020, which was Easter Sunday, during the COVID-19 lockdown. It was still a little dark at that time of the morning. Overhead, the sky was cloudy, threatening to pour. I stopped and turned my head to see who it was. Initially, I could not see his face well. In the past, apart from waving to each other and exchanging customary morning-greeting smiles, we had never spoken to each other. I stopped and shouted back, 'He is home. This one is for us; we'll reach home and then take him out for his walk.' He smiled and waved back. I waved back and continued jogging double-paced with my wife, Rekha, who walked briskly by my side.

In all these past years, morning walkers have become accustomed to seeing us with Sakha, our nine-year-old Siberian husky, walking right between the two of us, with his characteristic bushy tail raised. And many of them enquire about him when he is not with us for any reason, for example, when rain is imminent. In our suburb, we are called 'the couple with the husky'. Sakha attracts the attention of most morning walkers who go past us. They can't hide their smiles. Sometimes, dog lovers stop and ask if they can pat him. And we oblige. Sakha too complies; he enjoys the attention. Before COVID-19, I would run alone a few times a week after completing our usual four-kilometre walk with Sakha. A week ago, however, we decided to make some adjustments to our respective routines in order to maximise the benefits of our morning exercise.

Sakha's addiction to social media, interestingly, necessitated this change. He tries to stop and sniff every lamppost and every low bush he walks past, which I liken to reading messages on social media. At some locations, he also leaves his mark, which is not much different to posting on social media. In his younger days, he was much more obedient and would not visit every post and bush as he does now. To be fair to him and ourselves too, and after duly considering his relative seniority, we had to give in and let him have his own time to do his things his own way but, of course, without compromising on our morning exercise, which is so essential for our health during these days of lockdown, especially after starting to work from home about three weeks ago. In a nutshell, our exercise time has now doubled, thanks to Sakha and COVID-19. Regular physical exercise, apart from numerous other health benefits, is understood to keep the body's immunity levels high, which is paramount for fighting COVID-19.

Rekha and I voluntarily decided to work from home the week following the Australian government's first social-distancing announcement, precisely from Tuesday, 19 March 2020. I recall how guilty I had felt a day earlier at my workplace despite no such decision — to work from home — being taken by the office management. I decided to lead by example. On that day in the office, I felt as if I was letting down our global medical fraternity who had started exhorting people to 'stay home' and 'maintain social distancing' so as to check the spread of the deadly virus. When I decided to work from home, Rekha joined me, as it did not make any sense that one of us went out and got infected. Being an academic, she could do so, although within the next few weeks her university and most other universities in Australia started working online.

During the last three weeks, I have found myself working longer hours, albeit without experiencing any travel frustration or much work fatigue. I find much more time to do things than I would find before. My productivity as an engineering consultant, which is my day job, has increased considerably. My writing productivity, as a passionate writer, has also increased. I am gradually getting over the television and social media, which leaves me fresher to attend to the more important chores of life. My exercise time too has increased considerably. Rekha's experience is similar.

COVID-19 has not affected our characteristically simple lifestyle much except for (1) putting a stop to our Friday night movies at the cinema, which I really loved; and (2) clipping our wings. A weekly two-hour movie would bring much needed respite for me and was worth every cent we paid for it. It comprised a big chunk of my weekly entertainment. As for our travel, for a number of years we have frequently travelled both domestically within Australia and internationally, with work or otherwise, every two to three months.

During the last three weeks, our social life — in person — has taken a nosedive. But that has not made much of a difference to our lifestyles as, during the past few years, our work had kept us too busy to socialise except where absolutely necessary. On the whole, we find the 'new normal' has brought a number of positives for us and perhaps for many people around the globe who share our experiences and thoughts.

On Easter Sunday, a client called in relation to construction works being undertaken on a mining site. Construction works don't stop on weekends or holidays. Suddenly, towards the end of our technical discussion, he asked, 'Bill, what did you do this morning?' possibly referring to the traditional Easter services held in churches on this day. I replied gently, 'I did nothing, how about you?' With a tone of sadness, he replied, 'I attended the online service. We have never done anything like that in the past. How strange is the current time!' I concluded, 'We'll never forget Easter 2020 for the rest of our lives' and he sighed in the affirmative. Undoubtedly, life will never be the same after this.

The question is not 'when will this lockdown be lifted?' so that we can move around freely as we did before; the question that we all must ask ourselves and answer sincerely is 'what kind of life and living should we be going back to after the lockdown?' The new normal must be better than the old normal. That old normal has brought us to this stage. Our new normal must be more environmentally responsible, moral and conscientious, simpler and austere. This is the time to sit, reflect and develop good habits to help ourselves and our environment after this virus passes on. The lockdown provides us with the opportunity to make the necessary changes to our lifestyle and thinking so that our children can live in a better world.

About a month before the lockdown, while driving to work on a busy Monday morning, I recall saying to Rekha, with a mix of sadness, hopelessness and frustration:

'Look at this traffic. How much time do we all waste in these traffic jams? How much emissions do we produce that pollute our air and the environment? Look at the faces of these other drivers around you. Does anyone look happy? Some are clipping and painting their fingernails, some are busy with their mobile phones, some are putting make-up on their faces, some are having coffee or breakfast and some are even reading a book.

'When they reach the office, they will be quite tired — mentally and physically — and possibly frustrated. Before starting work, they will first rush to the kitchen and prepare a cup of tea or coffee for themselves. So much time is lost!

'The same thing happens in the evening on their return from work. Our peak hour has almost tripled during these past two decades. All this leads to an unrecoverable loss of productivity — due to the time wasted on the road while driving and then recovering at the workplace.

'Our country loses, our environment loses, we lose and our health loses. This lifestyle does not help anyone. But no one seems to be thinking. We need to push a reset button to slow down our lives. As one human race, globally, where are we all racing to? Most of us just exist. How many of us really know what it is like to live deliberately? Even at work, people cover their ears with headphones, disconnected from others. At their homes too their excessive use of social media and addiction to television disconnects most family members from one another.

'Nature must be watching us. Something will happen; something must happen to change how we live and perceive life.'

My, those words proved prophetic, sadly in retrospect, considering all those precious lives being lost in the process, even as we speak. It seems I may have been waiting for something to happen that would teach us all a lesson and bring us to our senses.

Certainly, we can't be myopic at this stage and mindlessly rush back to resuming what and how we were doing things before COVID-19. Because if we do, it will be our children and their generations who will pay for our wilful negligence, carelessness and irresponsibility. Nature will repeat itself, history will repeat itself. Our future generations will never forgive us. After all, we adults are only temporary custodians of the Mother Earth.

COVID-19 has taught us many lessons that should stand us in good stead but that much needed learning will happen only if we are wise. We have realised the adverse effects of a growing human footprint on our environment as well as a dire need to exercise global population control. At a national level, we have learnt the benefits of self-reliance, and on an individual level, a timely reminder to lead a more austere and simpler lifestyle. After COVID-19, it will look insane if nations keep on spending zillions of dollars on weapons and war. Instead, one would wish that nations come together earnestly — in peace, harmony and sincerity — and invest in human health, education and fighting poverty and hunger.

Are we wise? Have we woken up? If not now, then when? What more must happen before we change for the better? Nature will keep beating us until we don't improve.

I hope the lockdown and the human loss of lives around the world remind us humans about the pain and suffering that other species — animals and plants – suffer due to our sadistic, mindless and irresponsible actions. Is the pain and suffering of other animals and birds any less than human pain and suffering? After this virus passes on, shall we continue to cage them — for fun or consumption — under one pretext or another? We humans are known to be very clever and conniving in justifying our actions, howsoever immoral, unethical, barbaric and illegal those actions may be.

Next time we see a caged chicken or a sheep by the roadside, or a cooked piece of meat on our plate, let us first pause and think for a while before eating it. The same is the case with pigs and bovine animals that we consume without any hesitation or moral scruples, possibly because that is how we have grown up and been conditioned. These poor animals possibly suffer the same way as we are in this lockdown before they are slaughtered mercilessly so that we can eat a piece of them. Is the caging and killing of defenceless animals for human consumption morally and ethically justified if the world has an abundance of food from a variety of vegetarian sources?

The current pandemic and several past pandemics are known to have been caused by the transmission of viruses from animals to humans. Are these animals trying to warn us time and again? Hopefully, we will reflect deeply, realise our blunders and fallacies, repent sincerely, learn to empathise with animals and discover a more humane element in ourselves. This is my hope.

Chapter 1

MYSTERIOUS HUMANS

This chapter provides a general commentary about life on Earth and the human evolution; a philosophical commentary about general human nature and our fallibility, and how we humans have not changed much through our evolution; the human camouflage; importance of living selflessly; the big illusion; and a chat about Supreme Mind versus Human Mind. This chapter ends with a poem, *You Make Feel Delusional, O Life!*

Life on Earth

Earth was born around 4.5 billion years ago. Since then, it has been characterised by constant change. From the beginning, heat and gravity shaped its evolution. Plate tectonics shifted its continents, raised mountains and moved the ocean floor. Over time, its atmosphere also changed and processes not yet fully understood altered the climate on Earth. All those forces creating change somehow also led to the emergence of life on Earth. The Earth's atmosphere today bears little resemblance to the atmosphere of the early Earth, in which life developed.

Life on Earth is believed to have begun in the ocean, as far back as 3.5 billion years ago. The first organisms, single-celled microbes, represented life for about 2.3 billion years. Subsequently, about 1.2 billion years ago, more complex, multi-celled organisms evolved.

The microscopic organisms dating back 3.5 billion years were preserved in stromatolites (hard structures). Stromatolites, created as sticky mats of trapped microbes, bind sediments into layers, inside which minerals precipitate and create durable structures even as microbes die. Microbial life, being extremely resilient, could survive and thrive in extremely hostile conditions of acidity, alkalinity and salinity and concentrations of heavy metals, and at extremes of high and low temperature and pressure, as evidenced by life existing near the seafloor where, in the absence of sunlight, some organisms survive on chemical energy.

The Great Oxidation Event, which caused photosynthesis, took place about a billion years later. Thereafter, it still took hundreds of millions of years to build up the Earth's atmosphere and the ocean, which created enough oxygen on the planet to support evolving and complex life in the ocean.

Human Evolution

Modern humans evolved from primates, in particular from the genus *Homo* within the hominid family (the great apes), which led to the emergence of a distinct species of *Homo sapiens*. Genetic studies indicate that primates diverged from other mammals about 85 million years ago, in the Late Cretaceous period. The earliest fossils of first true primate-like mammals (proto-primates) to have been found are from the early Paleocene Epoch, around 55 to 66 million years ago, at the beginning of Cenozoic Era.

Anatomically, after separating from their last common ancestor with chimpanzees, the evolution of humans was characterised by a number of morphological, developmental, physiological and behavioural changes. A number of their distinct traits gradually developed, such as bipedalism (walking upright), increased brain size, language, lengthened ontogeny (gestation and infancy) and fewer pronounced differences between sexes of the same species, during which time various hominin species interbred with each other. Early humans also developed a powerful precision grip, which first occurred in *Homo erectus*.

Several hominins used fire and occupied much of Eurasia. Their lineage gave rise to *Homo sapiens* in Africa around 500,000 years ago, with the earliest fossil evidence placing *Homo sapiens* in Africa around 300,000 years ago. The earliest *Homo sapiens* fossils date back to about 315,000 years ago, and they were found in Jebel Irhoud, Morocco. The oldest known skeleton of an anatomically modern *Homo sapiens* (Omo Kibish I), dated to about 196,000 years ago, was discovered in southern Ethiopia.

Studies indicate that humans began exhibiting behavioural modernity about 100,000 to 70,000 years ago. More recent studies push that date to as far back as around 300,000 years ago, in the Middle Stone Age, a period of African prehistory. Some researchers associate the beginning of the Middle Stone Age with the discovery of stone tools that date as far back as 550,000 to 500,000 years ago.

The Early Stone Age spans from around 3 million years ago, as evidenced by the earliest stone tools and their use by hominins, to around 300,000 years ago. The Later Stone Age is believed to be associated with the advent of modern human behaviour in Africa. The transition from the Middle Stone Age to the Later Stone Age is thought to have begun between 50,000 and 39,000 years ago, when *Homo sapiens* and their technologies spread out from eastern Africa over several thousand years in several waves of migration, populating most of the world.

Through their evolutionary history, most of human existence was sustained by hunting and gathering in band societies. However, about 10,000 years ago, many human societies transitioned to sedentary agriculture, domesticating plants and animals, which led to human civilisation as we know it today. These human societies subsequently formed states and empires, and established various forms of governance, religion and culture around the world.

Hunting and gathering was humankind's first and most successful adaptation, spanning at least 90 percent of human history. A hunter-gatherer lived in a society which gained sustenance by foraging, collecting plants and pursuing animals.

Rapid advancement in the scientific and medical fields in the nineteenth and twentieth centuries considerably increased human lifespans, causing the human population to rise exponentially. In 2020, the global human population was estimated to be near 8 billion. In the last one hundred years, our number has quadrupled.

Humans Have Not Changed Over Time

Life has never been easy. Survival for humans has always been our greatest challenge. Since the cave-dwelling days of hunters and gatherers, humans have had to face and overcome numerous daily threats, not only from predatory animals who cohabit the planet, but also from their own kind. In addition, they have had to face and learn to accept and manage challenges from Nature, such as droughts, floods, wildfires, volcanoes, earthquakes and disease.

As humans learnt and improved their survival skills against other animals and natural calamities, challenges from their own kind became more frequent, especially in less hostile environments where they thrived and prospered, and their numbers began to increase. They started facing more hostile competition and threat from one another, in particular when natural resources could not keep up with their increasing consumption.

After the dawn of the Industrial Age — around 1760, characterised by the replacement of hand tools with power-driven machines, such as the power loom and the steam engine, — humans acquired numerous layers of sophistication and started portraying themselves as 'civilised'. Beginning in Great Britain and, later, some parts of Europe, the Industrial Revolution extended quickly to their colonies in the Americas and Australasia, and on to some parts of Asia and Africa, where mainly the occupying city-dwellers had access to the benefits of these historic developments. Many occupied populations would not have benefited at all, only the colonisers in these places would have. Notably, industrialisation furthered colonialism itself. So, it is very difficult to view occupation positively from the perspective of the people whose countries were invaded. Thereafter, a couple of centuries later, the arrival of the Information Age — also known as the Computer Age, Digital Age or New Media Age — in the late twentieth century characterised a rapid shift in the economy from industrialisation to computerisation. As a consequence of these developments, the average human life suddenly became much easier, in particular for the relatively privileged class.

Globally, the unprivileged and underprivileged have continued to slog physically for survival. Notably, in Kolkata, rather than rickshaws being pulled by mules, donkeys and buffaloes, as they are elsewhere in India, you will see humans pedalling cycle rickshaws for livelihood, even in 2020.

The Digital Age has greatly changed the lifestyle of the average city-dweller all over the world, especially those from the educated and relatively privileged class, by bringing in portable (laptop) computers, followed quickly by smart (mobile) phones, first into their homes and then into their personal lives. Since then, things have not been the same. *An idle mind is the devil's workshop*, as is generally believed. Social media has taken over as the prime source of entertainment and social interaction. As the relatively privileged class has found more time on its hands, family life has changed completely, as individual family members choose to live mostly with their mobile phones. Social media has made the differentiation of fact from fiction extremely difficult. Mental illness has increased as bullying, — or 'trolling', — has become rife on social media. Most political campaigning and socio-religious polarisation in humans takes place via mobile phones and social media.

Influenced by capitalism and materialism, the privileged class has found novel ways to retain its privilege, only possible if 'the others' —

the underprivileged and the unprivileged — remain at the bottom of the socioeconomic hierarchy. They create and actively nurture a class system — of *us and them*.

The fact is that humans have never ceased to be hunters and gatherers, only that their ways of taking advantage of others have changed and become much more sophisticated. Appearances are highly deceptive, as many a wolf prowls and hunts in sheep's clothing.

Intoxicated by materialism, selfishness and greed, — fuelled mainly by severe competition due to growing numbers, and driven and exacerbated by commercialism, many humans have stopped listening to their conscience and, in turn, their consciences have become silent.

The Human Camouflage

Humans, — like many other animals, — use many tactics to achieve their intended target or accomplish a mission — overtly or covertly — in both aggressive and defensive modes. One of their tested and proven tactics is their ability to camouflage. Unlike their counterparts in the animal kingdom, humans have become adept in both modes of camouflage: in — their appearance and in social behaviour.

Professional actors are paid to act, to appear and speak in a certain manner befitting the character they play, as dictated by the script and instructed by a director. Yet, in general, every human is a naturally good actor. Their behaviour, tone and body language change from one situation to another, from dealing with a person to dealing with another person. When they see themselves standing on a relatively weaker ground, their behaviour contrastingly mellows down, facial expressions reflect gentleness and innocence and tone becomes conciliatory and acquires softness. As soon as they become aware of being on stronger ground, everything changes suddenly. Their tone, facial expression, body language and words change.

Their physical camouflage goes in tandem with their behavioural camouflage. Given their conscious efforts to look younger and prettier than they actually are, it is not commonly easy to see their real and natural face. As part of the normal ageing process, invariably after they turn forty, most humans tend to lose hair from their head, and hair also starts turning grey. Facial hair — — also starts turning grey around this age. As if that was not alarming enough, they also start observing the growth of new hair in places such as nostrils, ears and eyebrows — that greatly challenges their intrinsic tendency to camouflage and keep up their fake — younger, attractive, prettier and stronger — appearance.

That is where grooming and make-up tools and cosmetics come to the rescue. Most people, — both men and women, — dye their hair in various shades of black and brown. Some men shave off their moustache, which they had nurtured (in many cases, as a sign of manliness) since their late teens. Many men completely shave their head when it starts balding and greying. There are also men who grow a moustache or beard and dye it black or brown to look younger. After all, it is all about looks, no matter how you do it, as long as it makes you look younger, attractive and stronger.

It is true that humans are adept at attracting and exploiting the weaknesses of other humans, — using a proven range of cosmetic and behavioural camouflage, — to achieve their objectives. It will not be surprising to find that not many people, especially above fifty, know or remember their true appearance or character. Many such people feel irritated, perhaps threatened too, to see other people, especially those younger than them, who wear their natural appearance, without any make-up or hair dye or any other kind of physical camouflage. Perhaps, the natural look of others makes them conscious of their own age and hidden appearance. A gentleman in his mid-to-late seventies recently said to me, 'I want to look young. It gives me confidence to think and act young.' And I whispered, 'And, perhaps, a little less mature too.'

In the last hundred years, during which time the global human population has quadrupled, the corrosive effects of capitalism and materialism have gradually eroded humans' empathetic and caring side. They have become more selfish and generally, as a default, look at one another as material commodities and the means to achieve their materialistic objectives. The world is polarised between the privileged and *the others*. Others, which comprise more than 80 percent of the population, work for the privileged. Among the others too, the bottom half is seen in terms of numbers. Their gods have forsaken them, perhaps for good. They have become tools and plants and brooms for the rest, godless and hopeless. The world has changed, it has perhaps returned to what humans would have been like thousands of years ago, as hunters and gatherers, always under threat from beasts in the guise of their own kind.

Even as the entire human race is currently reeling from a direct threat from an invisible bug, some of us don't hesitate in further polarising the human world — along lines of colour, power, wealth, ethnicity and religion — which is not only an extremely alarming realisation but also very sad and frustratingly disappointing in so far as overall human progress is concerned. Why do many of us choose to be stuck in our ignorant, distant past despite enjoying immense material benefit from an 'apparent' globalisation? This may be an absurd question, as that is how we have always been: the good, the bad and the ugly. We are both progressive and regressive.

It is baffling to see some individuals who don't shirk in exhibiting their disposition for religion and faith in God doing the most irreligious, inhuman acts, mostly out of their deep insecurity and fear. Humans who dwell in fear and suffer insecurity can be considered to be those who have actually no or little faith in God, because faith dispels fear, just as a match dispels darkness in a room when lit. Even a little faith in God should have been enough to assure one about God's protection. Can it be said, therefore, atheists and agnostics, especially those who may not feel as unsafe or insecure, have more faith in the Higher Being, albeit not on the conscious level, than the believers who feel perpetually insecure and unprotected and, therefore, keep praying to God, seemingly in vain?

Living selflessly

We humans are a mix of varying shades of the good, the bad and the ugly, complete with all three essential *gunas* — the *satva*, the *rajas* and the *tamas*. Unknowingly, over the course of a day, we tend to exhibit varying shades of all these three characteristics. Most of the time, we remain in control of ourselves and exhibit pragmatism and prudence in our thoughts and actions. However, when our moral and ethical guards are let down momentarily, due to the *tamas* ingrained in our very nature, we lose control over ourselves and are consumed by fear, anger and ego, which manifest in our greed, selfishness and arrogance, all of which trick us into doing unethical and selfish things, and sometimes immoral and illegal activities too.

As a direct consequence of these momentary lapses, we suffer one way or another. Invariably, our suffering becomes compounded by the price we pay for our actions. That is where the Four Noble Truths and the Eightfold Path of Buddhism offer to come to our rescue. The Four Noble Truths are: (i) the truth of suffering, (ii) the truth of the cause of suffering, (iii) the truth of the end of suffering, and (iv) the truth of the path that leads to the end of suffering. The Eightfold Path comprises: (i) right view, (ii) right resolve, (iii) right speech, (iv) right conduct, (v) right livelihood, (vi) right effort, (vii) right mindfulness and (viii) right Samadhi (i.e. *meditative absorption or spiritual union*).

At times, when logic fails to explain unimaginable, cruel and unjust situations or occurrences, natural or human-made, and with no timely justice in sight, nihilism may help one reconcile with what is happening, and some people may also use the traditional Indian concepts of destiny and karma to explain the cause of their miseries.

Where selfless actions, self-sacrifice, gender equity and caste equality are the need of the hour, Sikhism provides the necessary guide and inspiration. The life of Jesus Christ inspires one in negotiating difficult circumstances, especially when one suffers as a result of their own benevolent intentions and actions.

The life of Rama inspires every common person to be selfless and an ideal child and a caring sibling. Krishna's wisdom inspires one to act selflessly, live without expectations and never be a blind spectator to unethical and immoral actions done by others. Islamic teachings provide inspiration for doing charitable community work and observing austerity through fasting. Jainism inspires one against indulgence in cruelty and killing or consumption of animals, which is so important for the very survival and sustainability of the human race on the Earth. The Earth belongs to birds and other animals too as much as it belongs to humans. Let all other life forms now live and thrive, without fear and encroachment from humans, and as free as humans have been for the last couple of hundred thousand years.

We humans are very fortunate to be living in such a beautiful garden of varied flowers which give us all that we need to live a good, moral, meaningful and purposeful life. It is important all these flowers are given their own space to blossom and thrive, without encroachment or trespass from one another.

COVID-19 has provided us with a timely reminder about the importance of social distancing, as have many wise philosophers. Lest we forget! We may be in pain now but our gains will come later. The pain in our current fight against the bug will undoubtedly benefit our future generations but only if we learn from the present time. The bug may have woken us up just in time or else we could have possibly collapsed suddenly down the path of the 'old normal'. Paradoxically, the bug may look deadly at the moment but may have saved the entire human race if one looks at the bigger picture. The months of April to June 2020, during which we humans have retracted and confined ourselves to our homes, have proved beyond doubt the adverse effect of the human footprint on our environment. We have rediscovered a blue sky and cleaner water bodies. Birds and animals too have started breathing freely.

Our survival is dependent on a healthy environment for which we must control our number, our greed and our mindless consumption of natural resources. It will be an unpardonable blunder of gigantic proportions if we try to resume the 'old normal' once the lockdown is lifted. The second wave of the outbreak in the Australian state of Victoria, which triggered in early June 2020 and peaked in early August 2020, is a strong reminder against complacency. As of 27 August 2020, of the total 25,505 cases of infection, Victoria had recorded 18,608 cases (i.e. about 74%) and, of the total 549 deaths in Australia, Victoria had recorded 462 deaths (i.e. 84%), most of them occurring in the second Victorian wave. As a consequence of the deadly outbreak in Victoria, the state borders within Australia remained closed, people's movements hampered and businesses severely impacted, in particular, in Victoria.

The Big Illusion

What is the difference between reality and illusion if the former is ever changing in the same manner as the latter? If yesterday can't be retrieved and relived, was it real? What is real?

We all live in a Big Illusion, in a somewhat delusional state, believing it is all real. We consider the multidimensional layers of numerous illusions within the Big Illusion as subjective and relative realities. Some of those whom we call 'delusional' may perhaps be the only ones who are close to the Big Reality; some of those whom we call 'mad' may perhaps be the only ones who have the sanity to realise the Big Reality.

The Big Illusion transforms every moment. Every present moment elusively fades into the past in a jiffy, as if it never existed except in our memory. Our body dies every moment, little by little, and so does our environment. Our whimsical mind keeps flickering. Our weather and seasons keep changing as Earth keeps moving and the sun keeps burning to its death. One day, it will all merge back with the nothingness from which it all started. Given that sun has been burning for about four and a half billion years and its future life expectancy is predicted to be about five billion years more, we are halfway through the illusionary journey. One day, closer to its death, the sun will expand and gobble up everything that we see now and finally die into a small white dwarf.

The Supreme Mind versus the Human Mind

How much control do humans have over their lives? Does everything happen as per the will of God (referred to as the Supreme Mind or the Universal Intelligence)? Do humans actually create their own destiny or are they merely subservient to the will of God? Does Mother Nature act through humans, who we believe to be its best creation, though every day there is evidence to dispute this belief? At best, loose attempts to answer these questions, considering the absence of indisputable evidence, are generally made via religious belief systems. The perceptible world of Mother Nature can also be used to come to some realisation.

The following conversation, which took place in early June 2020, between the author and his esteemed friend, Vijay Narain Shanker, a veteran writer, philosopher and poet, provides some useful insight into this extremely abstract topic. This conversation is deemed important in the context of this book, in so far as the importance of human endeavour is concerned and how much control we really have on our lives. The author sincerely apologises to those readers who may find parts of this conversation a little blasphemous.

Vijay

A thought for you to mull over … Please respond with your ideas when you have time.

The Supreme Mind or the Intelligence of the Universe, what I see as the only God principle of Nature and Creation, is only to be known by us in brief moments of epiphany or fuller awareness. We have made all the forms, of course, to visualise better what is physically non-existent. It is only the Intelligence that came into self-existence that is everywhere.

The Hindu Vedanta believed in the Conscious Universe thousands of years ago. So too did the Indigenous peoples of many cultures. They created and worshipped forms but they always spoke of the Spirit, the Intelligence. And all that is conscious is part of that all-pervading Intelligence. And this is where we part company with theology and benign gods and benign Nature.

That Supreme Intelligence, almost like cells and other organisms, splits into billions of individual minds that then become independent and self-sufficient. The individual mind is contained by consciousness of the body and the ego. Both are absolutely necessary to the life of the individual. The cell, the Intelligence, has thus separated from the *central* source. Indeed, there is no central mother lode, for it is scattered and exists in all Nature and organic life.

If we see this thus far, then the Supreme Intelligence has no one home or an altar or a form; it is existent in dust and grass and tree and river and mountain and animal and man. And each form with its piece of Intelligence is free by itself and on its own. Each individual is driven by his piece of Intelligence or mind.

We come to the corollary then that the Supreme Intelligence has a 'connection of Being' with the individual but has no control or driving force on the individual mind. The mind that we have controls us and drives us.

The mind is everything, said the Buddha. It is the Energy of Creation.

The above thought developed today in response to a passage (*shloka*) from the Bhagwat Gita, where Lord Krishna says of the Evil and the Good: 'I am in all. I am in the Evil, but they are not in Me. So too I am in the Good and they are in Me. Behold my mystery.'

Bill

This thought is aligned with the thoughts of the famous Scottish philosopher, David Hume, from the Age of Enlightenment (eighteenth century). Hume greatly inspired many philosophers, including Einstein and Immanuel Kant, as understood from their own admissions.

It is indeed the human mind. I have always maintained that each one of us is a complete universe in ourselves — our mind contains everything and creates a reality for us, which is unique to us.

Buddha was correct.

Vijay

Thank you, I shall save both of our statements.

The moment we say the Supreme Mind or the Intelligence of the Universe is another entity after our mind has separated from it, we are also saying that the idea of a benign god is nothing. God or Nature is not always benign. It creates and also destroys. As we believe of Lord Shiva.

For the individual units of existence — I, you, the greatest sage, the innocent child, the loving mother — it does not matter; what matters are the rules and laws that came out of the necessity to sustain life.

Bill

These are genuine questions for a seeker.

I do agree with Lord Krishna to a good extent but I am not feeling comfortable with his assertion: 'He is in everyone and everything, but only good is in Him, and not bad.'

These assertions make Lord Krishna a 'good' God, which I (or perhaps both of us) do not fully accept without being able to realise the Absolute Truth in the bigger picture, unless we were to delve back into the controversial theories of karma and destiny, which are essentially based on the belief of reincarnation, and absolve God of everything bad that happens to us in this lifetime, for no obvious fault of our own, but instead puts blame on our (hypothetical) actions, mostly from our past lives. The hypothesis of karma etc. is a big hindrance in establishing accountability of people who must otherwise take full responsibility for the miseries that their actions and, equally, their inactions cause.

Irresponsible people tend to push things under the carpet and escape unpunished under the cover of karma and destiny.

Mother Nature — if perceived as the obvious reflection of God — as such is not always very kind. If we accept Mother Nature as a stark reflection of the Divinity — God (e.g. Shiva), then we must accept the destructive and angry side of God too, with a total disregard to our supposed 'karma' from our past lives.

I agree with your initial thoughts that Intelligence in everything; however, everything then acts independent of the Supreme Intelligence. The will, therefore, remains with humans — individually and collectively, both.

Vijay

Lord Krishna's *shloka*, 'I am in them but they are not in Me', matters … It is one of the *shlokas* worth pondering … Obviously, it is a philosophical theory put in the mouth of Sri Krishna by the author of the Bhagwat Gita. This expresses a continuation of Vedanta ideas of:

1. Energy or life force being immanent in different and in all forms: the *Nirakaar* (formless, invisible) *Brahma* is only that Intelligence and Life Energy.

2. Good and Evil are *one and the same energy* (the most important idea of Vedanta).

In fact, in other *shlokas* in the Bhagwat Gita, Lord Krishna says He is 'the Supreme and the Highest in the Good as well as the Bad'. I can paraphrase it roughly: he says he is the *Takshak Nag* among snakes, the worst of gamblers and criminals and so on. He is also the Best and the Top of good things.

What we have here is the seminal idea that the Life Energy is one, but it is given direction to good (humanity, love, kindness, compassion and so on) by the mind of the individual. The same is true of evil.

Men and gods and Nature and all beings prefer and want the good because it creates, gives joy and bliss and peace. There is no creation without joy and peace. No growth. Our word for the *Niraakar* is *Brahman*, from the root word *Brh* (meaning 'to grow').

So you see evil is not a moral category but a form of destruction. Growth is good as it creates.

Now Krishna, as an avatar, is a form of goodness because men want and worship goodness. He is seen as the embodiment of good. And the good in the world of humans is created by the mind. So when He says, 'The evil is in Me', it is simply that His Life Energy is in evil men too. When He says, 'I am not in them', I think He is saying that they (evil humans) have grown out of the goodness by the actions of their minds.

There is another thing: the destruction in Nature. It kills the innocent and the good but Nature's destruction is by its own natural laws, and not by the evil or hate in mind. All animals that kill do so without hate, or any mentally produced evil, but by natural processes.

It is we who have created only a good god. It is a human concept. Neither God nor Nature is always good to man because I see them entirely as Intelligence and Energies that are neither good nor bad.

Bill

I agree with you. I would like use the analogy of a professor of nuclear physics and his two bright students. Both students are brilliant, capable, intellectually gifted and keen to learn from their teacher. They learn same things from their teacher during the same period of time but, as per their individual natures, they use their intelligence and the knowledge they have acquired or discovered in two entirely different ways, both of which require intelligence. One student uses it for *constructive* purposes — to support life and ease human lives — in the fields of medicine and power generation. The other student uses it for *destructive* purposes — to destroy life — in the field of weapons generation and to cause as much destruction as possible of the human race. So the same knowledge is used by two students with intelligence, albeit with opposing intentions. This knowledge and intelligence are neutral on their own and have no such attributes as good or evil. We humans choose their use in accordance with our individual nature.

The current (global) moment for humans in the world is the net result (the sum total) of all creative (benign, positive) and destructive (malign, negative) acts of humans through their history since their inception — in all their cumulative shades of the good, the bad and the ugly.

Each human is a vector (as defined in physics) and, like vectors, humans have (1) *force* (positive and negative) and (2) *direction* (constructive or destructive), both of which define the state of our world — individually and collectively, locally and globally. Obviously, as the world still exists in this moment, as we perceive and understand it now, and may look to be relatively stable, albeit precariously due to humans' continual acts to undermine it — the positive (creative) side of humans has obviously prevailed, at least till now. But as soon as the scales tilt the other way, our human race may not take much time to disappear, or at least return to where we were a few thousand years ago.

It may be true that Lord Krishna lives in both our attributes — good and evil, as commonly defined — but how does it help us? If He is fighting on both sides, can we do anything about it? If He is fighting only on the side of the good, then who is fighting against Him? Is He fighting Himself, in a leaser form, where His victory is always certain?

The world is ridden with human issues, some existential. What is God doing about them? Did He help the Japanese when two nuclear bombs were dropped over them, consciously and knowing the apocalyptic consequences of their explosion? Is He helping the world community when it is fighting to survive against COVID-19 and we are fighting one another on racial grounds, such as in America?

I agree He exists in everything and everyone, just as water does, but how does His being or not being matter to us in our daily lives? We humans shall continue to act independently and make or break ourselves.

In the Mahabharata, He did not use any weapon but instigated Arjuna against his family. He did not even stop Yudhishtara from gambling away everything to Daryodhana. If Arjuna had not listened to Him in the Mahabharata, imagine how it would have all ended? History is written by the victors. Imagine how He would have been described now: perhaps, as an instigator, deceptive (*mayavi*) trickster or a coward (*ranchhod*).

Vijay

Very nice thoughts, thought provoking. My brief response:

God exists or not? Is God good or not? It makes NO difference to our lives and what happens to us.

It is or may be just Intelligence, not a human kind of intelligence though. There can be and are other kinds other natures and dimensions of intelligence. A tree, a snake, a tiger, a dog have different dimensions of thought and intelligence. It is man's age-old blunder that he sees himself as the centre of the universe and made his god in his own image.

The power the life force could be anything; perhaps a kind of nothing. An Energy that is Nothingness, as Hindus and Nagarjuna of the Buddhists believed. So the idea that there is a good god is only a human idea. The history of man's sufferings proves otherwise.

We know in science too now that matter is energy. Energy transforms to matter and back. Good and bad, suffering and happiness are human categories. Because we are physical beings, we like and enjoy pleasure and joy. But if we were pure energy or pure spirit, then the physical pleasure of foods or desires would not matter.

The individual mind is tied to the body and so we pick out the good and pleasurable. Body and mind work together all the time; they are extensions of each other. We have made our gods on the same model.

So it is always the individual with his mind who is creating his reality: good, bad, painful or blissful. And his mind always reacts/

responds to people, events, the environment and so on. Also, your genes, and the energy you are shaping and releasing around you, are the determining factors.

The greatest mistake that man has made historically is that, in a complex state of laziness of his mind and the fear of Nature, mainly due to his own weakness, he made his gods all powerful and omnipotent. For that, he has suffered through history, mainly because he has accepted suffering as an act of God. If man accepts pain and joy as realities of life, he will be better off and learn to deal with them. I suffer more, firstly, because I say it is God who makes me suffer due to my sins and, secondly, because I think it is my duty to accept suffering to please my God.

We must have gods and yet we must know we made them only as Ideals.

Bill

It all starts with the human mind and ends with the human mind. Nature has provided all what human mind needs but Nature does not think and decide for us, we humans do. Also, it is difficult to believe that it all happens by the will of God (Nature).

Nature did not give humans the wings to fly. Humans tried everything that they could to fly. Finally, due to our ever-inquisitive mind and endless endeavours, we humans did manage to learn how to fly, albeit at the cost of numerous human lives. The cumulative acquired knowledge, and our keen observations of Mother Nature, helped us to build machines that could fly like birds.

Similarly, numerous diseases that would kill hundreds of thousands of humans a hundred years ago — and were ignorantly considered by some a part of our karma or destiny, or the wrath of God on us — are now cured by simple medication, all due to human endeavour.

All knowledge is within us. We discover it within ourselves through contemplation and observations of Mother Nature and the universe around us. Through our contemplation, experience, observation and experimentation, we gradually uncover the layers of knowledge and discover what is already there in our cosmic existence.

We humans create our own destiny. Of course, there are laws of Nature. Where we act against Nature, we pay the price. So understanding and respecting Nature and keep making our best endeavours is what is required.

The ball may be in our court but the buck does not stop with us.

Human Fallibility

How often do we use a rational mind to deal with or judge a person or an act or a situation? Our personal bias and prejudices generally cloud our judgement, which makes us think and act irrationally. We discriminate between people for reasons of our bias and prejudices. Our ego and fear of potential loss of face make us myopically stick to our beliefs, and generally pay a heavy price for it, no matter how irrational and challengeable our beliefs may be. If we like someone or something, we find reasons to support our feelings. It is a similar case with our dislikes. In many, or rather most, matters of life, our personal likes and dislikes and prejudices — about a person or an action or a matter — become erratically subjective.

The Oxford dictionary defines the terms 'bias', 'prejudice' and 'discrimination' as:

- Bias: The action of supporting or opposing a particular person or thing in an unfair way, because of allowing personal opinions to influence your judgment.
- Prejudice: An unfair and unreasonable opinion or feeling, especially when formed without enough thought or knowledge.
- Discrimination: Treating a person or particular group of people differently, especially in a worse way from the way in which you treat other people, because of their skin colour, sex, sexuality, etc.

We love to believe even the ugliest lies if they fit into our beliefs. We hear what we want to hear, whether it comes from inside our head or from any other source, howsoever unreliable those sources may be. As a consequence, the many accused among us suffer for absolutely no fault, while the world watches silently and enjoys sadistically.

We humans are fallible. We choose to see what we want to see and ignore everything else that makes us uncomfortable and look small. We hear what we want to hear to give credibility and life to pre-existing seeds of bias, hate and prejudice within us against other people, situations and important matters of life. As they say, *Show me the face and I'll show you the rules.* We are capable of transforming white lies into Divine Truth and demonising angels if that satisfies our ego or intentions.

We humans are known for our strange behaviours. Varying degrees of jealousy and sadism are an intrinsic part of our character. Unbelievably, sometimes, our angels turn into our demons and also our foes magically turn into our best friends when it matters the most. As goes a Chinese proverb, *Our own teeth sometimes bite our tongue* — most pain comes to us from those who are closest to us and at such times when we need or expect it the least.

A dear colleague, Dr Farzad Habibbeygi, aptly puts it as follows: 'I can only say "humans" are the most complex creatures in the world. Our reactions are always affected by many factors. To name a few, as you truly mentioned: bias, prejudice, likes, hatred, benefit, fame, power, morals. They are like vectors in our life and their results make our decisions and judgement. Those factors that are more predominant than others dictate the course. How we "react" to a same "action" in the future will never be the same as we react now. The vectors keep changing with time and how we feel at that moment. Our age and circumstances and how life bends us has a marked effect on our judgement and behaviour.'

The following vignette illustrates varying elements of intrinsic human imperfections: irrationality and fallibility.

He looked after his pet just as he looked after his own child, with love, care and commitment. The pet was a cute husky, who was fed with the best and freshest pet food and taken out for a five-kilometre walk every morning along a scenic riverside pedestrian path. During the course of the day, whenever he found time, he would pat his pet with lots of love and affection, and offer him tasty snacks, including 'suitable' food from his own dinner plate before starting to eat. The pet was washed and groomed professionally at least once a month. With time, the pet grew older, and so did he. In a few years, however, his pet aged more than him (in biological terms) and became more stubborn, moody, demanding and increasingly defiant in following normal commands. He also started showing impatience and signs of laziness, asking for more food and attention. One day, when the pet became too difficult and defiant, he shouted at him angrily in protest, 'You son of a man, stop it!'

You Make Feel Delusional, O Life!

This poem illustrates some extreme shades of life, with its intrinsic multifarious and mysterious characteristics, that can easily confuse a human into believing and disbelieving things, which can potentially make them feel delusional. It also illustrates a complex and rather testing relationship between God and humankind, while highlighting the latter's general frustration at the perceived inability and helplessness of God in lessening numerous existential and mundane human sufferings, especially of the weak, downtrodden and the unprivileged. The human not only challenges God's role and intentions behind Creation but also appeals for His help to at least restore the dignity of the poor by making the wealthy more empathetic and caring towards them, thereby acknowledging and conceding that it is the wealthy and the powerful, and not God directly, who practically shape, make and break the lives of the poor.

*****

The illusion of life invariably made me delusional and I strayed; at times, I felt cold in the hot sun and, at times, I was scorched even by the moonlight. At times, my victory concealed my defeat and, at times, my defeat was hidden within my victory.

Sometimes, Life turns a gentle into a brute and a barbarian into a decent individual; sometimes, a giant is dwarfed and a dwarf becomes a giant. Life tricks us when we are wild and also when we are serene; sometimes consciously and sometimes unconsciously.

Life was passed mostly in exile, away from home, at times in prosperity and at times in poverty. Life tricks us, sometimes in togetherness (with our beloved) and sometimes in our separation; sometimes we have (lawful) authority and, sometimes, we are completely disenfranchised.

Life just passed by, in your longing and in your waiting, sometimes (blasphemously) ungratefully and sometimes in prostration. It is not that you don't exist but your silence makes me feel delusional and I stray, sometimes when I am in the sky and sometimes on the ground, sometimes at my home and sometimes at a place of worship.

Having witnessed thy mysterious nature, sometimes in the wilderness and sometimes in a garden, sometimes at the zenith and sometimes at the nadir; O Nature, I stray, sometimes in my dream state and sometimes in my waking state, sometimes in the din that surrounds me and sometimes in my solitude.

It is not that Life is not a garden of flowers, which contains flowers of varied types as well as some thorns; O Nature, thy mysterious images and reflections confuse me and make me feel speechless, both explicitly and implicitly, sometimes during a pitch dark night and sometimes at a glorious daybreak.

I kept straying, sometimes in my (unwise) thanklessness and sometimes in my gratitude and thankfulness, sometimes in a cultured way and sometimes in an uncultured way. O Life, I stray when you make me feel delusional, sometimes in my humiliation (by the world) and sometimes by my fame, both in my defeat as well as my victory.

With your benevolence and blessings, I received honour, wisdom and knowledge in abundance. I also sat in high council and addressed distinguished gatherings. As per your will and instructions, I befriended many a people, faithfully, while carrying out my allocated duties.

Your love not only protected me, I thrived and prospered too. Although I remained arrested (in your love), I remained (absolutely) free. In my yearning for you, at times, I lost my words and, at times, my thoughts.

Sometimes, your (divine) presence not only made me ecstatic but also intoxicated me like a drunken rogue.

O Lord, be kind and benevolent, charm me with your bright smile and drown me in your fragrant, effulgent divine form. Due to your silence, sometimes I have been lonely and sometimes dishonoured; sometimes I have become an infidel and sometimes a worshipper.

O Lord, how long will you keep quiet and let torture, oppression and injustice thrive in your world? If you are unable to punish culprits, at least make them humane, honest and spiritual, infuse wisdom in them and make them a little soft-hearted.

O Lord, if you are unable to do anything, why did you create this world in the first place, why did you become God? I request you, O Lord, don't deprive your children from your lustrous Divinity, your infinite Grace, your heavenly garden of flowers and your unbounded love.

Even if you are silent, there is not a place where you are not present; there is nothing that you can't do. O Lord, with your love and kindness now, restore the dignity of the poor, give them a respectful life and free them up and, if you can, make the wealthy a little soft-hearted and more humane.

*****

Behaka deti hai tu, ae Zindaghi

Behaka deti hai Zindaghi aksar tu, kabi dhoop mein aur kabhi chandni mein;
Kabi dhoop be lagi thandi aur kabi chandni nae be jalaya; kabi jeet nae chhupayee humaree haar, kabi haar nae chhupayee jeet humaree.

Kabi haleem bun gaye' wehshi, kabi wehshi bun gaye' mateen;
Behaka deti hai Zindaghi, kabi wehshat mein aur kabi sanjeedghi mein,
kabi hosh mein aur kabi behoshi mein.

Zinda thhey jub hum, hijrat mein rahe', kabi amiri mein, kabi muflassi
mein;
Behka deti hai Zindaghi, kabi zeist mein aur kabhi hijr mein, kabi hum
majaz rahe' aur kabi haq se bilkul mehroom.

Kat gayee Zindaghi aisae he, teri husrat mein aur tere initizar mein, kabi
kufr mein, kabi sajde' mein;
Aisa toh nahi ki tu nahi, par behaka deti hai khamoshi teri; kabi aasmaan
mein, kabi zameen par, kabi ghar mein aur kabi ibadat-khanne' mein.

Deekhi teri Kudrat kabi veeranae mein aur kabi gulzar mein, kabi urooj
mein aur kabi gehrayee mein;
O Kudrat, behaka deti hai tu, kabi khwab mein, kabi hoshyari mein; kabi
shorogul mein aur kabi tanhai mein.

Aisa toh nahi ki gulistan nahi hai Zindaghi, tarah tarah ke phool hai
jisme' aur kuchh kante' be;
O Kudrat, behaka deta hai tera har aks muje', zubaani be aur be-zu-
banee be, kabi shab main aur kabi subah mein.

Behaktae rahe' hum, kabi nashukri mein, kabi irfaani mein; kabi adab
se', kabi be-adabee se';
O Zindaghi, behaka deti hai tu, kabi zillat mein, kabi mahshoori mein;
kabi shikast mein, kabi fateh mein.

Teri barkat se humme' saadat be milae, irfani be milee; majlis mein be
baithe', ijlas mein be;

Teree hukam aur marzi se hummne' dosti be kee aur wafa be, naam be kiya aur apna karam be.

Teri mohabbat mein hum mehfooz be rahe', aabad be rahe'; giraftar be rahe' aur azad be rahe';
Teri justuju mei, kabi mere alfaaz be gaye', kabi khayalat be gaye'; tere soz-o-saaz mein kabi madhosh be rahe' aur kabi rind be bane'.

O Rabba, inayat kar de', dikha de' apna jalwa, apnee tabinda tabbsum, apnee mehak aur apna noor;
Teri khamoshi kee vajah se hum kabi tanha be rahe' and kabi ruswa be huae; kabi kufur be kiya aur kabi bandhagee be kee.

Kab tak khamosh rahega, O Rabba, kab tak teri duniya mein zulam-o-sitam rahega?;
Gunahgaroon ko agar saza de' nahi sakta, unhe' kum-se-kum insaaniyat de', imandari de', ruhanyat de', akal de', naram-dili de'.

Kuchh agar kar nahi sakta, Rabba, phir banayee kyon yeh duniya tumne', kyon bun gaya tu Khuda?
Guzarish hai tumse, O Rubba, buchoon ko mehroom na kar teri shaan se, tere gul-o-gulzar se, teri muhhobat se, teri noorani se.

Khamosh hai toh kya hua, koi aisee jagah nahi jahan tu nahi , koi aisa karm nahi jo tu nahi kar sakta;
O Rubba, ab shafqat kar, inayat kar, apne ulfat se gariboon ko izzatt de', zindaghee de', azadee de' aur, agar ho sake', amiroon ko be naram-dili de', insaaniyat de.

Chapter 2

HUMANS DURING THE COVID-19 PANDEMIC

This chapter discusses various shades of human nature, shocking death of George Floyd in the US and how the US and the rest of the world reacted to it, including the cries of Australian Indigenous people and Dalits of India. The world has shown its ugly side, characterised by many shades of polarisation along the lines of political power, racial and religious bias, and socioeconomic disparity — practical differences between the haves and have-nots, the privileged and unprivileged. This chapter ends with a short poem, *Alone*.

COVID-19 pandemic

The COVID-19, or coronavirus, pandemic has been caused by severe acute respiratory syndrome coronavirus 2 (SARS CoV 2) or novel coronavirus. Its outbreak was first reported in December 2019, in Wuhan, China. The World Health Organization declared a public health emergency of international concern on 30 January 2020 and subsequently a pandemic on 11 March 2020. As of 29 Aug 2020, more than 24.88 million cases of COVID-19 had been reported globally (more than 188 countries and territories), with more than 840,400 deaths. There is no known vaccine or any specific antiviral treatment for COVID-19. Its primary treatment is symptomatic and supportive therapy.

The common symptoms of COVID-19 infection include fever,

shortness of breath, cough, fatigue and loss of sense of smell. An acutely infected person may also develop pneumonia and acute respiratory distress syndrome. The typical time period between exposure and the onset of symptoms ranges between two and fourteen days, typically around five days. It is considered to be most contagious during the first three days after the appearance of symptoms, although its transmission is equally possible before any symptoms have even appeared. It can be contracted even from people who are asymptomatic.

The virus is primarily transmitted between humans in close contact, most often via small droplets produced during coughing, sneezing and even talking. People may also become infected by first touching a con-taminated surface and then their face. The recommended preventive measures, therefore, include regular handwashing, especially after going out or touching objects in public spaces; covering one's mouth while sneezing or coughing; maintaining physical distance from other people; wearing a face mask while in public areas; and self-isolating if you believe you have the virus.

The pandemic has caused a sudden and severe social and economic disruption on a global scale. Many countries have (temporarily) closed their borders, implemented travel restrictions, imposed lockdowns, introduced workplace hazard controls and closed public facilities. A sudden closure of educational institutions has affected the studies of most students in the world. The initial phase of the pandemic saw a widespread shortage of supplies exacerbated by people panic buying toilet paper, flour, hand sanitiser, mincemeat and other food items, as happened in Australia.

The pandemic has led to the postponement or cancellation of many international sporting events, including the Summer Olympics 2020 at Tokyo, ICC (The International Cricket Council) Men's T20 World Cup 2020, Wimbledon 2020, the French Open 2002 and the US Open 2020, as well as many annual religious, political and cultural events.

Misinformation about coronavirus, through social media and the mass media, has led to ugly incidents of xenophobia and discrimination against people of a particular race or a particular religion in many parts of the world.

On a positive note, however, the world witnessed the effects of decreased emissions of pollutants and greenhouse gases. Wildlife and Nature showed signs of recovery.

George Floyd and US race protests and riots

George Perry Floyd (1973–2020), a 46-year-old black American, was killed on 25 May 2020 in Minneapolis, United States, after a white police officer, Derek Chauvin, arrested him for allegedly using a counterfeit bill, and then pressing his knee against his neck. On 30 May 2020, ABC News reported Chauvin ignored onlookers' pleas to remove his knee, which he did not do until medics told him to do so: 'Chauvin had his knee on Floyd's neck for a total of eight minutes and 46 seconds, including two minutes and 53 seconds of which Floyd was non-responsive.'

On the evening of Memorial Day in the United States, Floyd had purchased cigarettes at Cup Foods, a grocery store in Powderhorn Park of Minneapolis, where a store employee thought Floyd had paid with a counterfeit $20 bill. Thereafter, two store employees approached him while he was sitting in the driver's seat of an SUV parked across the street in front of a restaurant, with two adult passengers also in the vehicle, and demanded that Floyd return the cigarettes, which he refused to do. Their interaction was filmed by the restaurant's security camera. A store employee then called police and reported that Floyd had passed a 'fake bill', and was 'awfully drunk' and 'not in control of himself'. According to the criminal complaints filed by the state prosecutors against the police officers, Floyd was 'calm' and had said, 'thank you'.

Floyd's last words, 'I can't breathe', have reverberated around the globe; they have been a rallying cry for protesters not only in the United States, but also in many other parts of the world, against racism in the

US police force and its lack of accountability. The incident has led to a serious debate in American society about racial discrimination. In a unanimous voice, people of all ethnic backgrounds and colours in over 2,000 US cities and in many large cities in Australia, Canada and the United Kingdom, have since been protesting under the banner of 'Black Lives Matter'.

The World Reaction to George Floyd's death

The image of George Floyd's face and his last words, 'I can't breathe', have become part of a rallying cry from a significant portion of the human world around the globe who have felt oppressed, persecuted, marginalised and discriminated or biased against on the basis of their colour, race, caste or religion, at the hands of a dominant and privileged section of society. Floyd has posthumously emerged as the face of immense human suffering due to racism, which has continued unabated, in various shapes and forms, all over the world.

On 12 June 2020, Indian newspaper the *Hindustan Times* reported on a video-conference between a former US diplomat, Nicholas Burns, and India's opposition leader, Rahul Gandhi, on a wide range of issues, including racism in the United States, in which the former is reported to have said: 'It was horrible, horrible murder of George Floyd, a young African-American man, by the police in Minneapolis. There are millions of Americans protesting peacefully as is our right. And yet, the President treats them like terrorists.' Burns is also reported to have said: Our greatest American in the last 100 years is Martin Luther King Junior. He fought peaceful and non-violent battles. His spiritual idol was Mahatma Gandhi. King led us to become a better country. We elected an African-American President Barack Obama. And yet, you see race come back now. You see African-American mistreated ... Countries sometimes have to go through a discussion, a political debate about who are we? At the core, what kind of nation are we? We are an immigrant nation, a tolerant nation.'

Disturbing video footage of violent clashes between the police and protesters in the US, as well as looting and destruction, was seen around the world after George Floyd's death, which prompted people to gather in their cities and join the US protesters in solidarity despite social distancing restrictions.

On 6 June 2020, the *New York Times* reported, 'Tens of thousands turned out in Australia, Britain, France, Germany and other nations in support of U.S. protests against the death of George Floyd, while denouncing racism in their own countries.'

In Australia, tens of thousands of Australians protested on 6 June 2020 despite social distancing restrictions. On the same day, despite cold weather and spitting rain, public demonstrations took place in London, Manchester and Birmingham, with protesters violating the rule that only six people from different households could gather outside. Reportedly, in London, tens of thousands of protesters had gathered in Parliament Square, where they shouted anti-racist slogans, carrying signs that paid homage to George Floyd. Despite most people wearing face masks, their collective chanting could clearly be heard: 'George Floyd', 'Black Lives Matter', 'No justice, no peace'. People were seen moving towards the US Embassy, both on foot and by car, honking and hooting.

As per The *New York Times*, Rahma Mohammad, a 37-year-old history teacher in the UK, said, 'It's been discussed historically, but it's never been resolved'. Another protestor in the UK, 42-year old Victoria Weakerly, said, 'I'm social distancing from my white privilege … I feel safe here among these people.'

That week also saw demonstrations in Paris, Berlin, Japan, Sweden and Zimbabwe. In Paris, despite being barred by the authorities from gathering in front of the US Embassy, thousands of people protested there as well as near the Eiffel Tower, reminiscent of a protest in memory of Adama Traoré, a Frenchman who died in 2016 in police custody.

Germany too saw a week of demonstrations in Hamburg and Frankfurt as well as Berlin. Chancellor Angela Merkel reportedly called the death of George Floyd 'a murder', adding: 'It is racist ... But I trust in the power of democracy in the United States, that they are able to come through this difficult situation.'

The President of Ghana, Nana Akufo-Addo, is reported to have tweeted: 'tragic death of George Floyd will inspire a lasting change in how America confronts head on the problems of hate and racism'. In Nairobi, many Kenyans and Americans, wearing masks, reportedly gathered outside the US Embassy, chanting 'Down with police brutality' and carrying posters, 'Silence is violence'.

As per the *New York Times*, dated 13 June 2020, after the protests started in Minneapolis — in the Saint Paul metropolitan area of Minnesota — the unrest quickly spread across the United States, in over 2,000 cities and towns. Demonstrations and protests in support of the Black Lives Matter movement were also seen in over sixty countries.

An Elderly Man Knocked Down by Police

Humans are vulnerable to emotions and become blinded by rage. The following story not only illustrates a case of racial bias but also a lack of empathy and care on the part of some police officers in the US while dealing with volatile situations where tempers needed to be cool on all sides and inherent human dignity needed to be upheld. In the first week of June 2020, the US and the world media reported that a 75-year-old man had been pushed by Buffalo police during the people's protest against the death of George Floyd.

On 5 June 2020, News Channel 9 reported: 'A graphic video of an elderly man being pushed to the ground by riot police in New York has prompted an internal investigation ... Approximately two hours ago, police were marching through Niagara Square in Buffalo, New York, when they were approached by the man. The man appears to have been knocked unconscious on the pavement and blood can be seen pouring from one ear. After being shared on Twitter by Buffalo radio Station WBFO FM 88.7 ... The injured man was taken to ECMC Hospital in

Buffalo and is receiving treatment for a head injury."

This incident raises a number of simple questions, albeit not with simple answers: shouldn't police have considered the age of this elderly gentleman before knocking him down? Shouldn't police exercise self-restraint in such situations? Is it possible that a human can control themselves in the midst of a seeming street battle? In that moment of rage, did the US policemen involved in the shocking incident become too blind to see a fellow American, and a senior one at that, who was only exercising his democratic right to protest? In him, did the police only see a foe that visibly challenged their authority as police?

Humans, whether rioters or police, are invariably vulnerable to emotions and react aggressively when they find themselves under a direct physical threat, such as during riots and violent protest, or when their authority is challenged, for right or wrong reasons. In volatile situations, such as peaceful protests that suddenly turn into violent riots, rage invariably gets the better of humans, both protesters and police.

In inflammable and volatile situations, civility, discretion, restraint and discrimination vanish in a moment and anger comes out. But does that mean that humans, both in the position of power and on the ground, should do nothing and unquestionably accept such irresponsible behaviour from the very same people who are responsible for upholding and maintaining law and order in the first place? No, they must protest and fight to make the system fair and just.

Misleading Briefings by the Police

The 'pushing' incident was not owned up to initially by the police; they called it a case of 'tripping'. However, when video footage circulated on social media which revealed the reality, the police had to accept it was their doing and prepare to face the consequences. Unfortunately, in many similar cases, justice is either not always delivered, due to misleading reporting by the police, or delayed due to a complete lack of evidence despite the incident having become common knowledge.

On 7 June 2020, Matthew Guariglia of NBC News highlighted the issue of systemic falsification of reports released by police (in the US) to media and authorities, especially in situations where black Americans are involved. This article was critical of Melvin Carter, the mayor of Saint Paul (Minnesota), who had declared with certainty in front of the public and the nation's press: 'Every single person we arrested last night, I'm told, was from out of state.' When he was later proved wrong, he said he had been given faulty information by the police. A similar incident happened a few days later in New York, when police briefed the *New York Post* that US $2.4 million worth of watches had been stolen out from a Rolex store, which was later completely denied by the store's spokesperson.

In his article Guariglia noted, 'The common thread? Faulty information spread by law enforcement sources ... In reality, the police as an institution and policing as a practice are not fair, balanced or objective ... There are many reasons why police would misinterpret, exaggerate, play ignorant or outright lie.'

He claimed that, in general, little evidence was available, perhaps 'by design', to contradict the police reports and the press also tended to devalue whatever testimony was available, perhaps due to an unsympathetic white audience. The following excerpt from his article provides a grim insight into American history:

> For over a century, Black activists and other victims of police violence have tried to address not just the physical violence, but the narrative erasure of their trauma ... For three days in August of 1900, police and a white mob terrorized Manhattan's largest Black neighbourhood. When the dust had settled and it was clear that a vast majority of the people that had been arrested were Black, even as their white assailants went free, activists went to work. Their goals were not only accountability and justice, but also to fight against what they called the 'whitewashing' of events ... In the aftermath, the community collected stories from

people who had been brutalized by the mob, police or both. They published them, disseminated them and held rallies to read and share them. That is what African Americans still have to do: build a counter-archive of stories to combat police spin.

Guariglia believes and hopes, due to mobile phone footage provided by onlookers, there will be a positive change going forward: 'Cell phone footage has become a new form of testimony'. However, at the same time, he sounds frustrated and a little hopeless when he says: 'despite a century in which there has existed a chasm between what police have said and what communities have known — police departments are still relied upon to be the arbiters of what did and did not happen'.

Reaction in Australia

The *New York Times* reported on 6 June 2020:

In Australia, even as Mr. Morrison, the prime minister, advised against attending the Black Lives Matter marches on Saturday for fear of new outbreaks in a country that has managed to beat back the virus, huge crowds turned out in cities like Sydney and Melbourne, calling for an end to systemic racism and Aboriginal deaths in police custody. Anger has grown for years over the deaths: There have been more than 400 such fatalities since 1991, without a single officer having been convicted.

Police officers surrounded many Australian protests but did not engage with the demonstrators. In many cases, the protests were larger than expected. Reportedly, the protests were the largest since 2000, when 250,000 people had marched for reconciliation over Australia's treatment of Aboriginal people. Indigenous activists spoke in sombre but impassioned tones, as many protesters held signs with the names and photographs of people who had died in police and prison custody.

In Melbourne, many protesters holding Aboriginal flags, signs and clapsticks chanted, 'I can't breathe', in support of David Dungay, an Aboriginal man who died in Sydney's Long Bay on 29 December 2015 at the hands of prison officers who tried to stop him from eating biscuits. The prison guards held him with his face down and injected him with a sedative. Before his death, he is known to have said that he could not breathe, not once but 12 times. In Sydney, initially there was tension and uncertainty about the protests, as a court had ruled the day before that it would not be allowed for social distancing reasons. But after the protest organisers appealed, a higher court allowed it to go ahead just minutes before it was scheduled to start. Many protesters thought the attempt to cancel the event exemplified racism. As such, the crowd's anger seemed to be mixed with resolve. 'No justice, no peace, no racist police,' they shouted.

The *New York Times* also reported:

Margret Campbell, an Aboriginal elder, is reported to have said, 'I've never seen so many emotions expressed by so many people in my whole lifetime of protesting ... What really matters is what happens when people have to make decisions — how will they vote, how will they keep it up?' The *New York Times* also quoted Dr Ron Baird, an African-American who lives and teaches in Australia: 'No Mr. Morrison, Australia is not the United States, but Australia does have its own long, dark, brutal past of oppression.'

On 13 June 2020, Australian ABC news reported, 'Australians join Black Lives Matter protests in Perth and Darwin as refugee rallies held in Sydney, Brisbane and Melbourne.'

In Perth, the capital city of Western Australia, despite Premier Mark McGowan's advice and the City of Perth's refusal to grant permission for the protest, around 7000 people demonstrated in a Black Lives Matter protest. The organisers called for an end to racial violence, including systemic racism and the removal of Aboriginal children from families, and for a reduced Indigenous incarceration rate as well as 'sovereignty now'. The crowd followed behind the event organisers carrying a large Aboriginal flag.

About 11,000 face masks and hand sanitiser were made available to the protesters, via hygiene stations spread across the venue, and the organisers encouraged physical distancing. One of the event organisers, Jacinta Taylor, hoped the event would bring about long-lasting change: 'There have been people like my dad who have been pushing for change since they were my age ... I don't want to have to be 80 years old and still pushing for this kind of change.' Her father, Ben Taylor — a 79-year-old Noongar elder — is the recipient of the Medal of the Order of Australia for his work for Aboriginal and Torres Strait Islander rights.

In Darwin about one thousand people protested and four young Aboriginal women gave speeches. In the Far North Queensland town of Innisfail, around 300 people joined a march, undeterred by rain, and highlighted Indigenous people's deaths in custody. The organiser, Brett Ambrun, said the rally demonstrated 'standing up as a community'. In Adelaide, a small number of Black Lives Matter protesters demonstrated despite the cancellation of the event (by organisers) earlier that week.

In Sydney, Brisbane and Melbourne, the Refugee Action Coalition organised asylum-seeker rights rallies in tandem with the Black Lives Matter protests. In Sydney, about sixty people marched around the Town Hall despite a court order prohibiting the protests (due to coronavirus restrictions) and a warning from police that 'appropriate action' would be taken against protesters. In a Brisbane suburb, crowds grew outside Kangaroo Point Central Hotel and Apartments, where many asylum seekers were reportedly being held. In Melbourne, many people gathered outside Mantra Hotel and chanted 'free, free the refugees'. The hotel was reportedly holding several asylum seekers and refugees who had been evacuated from offshore detention centres for medical reasons. A similar sized crowd also protested at the Melbourne Immigration Transit Accommodation detention facility in Broadmeadows.

Following the countrywide protests, Australian authorities reminded people of the seriousness of the pandemic and issued health advice against holding any more protests. In response, Terry Slevin, the chief executive of the Public Health Association of Australia, said: 'Two hugely important public health objectives — Black Lives Matter and COVID-19 — have been framed as competing imperatives. They are not ... If the same commitment made by Australians and their governments to control COVID-19 was applied to eradicating racism and improving the circumstances of our First People, Australia would be an enormously advanced nation.' The public health body urged governments and police to support the people's right to protest and assist in mitigating coronavirus transmission risks by supplying face masks to protesters.

The Cry of Indigenous Australians

Julia Hollingsworth discussed the historic race issue in Australia in an article published in CNN, dated 10 June 2020.

She claimed that those thousands of people who had taken part in the Black Lives Matter protests across Australia on 6 June 2020 did not voice their anger only about the mistreatment of African Americans in the US, but also to end discrimination against Australia's own Indigenous population. The protests also came after video footage from Sydney taken by onlookers showed a police officer kicking a 17-year-old Indigenous Australian boy's legs out from underneath him and then pinning him to the ground with the help of two other policer officers.

From the article, it is noteworthy that, while Indigenous Australians comprise just 3.3 percent of the country's population (which is about 25 million people), they disproportionately make up more than 25 percent of its prisoners. In addition, Indigenous Australians' life expectancy is about nine years lower than that of non-Indigenous Australians, with relatively higher infant mortality. Indigenous Australians are also twice as likely to commit suicide than non-Indigenous Australians.

The Guardian on 9 June 2020 reported on a study by Australian National University's Siddharth Shirodkar that found that 75 percent of

Australians held a negative view of Indigenous Australians. Shirodkar is reported to have said, 'This study presents stark evidence of the solid invisible barrier that Indigenous people face in society ... But the data is actually not about Indigenous Australians, it's about the rest of us.' He also said, 'implicit bias isn't itself a measure of racism but can potentially cause it or discriminatory actions'.

Aboriginal Australians are considered to be one of the world's oldest known civilisations. They are believed to have arrived on the continent at least 45,000 years ago. About one million Aboriginal Australians are estimated to have lived in Australia at the time of its invasion and colonisation by the British in 1788. According to the Australian Institute of Aboriginal and Torres Strait Islander Studies (AIATSIS), there are currently more than 250 Indigenous language groups. Their diversity is reflected by their distinct belief systems and their regional knowledge of the country's landscape. Despite those facts, the British colonisers saw Australia as a *terra nullius*, meaning 'nobody's land'.

As such, the British government didn't recognise Indigenous ownership of the land. After colonisation, huge numbers of Indigenous Australians are known to have died after being exposed to a number of new diseases imported by the colonisers, such as influenza, tuberculosis, typhoid, measles, venereal diseases, pneumonia and whooping cough. In addition, according to AIATSIS, about 2000 British colonisers and more than 20,000 Indigenous Australians are known to have been killed in violent conflicts between the 1790s and the 1930s.

Indigenous Australians were not allowed to vote in federal elections till 1962. From 1910 to 1970, as part of the government's policy of assimilation, around one-third of all Indigenous Australian children were forcefully separated from their families and housed in white households or government institutions. In 2008, Kevin Rudd, the then Prime Minister of Australia, apologised to these Stolen Generations, saying that Parliament 'resolves that the injustices of the past must never, never happen again'.

In contrast to other Commonwealth countries, such as New Zealand and Canada, Australia doesn't have a treaty between the government and Indigenous people. Similar to the US, there are concerns about the manner in which Indigenous Australians are generally treated by the police. After protests led by Aboriginal Australians, in 1987 the Australian government launched a royal commission into the deaths of Aboriginal people in custody.

An Indigenous-led justice coalition, Change the Record, has found that, between 1980 and 2011, there were 449 deaths of Indigenous Australians in custody, which represented about 24 percent of all deaths in custody during that period. Notably, no police officer was ever convicted for any of those deaths.

Prime Minister Scott Morrison is reported to have said, 'But what I do say is that Australia is not other places … So let's deal with this as Australians …' while acknowledging that Indigenous deaths in custody was an issue and that the government was working to address it.

The Dalit Cry from India

Al Jazeera reported on 11 June 2020 that, 'US protests trigger calls by India's Dalits to end discrimination — Dalit campaigners support Black Lives Matter protests and hope it ignites a similar conversation in India'.

Al Jazeera reported that the Dalit community, a socially marginalised community that was once referred to as 'the untouchables', was spurred on by the anti-racism protests in the US and called on India to acknowledge the centuries of oppression they have endured at the hands of the upper castes and the overall social system.

Mr Omprakash Mahato, president of the Birsa Ambedkar Phule Students Association at Jawaharlal Nehru University, is reported to have said: 'We extend our solidarity because we feel them and we have faced discrimination ourselves … In India, people need to admit their role in everyday discrimination faced by Dalits and only then can a dialogue for change be initiated. We hope what they are seeing unfolding globally will lead to soul searching ... People need to understand that every life matters.'

As per *Al Jazeera*, Ruth Manorama, who works for the rights of Dalit women, told the Reuters news agency that Dalits were among the worst-hit by India's strict lockdown, often having to wait longer for their turn to receive food or financial aid at local distribution points, and even being turned away. In her words:

Indian Dalits have historically learned a lot from the struggle of the African Americans ... This is a good moment to challenge the narrative in India also and talk about the age-old repression of Dalits, which is visible even during the COVID-19 pandemic with discrimination denying people aid ... About 300 people have signed a Change.org petition emphasising that the 'lives of Dalits and minorities matter too' and urging Indian Prime Minister Narendra Modi to 'admit ... that caste discrimination is included in racial discrimination'.

Henri Tiphagne of People's Watch, which is a charity backing the petition, is reported to have added: 'It is a good time for people in India to understand and to point out to the government that racial discrimination is not only what you see in America. It is the same as how so-called "untouchables" are treated in India.'

Historically, in India, Dalits were called *Achhoot* (untouchables). To correct the historical wrong, Mahatma Gandhi called them *Harijan* (God's people). Over centuries, they are known to have faced physical segregation, discrimination, intolerance, contempt, humiliation and even violence, which they have resisted. Dalits have historically been forced to perform those tasks which the people from the upper classes would refuse to, such as disposing of corpses and cleaning toilets and streets. They make up about a quarter of India's population of 1.4 billion. A strong traditional bias against Dalits and members of other, less privileged caste groups remains alive in India, making it harder for them to access education and jobs or to buy homes.

People from the upper castes have been known to bar them from entering temples and using public facilities, such as water wells and ponds. When they would get caught violating the social norm, they would invariably be made to pay the ultimate price. As inhuman as it gets, their shadows too were not allowed to touch people from the upper castes. Notably, in the hierarchy of the Hindu caste system, a person's caste is determined by birth, from the caste of the family in which one is born.

The term 'caste' seems to be derived from the Spanish and Portuguese word *casta*, which refers to the institutionalised system of racial and social stratification in seventeenth-century Mexico. The online dictionary *Definitions* further explains *casta* as follows:

Casta is a Spanish and Portuguese term used in the 17th and 18th centuries mainly in Spanish America to describe as a whole the mixed-race people which appeared in the post-Conquest period. A parallel system of categorization based on the degree of acculturation to Hispanic culture ... inspired by the assumption that the character and quality of people varied according to their birth, colour, race and origin of ethnic types. The system of *castas* was more than socio-racial classification. It impacted every aspect of life, including economics and taxation. Both the Spanish colonial state and the Church expected more tax and tribute payments from those of lower socio-racial categories.

It seems the Indian system, which comprises two different concepts, *varna* and *jati*, as described below, is not the only system in the world that has differentiated humans based on their birth, colour, race and origin of ethnic type.

- *Varna* comprises a system with a framework for grouping people into four distinct classes — based on type, order, colour or class — believed to have evolved based on religious ideas and practices followed by the Indo-Aryan peoples, living in the western Gangetic plain of ancient India during the Vedic period (1500 BC to 500 BC). The four classes were: the *Brahmins* (scholarly and priestly people), the *Kshatriyas* (rulers, administrators and warriors), the *Vaishyas* (artisans, merchants, tradesmen and farmers) and the *Shudras* (general workers and labourers). Implicitly, the *varna* classification had a fifth category, which grouped all people outside the above four classes as *tribals* and the *untouchables*.

- *Jati* literally means 'birth'. In addition to the four *varnas*, there are thousands of *jatis* in India, which are complex social groups, more flexible and diverse than *varnas*, without the rigid boundaries and distinct characteristics of *varnas*. Seemingly, *jatis* may have evolved due to a more practical necessity to allow people freedom to work in areas outside their *varnas* and not prevent a member of one caste from working in another caste's occupation. *Jatis* have existed in India among Hindus, Muslims, Christians and tribal people, and, as such, there is no clear linear order among them.

The Indian caste system is understood to have originated in ancient India. It has transformed over time, especially in the last 500 years, during the reign of the Mughal Empire (1526–1540 and 1555–1857) and the British Raj (1858–1947). Its current form is thought to be a result of the collapse of the Mughal Empire and the rise of the British Raj. The gradual demise of the Mughal Empire was accompanied by the rise of powerful men in India who, by association with kings and priests, established the superiority of the Brahmins and the regal and martial form of the castes, thereby reshaping and regrouping many casteless groups into differentiated castes. After taking over from the Mughals, the British Raj exploited the caste system to their advantage. They made rigid caste structure a central mechanism of their administration and, from 1860 to 1920, segregated their Indian subjects by caste. They granted senior appointments and administrative jobs only to Christians and the people belonging to certain upper castes. Following social unrest during the 1920s, they introduced quotas for people from lower castes in government jobs.

After gaining independence in 1947, India formalised the caste-based reservation system of jobs with lists of scheduled castes and scheduled tribes, enacting many laws to improve the lives of people from lower castes. Yet, despite a constitutional ban on discrimination based on caste, the caste system continues to thrive in India, with devastating social effects. It seems to also be ingrained in other regions and religions in the Indian subcontinent, such as Nepalese Buddhism, Christianity, Islam, Judaism and Sikhism, despite been challenged from time to time by many reformists from all these religions.

Alone (a short poem)

You stood alone, you fell alone.
You grew alone, you suffered alone.
You triumphed alone, you failed alone.
You dreamt alone, you realised alone.
You crawled alone, you walked alone.
You came alone, alone you shall depart.
Alone, from nothing back to nothing.

Chapter 3

OUR GOOD, BAD AND THE UGLY

This chapter tries to decipher the mysterious human behaviour on an individual level, as well as country and political leadership levels, with several real life vignettes and anecdotes. It also provides a commentary on sickening gender division and a discussion on 'missing' females. This chapter discusses the many ugly shades of the human character which have been brought to the fore by the COVID-19 pandemic, including a few vignettes about human behaviour against animals; panic buying in Australia; migrant workers crisis in India; Islamophobia in India; Xenophobia in Australia and China; political scenario in India; and an attempt to decipher the unusual behaviour of some world leaders.

On the one side, doctors and medical professionals, researchers and health workers have worked virtually day and night to save human lives in whichever way they can, in the process, many sacrificing their own lives to save others. On the other extreme, many other humans, especially those in positions of power and authority, have exhibited strange behaviours, acting in the opposite way to how the former group has.

The global media has reported numerous stories about humans suffering during the pandemic, some due to lack of facilities and some due to the mass return of migrant workers, most of whom have had to endure unbelievable and unprecedented hardships to get back home, many dying on the way, and many new lives too born on the way. Many political leaders have shown a lack of empathy or real care towards the people who have suffered and died. Opening economies has taken precedence over saving human lives. Interracial and religious tensions have been fuelled in some countries. Some countries used the COVID-19 lockdown to allow oppressive activities against minorities.

This chapter ends with a poem, *A Plea to Death*.

Our mysterious behaviours

We humans come in all kinds and shapes, and so do our families. We also act in mysterious ways, as does Mother Nature, which may appear to be amusingly or grotesquely strange or unusual in some cases, and baffling and completely inexplicable in other times. This chapter illustrates varying shades of our good, bad and ugly sides in general – as man versus woman, as humans versus animals – as well as a few real-life vignettes the author was a witness to or a part of.

In many cases, our 'good' side is unequivocally perceived and acknowledged as such by one and all, unless some of us have a religious, ethnic or nationalistic bias. The term 'good' can be also defined by various attributes such as benevolence, altruism, care, empathy and compassion, individually or collectively. To illustrate this undisputed form of 'goodness', let us take the example of a non-swimmer jumping into a river to save a drowning person. Similarly, in many cases, our 'bad' and 'ugly' sides can unequivocally be termed as such and considered as deplorable and horrendous.

Where a bias of any kind, religious, ethnic, socioeconomic or nationalistic, corrupts the judgement of a community, that community will condone 'bad' and 'ugly' acts undertaken by an individual or some members of that community against the interests of rival communities as acts of bravery and heroism, which would otherwise be deemed deplorable and horrendous. So the voice of the people is not always the voice of God, contrary to what some people believe.

Appearances can be deceptive, at least on an individual level. At times, upon sincere reflection, we realise a seemingly bad act or behaviour by some people — including our closest family members — towards us in the past had a completely selfless, noble intent and was actually meant for our own good, for example, the punishment that we may have received from our parents for our bad behaviours. Equally, there must have been times when we were completely taken in and deceived by the very same people, usually sweet-tongued, whom we had trusted the most.

Life and people, however, don't generally come in black and white, easily identifiable shades. In most cases, an overwhelming number of us show the full assortment of the good, the bad and the ugly, which makes us what we are — the *humans* — as Nature created us.

Expectation of perfection in humans is a fallacy. For that matter, the term 'perfection' is also a subjective word. What may appear as perfect to one person may not necessarily appear as perfect to another person. Importantly, also, what may appear as perfect to us today, based on the current state of our mind — or, rather, the momentary state of our mind — may not appear to be perfect after some time when we perceive things in another state of our mind, which is ever fluctuating, flickering and whimsical.

Thus, if the measuring yardstick — our mind — is ever changing, how can the measurement —our judgement — about a person or a situation be considered valid?

Like perfection in humans, idealism too is a fallacy. Idealism can be extremely misleading; it can make an idealist person strive for and chase something that simply does not exist, rendering them perpetually unhappy and miserable. Of course, in the future, when humans may be conceived, designed and raised as programmable robots, the behaviour of those *robotic humans*, or humanoids, may be considered to be predictable. Those robotic humans will be custom-made, in accordance with our pursuit of perfection, to meet our individual requirements. Importantly, they will not surprise and disappoint us, with their 'bad' and 'ugly' behaviours, in the same way as humans today do.

But who knows what artificial intelligence will bring forth? Perhaps those robotic humans may also evolve and learn to be as conniving and manipulative as today's humans are, or they may become as corruptible as we humans are.

As a realisation, therefore, let us accept and the embrace the mysterious, rather enigmatic, humans as they are — with their good, bad and ugly — rather than create something hypothetically perfect that we may have absolutely no idea about. It is prudent to cherish humans, with their feelings and emotions — in all their good, bad and ugly shades of nature — rather than create cold-hearted, unemotional humanoids.

As an argument, if we can accept the perceived imperfection of Mother Nature, with its temperamental moods and whimsicality, why should we not be able to accept humans, with all their imperfections and unpredictability, and alleviate the sufferings brought on by our disappointment with their unexpected behaviours? Why should we nurture hatred and anger against the people who may have deceived or disappointed us in the past? Isn't it prudent, therefore, to embrace human imperfection as it is and lighten ourselves of a toxic load of bad memories that otherwise we may carry in our minds our whole lives?

Man versus woman — why one more division?
Humans like divisions. Over our history, we have divided ourselves along numerous lines: religions and sub-religious sects, castes and sub-castes, gender identities, colours, races and geographical locations, eating habits and dietary preferences, professions and class. Not many people will identify themselves first as a 'human' because most people think that is a given. Being human is taken for granted but most forget that when they see others differently and, unconsciously or consciously, discriminate against them.

Ask any stranger who you happen to meet randomly at a social gathering or in a public place, 'Who are you?' Invariably, the answer will be the person's name. But don't be surprised to hear the answer as the person's religion and/or nationality, particularly if this question is asked on the subcontinent, particularly in multicultural, multi-ethnic, multi-faith India. Probe further: 'What are you?' The answer would invariably be the person's profession but, again, don't be surprised to hear a different answer, including the person's religion or caste or race or nationality, particularly on the subcontinent.

Common people in a Western developed country, such as Australia, will generally identify themselves in the following order, with some variations: name, profession (including 'student'), nationality, perhaps race (Caucasian, African, Indian etc.), gender orientation (straight, gay etc.), food preference and religion (including atheism, agnosticism). However, common people in a developing country, such as India, will generally identify themselves in the following order: name, religion (Hindu, Muslim, Christian, Sikh etc.), ethnicity (Tamil, Bengali, Guajarati, Punjabi etc.), profession (including 'student'), nationality and food preference (vegetarian or non-vegetarian).

While the world has historically been fighting itself based on religious faiths, such as Christianity, Buddhism, Islam, Hinduism, Sikhism and Jainism, humans have also divided themselves by creating numerous sub-religious faiths and sects, for example Sunni, Shia and Ahmadiyyas (in Islam); Catholics, Protestants and Anglicans (in Christianity); Mahayana, Theravada and Vajrayana and their variants (in Buddhism); Vaishnavism, Shaivism, Shaktism and Smartaism and their variants (in Hinduism); Nirankaris and Nam-Dharis, or Kuka Sikhs and their variants (in Sikhism); and Digambara and the Svetambara (in Jainism). In addition, as discussed in Chapter 2, Hindus have also divided themselves along castes.

Geographically and ethnically, humans divide themselves as northerners, southerners, easterners and westerners, and more specifically as South Asian, South-East Asian, East European, West European, North American, South American, South African, West Africans and so on. Nationally, humans divide themselves as Australians, Kiwis, Indians, Pakistanis, Chinese, British Irish, Scottish, French, Russian, Italian, Spanish, German and the list goes on. Politically, there are 195 countries, which include 193 member states of the United Nations and two non-member observers (Vatican City and the state of Palestine). From a technical point of view, however, there are 197 countries and from a travel standpoint there are 217 countries.

On the basis of dietary preference, humans identify themselves as omnivores, meat-eaters and vegetarians. Vegetarians are subdivided as vegans (who eat only plants); ovo-vegetarians (who eat plants and eggs, but not dairy products, meat or fish); lacto-vegetarians (who eat plants and dairy products, but not eggs, meat or fish); lacto-ovo vegetarians (who eat plants, dairy products and eggs, but not eat meat or fish); and pescetarians (who eat fish but not meat). Food allergies that further divide humans and their diets come generally from peanuts, dairy products, eggs, wheat, soy, fish, shellfish and other seafood.

In addition, religious restrictions on certain foods are practised by people from all religious faiths — for example, Jews eat kosher food only, Muslims eat halal food only; and Hindus prefer lacto-vegetarian food but can eat lacto-ovo vegetarian and pescetarian food too.

Socioeconomically, humans divide themselves as upper class (rich), upper-middle class, middle class, lower-middle class and lower class (poor). In terms of work, humans divide themselves as professionals and workers, or rather as white-collared professionals and blue-collared workers. White-collared workers generally describe themselves by their day's work: as manager, politician, doctor, engineer, lawyer, academic, nurse or banker, for example. Similarly, blue-collared workers describe themselves as mechanic, carpenter, electrician or driver, as example.

Colourism is a new division, as if there were not already enough divisions giving people reasons to differentiate between themselves and discriminate where possible. On the subcontinent, the myth goes that a fair complexion is a ladder to success. As such, beauty, especially by women, is associated with a fair complexion, with men not far behind and catching up fast. All world-renowned cosmetic companies have invested heavily in the subcontinent to promote their beauty and 'fair-complexion' products and many renowned actors and models from the West and the subcontinent shamelessly promote them in exchange for a hefty fee. Strangely, these models don't even realise that they indirectly promote racism and disadvantage those people whose complexion may be on the darker side, even though they may actually be much more beautiful than their fair-complexioned contemporaries. Seemingly, not many people feel comfortable in their skin colour. Many Caucasians will give themselves sun tans, whether under the sun or in solariums, to give some colour to their pale complexions.

Now that there are so many divisions among humans, why create another division, between sexes and genders? The binary of male and female splits the human race into two distinct divisions. If all humans are seen as 'equal', with no one considered superior to the other, the world would not need feminism. It is time to deconstruct outdated social beliefs and myths about the social differences between the sexes.

Man and woman, both are humans. How can they be different? Their body shapes may look a little different, as they have differing anatomies in terms of their reproductive organs, but how can their minds be different? Together, they lay the foundation of the human race, the building blocks. Without the other, one is incomplete. Nature needed both to complete the human race and ensure its survival. Their mutual attraction is the reason humans have survived and thrived, with about 9 billion of us living on this planet after having multiplied nearly eight times in the last 400 years and four times in the last 100 years. It is only the social construct that has made us look at each differently, otherwise we are no less than each other in intelligence, wisdom and skills, including love, nurturing, compassion and empathy as well as our fighting abilities.

As for gender, it is rather complex. People define themselves in different ways as they gain a deeper understanding of their bodies and emotions. It is about one's body chemistry and innate feelings about how one identifies. There are more than the two genders that are most commonly recognised (male and female, the gender binary), such as transgender, gender neutral, non-binary, agender, pangender, gender-queer, two-spirit, third gender, and all, none or a combination of these.

Missing females — a shame on humanity

The human world may be living in 2020 but it has not progressed much in the core areas. Despite boasting material progress, especially during the last 300 years, and toying with fancy ideas for the future, such as landing humans on Mars, how long will one half of humanity be made to suffer and made to feel inferior, and for what reason?

This section covers briefly only one aspect of the ugly side of the human race. A United Nations study has revealed that, over the past fifty years, there have been 142.6 million 'missing females' in the world. India accounts for 45.8 million (approximately one-third) of them. 'Missing females' are defined as women who are 'missing from the population at given dates due to the cumulative effect of postnatal and prenatal sex selection in the past'.

The United Nations Population Fund (UNFPA), the world organisation's sexual and reproductive health agency, reports that the number of 'missing women' has increased from 61 million in 1970 to a cumulative 142.6 million in 2020. As per the report:

- Preference for male children has led to long-term changes in the percentages of women and men in some countries. The demographic imbalance could potentially impact on marriage systems in these countries, leading to 'marriage squeeze', where prospective grooms will outnumber prospective brides. For example, in India, the 'marriage squeeze' is expected to peak in 2055 when the proportion of single men, even at the age of fifty, may rise to 10 percent. Affecting mostly young men from lower economic strata, many men will be made to delay or forgo marriage because they will be unable to find a spouse. At the same time, the marriage squeeze could result in more child marriages.

- Every year, on a global level, with the full knowledge and consent of their own families, millions of girls are subjected to practices that harm them physically and emotionally. In addition to child marriages, these practices include female genital mutilation, breast ironing and virginity testing, which construe human rights violations.
- About 4.1 million girls are expected to be subjected to female genital mutilation in a year.
- About 33,000 girls under the age of eighteen will possibly be forced into marriages, usually to much older men, in a day.
- The world's two most populous countries, China and India, account for about 90–95 percent of the estimated 1.2–1.5 million 'missing females' at birth due to gender-biased (prenatal) sex selection.
- In India, gender-biased sex selection accounts for about two-thirds of the total missing girls. Each year, from 2013 to 2017, about 460,000 girls were 'missing' at birth in India.
- India has the highest rate of excess female deaths, 13.5 per 1000 female births, which suggests about one in nine deaths of females below the age of five may be due to postnatal sex selection.

As per the report, upscaling ongoing global efforts to keep girls in school longer and teach them life skills, and to engage men and boys in social change can possibly end child marriage and female genital mutilation within ten years.

UNFPA's executive director says, 'Harmful practices against girls cause profound and lasting trauma, robbing them of their right to reach their full potential … The pandemic both makes our job harder and more urgent as so many more girls are now at risk.'

Reportedly, if UN services and programs remain paralysed for six months due to the COVID-19 pandemic, an additional 13 million girls worldwide may be forced into marriage and, alarmingly, 2 million more girls may be subjected to female genital mutilation by 2030.

Humans versus animals

During the pandemic, many stories have emerged from India which illustrate various shades of humans' relationship with other animals, some sad and some heartening.

A pregnant elephant's murder

This story illustrates an inhuman shade of humans where they can do anything, including commit horrendous and despicable acts against innocent animals, in situations where their interests — in this case, crops — are threatened by the latter. Sadly, animals find themselves in such situations for lack of food in their natural habitat due to human encroachment, which has been exacerbated by an explosion in human numbers. Where humans and animals fight for food, the latter pays the ultimate price.

The *Hindu* reported on 4 June 2020 that, in the southern Indian state of Kerala, a wild elephant had left the Silent Valley forest and wandered into a nearby village in search of food, where a man reportedly offered her a pineapple filled with powerful crackers. The fruit exploded in her mouth, breaking her jaw. She then entered a river where, after standing in the water for hours, she died despite efforts to rescue her.

On 4 June 2020, the BBC reported that there was outrage in India after a pregnant elephant died eating a 'firecracker' fruit and that wildlife officials were investigating the death. The elephant had reportedly spent days in pain before dying despite vets trying to save her. The incident sparked outrage on social media. On Twitter, Ratan Tata, chair of Tata Sons and one of India's leading businesspeople, condemned the act: 'I am grieved and shocked to know that a group of people caused the death of an innocent, passive pregnant elephant by feeding the elephant with a pineapple filled with firecrackers. Such criminal acts against innocent animals are no different than acts of meditated murder against other humans. Justice needs to prevail.'

The elephant's death sparked controversy in India along socio-religious and political lines. Angry and controversial statements by prominent politicians triggered a storm on social media. *Al Jazeera* reported, on 4 June 2020, that the fifteen-year-old pregnant elephant's death had triggered a 'hate campaign' against Muslims by right-wing Hindu forces.

Parliamentarian of India's ruling party BJP, Maneka Gandhi, also an animal rights activist, had (wrongly) claimed that the incident happened in Malappuram district, which is about eighty-five kilo-metres to the west of Palakkad where it had actually happened. Her controversial statement, 'It's murder. Malappuram is famous for such incidents, it's India's most violent district … For instance, they throw poison on roads so that 300–400 birds and dogs die at one time', stirred strong controversy across India, as it did not define who 'they' are. Hundreds of posts on social media suggested the perpetrator could be a Muslim. No one knows if Ms Gandhi's mistake was due to ignorance or was deliberate, but naming Malappuram as the place of the incident, where 70 percent of the population are Muslim, suggested to most people across India that the culprit was a Muslim.

As per *Al Jazeera*, Mr Dhanya Rajendran, editor-in-chief of *The News Minute*, tweeted: 'Seeing all the hatred on the pregnant elephant's killing in Kerala, need to add something. The elephant was found dead in the Velliyar River which flows through Palakkad district.'

As per *Al Jazeera*, Mr Vijayan, Chief Minister of Kerala, tweeted: 'Some people have tried to import bigotry into the narrative … [We] are saddened by the fact some have used this tragedy to unleash a hate campaign. Lies built upon inaccurate descriptions and half-truths were employed to obliterate the truth.'

It is saddening to note that, instead of one and all expressing deep remorse, followed by proactive action to prevent any similar incidents in the future, even the painful murder of an innocent, trusting elephant by a human being was not spared from being exploited for political leverage and finger-pointing towards a particular community, despite evidence showing otherwise. Sadly, in an environment of socio-religious tensions, the core issues — animal rights and the livelihoods of poor farmers — get buried because their solutions do not help the politicians.

The following excerpt from *Al Jazeera* reports alarming occurrences of animal cruelty:

Poor villagers … often use firecracker or explosive-filled pineapples — which act like pressure-activated landmines — to protect their fields and homes from wild animals. A similar incident was reported last month in a nearby district in Kerala where a female elephant was found with serious mouth injuries. About 2,361 people were killed in attacks by elephants between 2014 and 2019, according to data recorded by the Indian government. In the same period, about 510 elephants died, including 333 from electrocution and about another 100 from poaching and poisoning, the figures stated.

A man raises two elephants as his family

On the one side, while heart-rending stories keep emerging about human cruelty towards animals, another story during the pandemic, again from India, is quite heartening. This illustrates the other side of humans — the side of goodness, gratitude and extreme benevolence. On 11 June 2020 it was reported that an Indian man had upset his wife by bequeathing his land to his two domesticated elephants.

The story is about one Mr Akhtar Imam, fifty, from a village in the eastern state of Bihar, who also runs a wildlife trust, and his love for his two elephants, siblings Moti (twenty) and Rani (fifteen), whom he has raised from their birth. Mr Imam announced that he had changed his will to bequeath 2.5 hectares of his land to the two gentle giants. The elephants, who roam his property freely, also have two dedicated staff to look after them round the clock.

In his words to the *AFP*, Mr Iman said: 'I simply don't want hardship for my Moti and Rani, who are no less than my family … I don't want my elephants to face the fate of orphaned or abandoned captive elephants who die on the streets or in deserted fields due to lack of proper care.'

Last year, the elephants had saved his life from armed attackers while he slept. 'When I opened my door to see why the elephants were trumpeting, I saw they were chasing criminals nearby … I am alive due to my elephants who had worked like bodyguards to me.'

On being asked why his family was not happy with his will to bequeath the larger portion of land to his elephants, he is reported to have said: 'They don't understand that the elephants are not a showpiece for me … My relationship with elephants is lifelong. We love each other.'

The *Guardian* reported that Asian elephants, some of whom live well into their seventies, are listed as endangered on the Red List of the International Union for the Conservation of Nature. Due to the continued encroachment into forests by humans, their number is understood to have been reduced to about 45,000, of which about one-third live in captivity, and their habitat has also been reduced to about 15 percent of their original territorial range.

A man stabbed to death for feeding stray dogs
This story illustrates both the humane and ugly side of humans. On 21 June 2020, in Delhi, India, a 57-year-old man was stabbed to death after an argument with a 22-year-old over feeding stray dogs.

Reportedly, according to the police, the victim would often feed stray dogs. On 21 June, at around 10 pm, he was feeding stray dogs near a park in his area when the 22-year-old arrived at the scene. When the accused started arguing with the victim, the street dogs started barking at him, which made him angry. Thereafter, he went back to his house and returned with a knife and attacked the victim. The police arrested him later.

This story is about a young, hot-headed person, without much empathy or compassion for animals and scant respect for age, killing a person at least one generation older than him in pure rage.

Ironically, it was the empathy and care for stray and abandoned animals that cost this man his life. Unfortunately, it has also been reported that many pet owners in India have abandoned their pets during the pandemic upon hearing baseless rumours that animals can spread the coronavirus.

A monkey was hanged

This story illustrates the ugly and sadistic side of humans. On 30 June 2002, a monkey was found hanged to death from a tree in Ammapelam village, in Kammam district of the southern Indian state of Telangana. Allegedly, the monkey had entered a farmer's field. A video showing the monkey struggling for its life, with two dogs barking over it and some locals with *lathis* (long wooden rods) in their hands, had gone viral, which caused the uproar. Three people have been detained in connection to the case.

The Federation of Indian Animal Protection Organisations (FIAPO) condemned the act and demanded the accused be arrested. FIAPO has also called on the government 'to act on its social responsibility towards animals across the country, to ensure their rights be recognised and secured'. It also said that the state must 'holistically address the issue and must strike a balance between the rights of animals and human beings'.

A 'developed' country is a myth

It is a myth to call any country a 'developed' country. No country can ever claim to be a developed country, as 'development' never ceases. As such, it is not correct to divide the world into 'developed' and 'developing' countries. Interestingly, the 'developed' and 'developing' dichotomy was represented earlier by the so-called 'first' and 'third' world terminology.

All countries must be termed as 'developing' countries. All countries — the so-called developed or developing — need to keep doing things to improve their infrastructure, keep their economies going and generate work for their people, improve people's overall life and happiness, and address age-old human issues, such as disease, poverty, unemployment and racism.

COVID-19 has clearly and unquestionably illustrated, through the available data about infection and death rates, that the so-called developed countries carry that tag mistakenly. The questionable performance of the UK and many European countries at the start of the pandemic proves the point and highlights the scope for development in those countries. In the USA — the world's strongest country (on paper) in terms of economy and defence, which has long bragged about its democratic status and its being a champion of the weak in the world — we have seen race and gun issues, and one of the highest infection rates of COVID-19. These examples show how much scope there is for the USA to develop further. Just by being boisterous about what a great democracy it is does not give it much credibility in allowing its citizens to carry guns.

Economies can't be ethically run by instigating socio-political and military conflict in other countries so we can sell weapons to them, or by exploiting the natural or human resources of other countries to benefit our own people. Economies must be run based on internal — natural and human — resources, with ongoing humane economic and development projects. Projects undertaken with other countries must be based on a win–win outcome, founded on a principle that all people in the world belong to one large global family. How do we divide the Earth's atmosphere, the sun, the moon and the stars between us?

Ill-gotten wealth from elsewhere used to feed oneself and one's family members invariably brings misery and disease to one's family. It is not ethical to snatch bread from others or cleverly steal their bread and offer them just breadcrumbs in return. It is not ethical to keep scheming and scripting conflict in the world, where generations of humans die on all sides, just to fill your coffers. The two proverbs *What goes around, comes around* and *As you sow, so shall you reap* are born out of human wisdom and experience.

History bears witness to the law of nature that 'a fall follows a rise'. What goes up must come down, so does pride and arrogance, unless one is grateful and humble. Even the unsinkable *Titanic* sank, and that too for unthinkable, trivial reasons. Inflicting irreversible suffering on other people, to maintain dominance over them and keep exploiting them and their resources, comes back sooner or later, when Nature hits back.

A great nation truly becomes great when it does not claim greatness or calls itself the best country in the world. Greatness of a nation, any nation, lies in its benevolence and how it respects and cares for all people, including its own citizens and the citizens of all other countries. A mighty nation truly becomes great when it reflects humility and speaks in humble tones. By claiming to be mighty, one does not become great. An individual or a nation that talks the loudest, without the courtesy to listen to others, is the weakest of all; it is hollow. *Empty vessels make much noise*, as the saying goes. Nature provides everything that we use and live on, but Nature never claims it is great. How many mountains do we see roaring? How many tall trees make you feel small?

Deciphering the unusual behaviour of some world leaders

Some countries with struggling economies, high unemployment rates and considerable populations living in poverty have had these issues exacerbated by the pandemic. The governments of many such countries potentially face anger — at the ballot box or in the streets — from a sizeable percentage of their population, especially those from relatively lower socioeconomic strata, if they continue to impose pandemic-driven lockdowns for prolonged periods of time.

It may be true that many such leaders have inherited the issues in their countries and, therefore, it would not be fair to blame them for creating the problems. But it won't be wrong either to say that, during their time in power, most of these leaders remain embroiled in party politics and spend most of their time and energy fending off challenges from formidable members within their own political parties and, without doubt, from the opposition.

Practically, therefore, in most democracies, for a cumulatively considerable period of time, the parliament is occupied with arguments and counter-arguments, allegations and counter-allegations and even mud-slinging, all at the taxpayer's cost. The core aim of the parliamentarian is effectively narrowed to retaining power as many plans and schemes hang in the air due to stalemates. Meanwhile, the people's issues are exacerbated and their frustration grows. For fear of getting routed at the ballot box, many clever politicians adopt proven psychological and management tactics to engage people.

It is not surprising some governments have reacted to the COVID-19 pandemic in unusual and strange ways, raising many eyebrows globally, unlike their counterparts in other countries who have generally followed the WHO guidelines and got along with the business of dealing with the pandemic as they should have. The leaders of Belarus, Brazil and the USA were defiant in not following the WHO guidelines, such as physical distancing and wearing a face mask. The leaders of Japan, Sweden and the UK, on the other hand, took a bit of time to realise the importance of physical distancing and face masks. By the time they understood, infections had already risen alarmingly. Sweden and Japan decided initially to let life continue as is but that resulted in a high number of infections. Once they woke up to the reality, these countries were able to control the spread and keep infections at a reasonable rate. The British prime minister tested positive to COVID-19 and initially self-isolated before being moved to intensive care in hospital.

The country heads whose actions are markedly different from most other leaders are not fools; they know exactly what they are doing and the reasons why. One such leader is the Belarus president, 65-year-old Alexander Lukashenko, who has been in office for more than a quarter of a century, since 1994. Defying the WHO and his own health ministry, he refused to impose major restrictions in his country against the coronavirus pandemic.

- On 16 March 2020, as per *The Hour*, President Lukashenko advised people not to worry about the virus, but instead to work in the fields and sow crops: 'People are working in tractors. No one is talking about the virus … There, the tractor will heal everyone. The fields heal everyone.' He advised to use vodka to fight the virus: 'I don't drink, but recently I've been saying that people should not only wash their hands with vodka, but also poison the virus with it. You should drink the equivalent of 40–50 ml of rectified spirit daily, but not at work.' He also recommended: 'Wash your hands more often, have breakfast on time, have lunch and dinner.'
- On 29 March 2020, *The Guardian* reported that, while playing in an ice hockey game with his presidential team against a side from the Grodno region, President Lukashenko said: 'There are no viruses here', adding that ice hockey is an 'anti-virus remedy'.
- On 17 April 2020, *The Guardian* reported that Belarus had shown a delayed response to the pandemic and continued to host Europe's only active football league at that time. Dismissing

the pandemic as a 'frenzy and psychosis', President Lukashenko had publicly declared in that week, 'No one in the country will die from coronavirus'.

- On 2 May 2020, *The Washington Post* reported that coronavirus was spreading rapidly in Belarus, but its leader still denied there was a problem. He said: 'WHO doesn't really love us. This is an international organisation, which always involves a lot of politics.' He seeks a sixth term in office in the upcoming presidential elections, which will be held no later than 30 August 2020. Reportedly, he faces little opposition, although his country's relations with Russia are strained, leading him to develop closer ties with the US and Europe. The initial domestic disapproval of his coronavirus response is unlikely to loosen his grip on power.

On 29 August 2020, Belarus had 71,346 infections and 667 deaths, so it seems the country has not done so badly despite Lukashenko's stance. The death rate was 71 per million of population, i.e. 0.007 percent of the total population of Belarus, which is understood to be about 9.45 million. History may not judge the president of Belarus as harshly as the president of the country which has the highest number of COVID-19 infections and deaths — US President Donald Trump.

Meanwhile, in Brazil, South America's largest country by geographical area and by population, with around 212 million people, President Jair Bolsonaro has been criticised by the world media for his performance during COVID-19. This criticism seems to be premature.

On 29 August 2020, the US led the world, with about 6.09 million total infected cases, 3.37 million recovered cases and more than 185,000 deaths, with a death rate of 561 deaths per million people and more than 242,000 tests per million. Brazil was just behind the US, with about 3.82 million total infections, 2.97 million recovered cases and more than 119,000 deaths. Brazil had conducted 66,602 tests per million people and its death rate was 562 per million, which was comparable to death rate of 561 per million in the US. Despite the large number of deaths, its death rate was below that of Peru (856) and Chile (582), and many European countries — Spain (620), the UK (611), Italy (587), Sweden (576), Belgium (852), Andorra (686) and San Marino (1237).

Bolsonaro tested positive for COVID-19 on 6 July. Reportedly, he appeared on live television, indoors without a face mask, in close proximity to a group of reporters to announce his test results, boldly assuring people: 'There's no reason for fear. That's life. Life goes on.' After constantly downplaying the pandemic over the previous few months, he also said: 'I thank God for my life and the role I've been given to decide the future of this great nation that is called Brazil.'

Bolsonaro was the chief guest at India's Republic Day function in January 2020, and is seen as a close friend of Prime Minister Modi. He ordered Brazil's military to start mass producing the antimalarial drug hydroxychloroquine, as a COVID-19 treatment, and spent millions ordering its ingredients from India. Without any evidence of its effectiveness, he claimed: 'God is Brazilian! The cure is right here', and criticised those scientists who did not support the drug.

They say, *A drowning man will clutch a straw*. Did President Bolsonaro have any other choice? Yes, he had, he could also have followed the WHO guidelines like most other countries did. But a strict lockdown for an initial couple of months, such as in India, could potentially have crippled his country's economy and send the unemployment rate to unacceptable and possibly unmanageable levels. He would also have wanted the best for his people, whatever best was available at that time. Was there any cure for the virus at that time? No, there was none and the world was panicking, but he did not panic. Hydroxychloroquine provided a faint hope for the world at that time. At the end of April, when the death toll in Brazil topped 5,000, he was seemingly sincere when he said: 'So what? I'm sorry, but what do you want me to do? I'm not a miracle worker.'

Apart from establishing national emergency funds for laid-off workers and boosting public health systems by relocating millions of doctors and nurses, he has been criticised for his scorn of local and state shelter-in-place orders. He fired his health minister for calling for social distancing and self-isolation, as he knew the consequences for the economy, which he thought would have caused much greater damage and ultimately killed many more people.

All throughout the pandemic, Bolsonaro has put up a bold front, as a good and inspiring leader should do. He posted videos showing him shopping during the lockdown, without a face mask, looking happily sociable to instil confidence in people, for which he was criticised. He also joined an anti-lockdown protest, where he is understood to have hugged supporters and held babies. One day, when he stopped to eat a hot dog in a town square during lockdown, one woman is reported to have shouted at him: 'Killer! You're a killer!'

As he opened the economy and expanded the list of essential businesses, he told reporters: 'Banning this and that isn't going to contain the spread … When you ban football and other things, you fall into hysteria.'

According to CNN, he had tested negative three times before. While awaiting the results of his fourth test, he took both hydroxychloroquine and azithromycin. Like Trump, he has promoted hydroxychloroquine as a potential treatment for the virus, despite it being consistently proven ineffective, with WHO discontinuing a major trial of the drug.

Following months of downplaying the virus, in early July 2020, President Bolsonaro spoke on Brazilian TV about the pandemic:

- He conceded, 'Everyone knew that it would reach a considerable part of the population sooner or later. It was positive for me. We know the fatality of the virus for those of a certain age, like me, above sixty-five, as well as for those with comorbidities, diseases, other issues. In those cases, the virus could be decisive and lead to death — everyone knew that.'
- Defending his close interaction with the public, he said: 'I have

to admit, I thought I had gotten it earlier, considering my very dynamic activity in the face of the people … And I can tell you more, I am the president and I am on the front line, I don't run away from my responsibility nor do I shy away from the people.'

- Defending his government's management of the pandemic, he said: 'No country in the world has managed to prevent deaths … the whole world was unanimous in saying that the purpose of the isolation measures … was not to prevent people from contracting the virus but that the contraction was inevitable and it should happen over a longer time for hospitals to be equipped with ICU beds and respirators.'

- Emphasising that his priority was to restart Brazil's lagging economy, he said: 'I know that nobody can recover from dying, but the economy not working leads to other causes of death and suicide … We have suffered very harsh criticism in this regard, but today it shows that we are right. The fact that I am infected shows that I am a human being like any other.'

- Thanking his well-wishers, he said: 'I'll get away a little. Just so you all can see my face. I'm fine, I'm fine, thank God. Everything is okay … Thank you to those who prayed for me. Those who criticised, no problem, they can continue to criticise if they want. After all, we preserve the freedom of speech and understand it as one of the pillars of our democracy.'

- Reminding younger people of their responsibility to take care of elderly people, he said: 'So let's take special care of the elderly, of course. Younger people: take care, but if you are affected by the virus, be assured that for you, the possibility of something more serious is close to zero.'

To conclude, Bolsonaro's response to the pandemic could be analysed in several ways and he can be judged both ways — kindly and harshly. People with little experience in heading a family or leading a team, not to speak of leading a developing country like Brazil, may severely criticise his actions and words. One thing that seems to be loud and clear, post his positive test results and his (honest) statements thereafter, is that he has known all along the severity of coronavirus and its potentially crippling effects on the economy and, therefore, was trying to put up a brave face for his people — to instil fearlessness and confidence while dealing with the virus — and trying to save their jobs. In hindsight, his speech broadcast on national television and radio on 24 March 2020 sums it up: 'Our life has to go on. Jobs should be maintained.'

WHO Director-General Tedros Adhanom Ghebreyesus wished President Bolsonaro a 'speedy recovery' and reminded the world: 'It's very important to understand the seriousness of this virus and to be really serious … No country is immune, and no country is safe, and no individual can be safe.'

That brings us finally to US President Donald Trump. Instead of unifying his country, Trump will be remembered for polarising people and dividing his country, functioning more in dictatorial mode and un-democratically firing anyone who doesn't agree with him, terming any challenge from his opponents as 'a witch hunt' and calling them 'far-left fascists', claiming the US is 'under siege from new far-left fascism'.

On the economic front, prior to COVID-19, his performance may have been deemed fine but the pandemic, and the racial issues occurring during this time, have clearly tested his acumen and leadership skills. He has been found wanting on several occasions, falling short (at best, well below average) of the leadership expected during a global health crisis. Instead of getting down to work to control the spread of the virus in his country, he appeared to be wasting his time and energy in criticising the WHO and China, while more and more people got infected. It can be said that he has actually fuelled the spread of the virus in his country by being a strong opponent of lockdown and physical distancing, and his open defiance against wearing a face mask in public. On the surface, President Bolsonaro may appear to have taken a similar approach as

President Trump to deal with the pandemic but, on a closer look, the former did not much room to manoeuvre as compared to the latter. At the start of the pandemic, Brazil's economy and employment rate was not as healthy and robust as that of the US. The damaging effects of a strict lockdown in Brazil, such as done by India, could possibly have resulted in many more casualties in that country that what actually happened.

Many books can be, and will be, written on President Trump. At the end of 2019, impeachment proceedings against him were initiated based on charges of abuse of power and obstruction of Congress. In February 2020, he was acquitted on both counts. He was alleged to have solicited foreign help in the forthcoming 2020 election and then obstructed the inquiry itself by instructing his administration officials to ignore subpoenas for documents and testimony. He is alleged to have withheld military aid to Ukraine and has not invited the Ukrainian president to the White House as a tactic to pressure Ukraine into investigating his Democrat rival, Joe Biden.

The pandemic has rigorously tested Trump's leadership and may not have helped his chances for re-election in November 2020. In addition, his response to the race riots and protests following George Floyd's death, as covered in Chapter 2, can be deemed questionable by any measure. His performance has been criticised by even his own Republican Party members, many of whom have decided to support Joe Biden in the election.

Right from the start of pandemic, Trump appeared to be defiant, perhaps copying President Bolsonaro; however, he did not realise the difference between the economies and the challenges faced by the two countries. Like Bolsonaro, he has been a great chum of Indian Prime Minister Modi. He has also been a great promotor of hydroxychloroquine to treat coronavirus and has imported huge quantities of the drug from India. The US had already received the drug by April and it was being tested on more than 1500 coronavirus patients in New York, as the US Food and Drug Administration had identified it as a possible treatment for COVID-19. (Demand for the drug had rapidly spiked after India decided to lift a ban on its export.)

On 29 August 2020, US cases were at 6.09 million, about 24.5 percent of the global coronavirus cases (about 24.89 million). Total global deaths were about 840,400, of which 185,800 (about 22 percent) had occurred in the US, with a death rate of 561 per million people.

Trump blames the high death and infection rate in the US to a high number of tests being undertaken. That may be a valid point; however, it would also be useful to take a look at other countries with a comparable test rate to assess the veracity of President Trump's claim. On 29 August 2020, the US had carried out about 80.21 million tests, with a testing rate of 242,107 tests per million people. In comparison, Russia, with 116 deaths per million, had undertaken about 35.75 million tests, with a higher testing rate of 244,968 tests per million people than the US. The UK, with 611 deaths per million, had conducted about 16.27 million tests, with a testing rate of 239,511 tests per million people.

Other countries, with a testing rate of more than 200,000 tests per million people and a much lesser death rate than the US include: Qatar (218,802 tests per million people and 70 deaths per million people), Israel (241,135 tests per million people and 97 deaths per million people), the UAE (689,773 tests per million people and 38 deaths per million people), Singapore (312,890 tests per million people and 5 deaths per million people), Bahrain (636,411 tests per million people and 111 deaths per million people), Australia (236,909 tests per million people and 23 deaths per million people), Denmark (407,270 tests per million people and 108 deaths per million people), Maldives (201,321 tests per million people and 52 deaths per million people), Luxembourg (998,982 tests per million people and 198 deaths per million people), Lithuania (231,766 tests per million people and 32 deaths per million people), Iceland (615,411 tests per million people and 29 deaths per million people), Malta (417,342 tests per million people and

23 deaths per million people, Cyprus (237,214 tests per million people and 17 deaths per million people), Cayman Island (528,750 tests per million people and 15 deaths per million people), Bermuda (672,600 tests per million people and 145 deaths per million people), Monaco (1,322,397 tests per million people and 25 deaths per million people).

In keeping with his tendency never to accept the blame for any debacle but to put it on someone else or blame procedures, Trump has claimed that gun crime will plummet in the US due to a new policy under which gun-related deaths will not be recorded. He is reported to have said, 'I have ordered for authorities to slow down the measurement of gun crime because it is adding to the number of deaths ... The more you measure gun deaths, the more people are going to die. It's as simple as that.' The National Rifle Association has reportedly backed his move, saying 'Guns don't kill people. Gun statistics kill people.'

Trump has been critical of the WHO on several counts and has refused to support any of its guidelines, including physical distancing, self-isolation and wearing face masks in public. He has accused the WHO of colluding with China, severing US ties with the organisation just as coronavirus cases have sharply jumped across the country (and around the world). The US is formally withdrawing from the WHO, with effect from July 2021. This move has drawn wide criticism from bipartisan US lawmakers, medical associations and advocacy organisations. Joe Biden has vowed to reverse the decision on his first day in office, if elected.

Trump has constantly been embroiled in allegations that he sought Russian help to be elected president and that, more recently, he has sought Chinese help to be re-elected. In 2018, according to reporting of Trump's remarks at a closed-door fundraiser in Florida, he praised Chinese President Xi Jinping after the Chinese ruling Communist Party announced that it was eliminating the two-term limit for the presidency, paving the way for President Xi to serve indefinitely. Amid cheers and applause from his supporters, Trump appeared to have wished for a similar process in the US when he said, 'He's now president for life, president for life. And he's great. And look, he was able to do that. I think it's great. Maybe we'll have to give that a shot someday.'

He is also understood to have praised President Xi for treating him 'tremendously well' during his three-day visit to China in 2017 and called him 'a great gentleman', adding 'He's the most powerful (Chinese) president in a hundred years'.

As reported in *Politico*, Trump lambasted the WHO for accepting China's assurances about the pandemic, even while, over a period of five weeks in January and February 2020 (before the US recorded its first death due to coronavirus on 1 March 2020), he touted the Chinese government on Twitter fifteen times for its transparency and hard work to defeat the coronavirus, praising and thanking President Xi in particular.

The US Navy has deployed two aircraft carriers to the strategic South China Sea to boost its presence in the region, with Republican Senator Tom Cotton saying, 'No country on China's periphery, right now, is safe from Chinese aggression' .

In addition, the US has imposed sanctions on three senior officials of the Chinese Communist Party for alleged human rights abuses against Uighurs, ethnic Kazakhs and members of other minority groups in Xinjiang. As reported by *The Guardian* on 10 July 2020, Secretary of State Mike Pompeo said: 'The United States will not stand idly by as the Chinese Communist party carries out human rights abuses ... to include forced labour, arbitrary mass detention, and forced population control, and attempts to erase their culture and Muslim faith.' China said it would impose reciprocal measures and that the US action 'marked a serious interference in China's affairs and was deeply detrimental to bilateral relations'.

Obviously, the US government is trying its best to do something 'heroic' to help Trump win re-election. China seems to be in its crosshair, the same China which Trump had praised just a few months ago. If not for the pandemic and the US's dismal performance during the last few months, everything would have been hunky-dory between the two countries and the bonhomie between the two presidents could have continued. Trump is trying hard to provoke China, as only a decisive military victory may help him in getting re-elected, but there is a significant risk in this move. Both countries are nuclear powers. Will the world witness a nuclear catastrophe and pay an unprecedented price just for the ego of two individuals, a disaster not even matched by COVID-19? The world will wait anxiously for 3 November 2020 to pass.

After President Obama, the US has undoubtedly changed a lot in the last four years during the Trump presidency. More change is anticipated whether Trump is re-elected or not — the only difference is the direction in which that change will occur over the next four years.

Leading a country is not child's play

It cannot be easy to lead and govern a country when there are many unemployed people and many hungry mouths to feed. The main issue is the growing global population. It is not easy to keep generating jobs and fuelling the economy. Hard decisions need to be taken every now and then, some of which may not be easy on some people.

All the people in any one country are never happy at the same time. You are damned if you make any hard decision that may severely impact some people and you are equally damned if you don't make it, as your hesitation or reluctance may impact many more people. To keep a country going and do the best for most people unfortunately means that some people end up becoming sacrificial. That is the truth of the matter, which is bitter of course. The fitter ones usually survive. COVID-19 has clearly proven that. The coronavirus infection rate in youth (generally younger than thirty years) has been seen to be much higher than in elderly people (generally older than sixty years) but their mortality rate has contrastingly been much lower than in older people.

The economy of a country is driven mainly by relatively younger workers. A lockdown not only puts a brake on the economy, it also impacts on jobs, leading to youth frustration and mental illness, with a much more damaging effect on the country as a whole. Taking calculated risks becomes unavoidable for world leaders. You take a calculated risk with some portion of the population for the greater good. Otherwise, a prolonged lockdown in any country has the potential to kill many more people due to hunger and starvation.

This problem especially plagues countries with a large population, for example India. The Indian government had no other viable option but to open up the country, gradually in stages, after imposing one of world's strictest lockdowns for several weeks. India imposed a country-wide lockdown on 25 March 2020 and announced plans to reopen the country on 30 May. Understandably the cost is also high, as infection rates suddenly started rising after the country being reopened.

At the time India went into lockdown, it had 519 confirmed cases and ten deaths. By the time it reopened, the case tally had passed 173,000, with 4971 deaths. It added nearly 8000 new cases on the day it reopened alone.

As per *Trading Economics*, India's unemployment rate was at 8.7 percent at the beginning of the lockdown, alarmingly spiking to 23.5 percent in the months of April and May, and falling to about 11 percent in June after the country was reopened.

On 10 July 2020, infections in India were reported to be close to 800,000, with more than 21,000 deaths. That is, in the six weeks since it reopened, India recorded a fivefold increase in coronavirus infections and deaths, while unemployment more than halved, proving there is a significant cost to be paid to keep people employed and the country running. Unfortunately, that cost is 'human lives'. The stark truth is staring us in the face — to save the most, you can't help but sacrifice some.

It all boils down to the management of the virus, as prolonged lockdowns are no solution. Even in Melbourne, due to a recent sudden spike in infections, the government had to close the Victorian borders on 8 July and reimpose a lockdown on five million people for the following six weeks. A hard decision indeed but was there any other option? No. The lockdown will impact on all other Australian states and is understood to be costing the Australian economy about A$1 billion per week. Australia being a much wealthier country (per capita) than India, with about 25 million people (about 1.8 percent of India's population), may be able to afford the lockdown, but India can't do so beyond what it has already done for nearly two months. The Indian prime minister does not have the same luxury as the premier of the Australian state of Victoria. In Australia, the lockdown is a state decision and decided by the state premier and not by the Australian prime minister. The same is the case with the Brazilian president who decided against the lockdown and all for valid reasons.

Brazil's s unemployment rate was at 12.2 percent in March and peaked at 12.9 percent in May. Had President Bolsonaro imposed a countrywide lockdown over the same period, the unemployment rate in his country would also have spiked about 3 to 4 times and been much higher than India's peak of 23.5 percent. Bolsonaro may be criticised by some but has done the best for his country and carried out a delicate balancing act between two extreme scenarios, one of which — total paralysis of the country, with unmanageably high unemployment, fear and depression — would not be acceptable to any leader at any point in time. It would, therefore, be quite unfair to criticise him. As the pandemic has not yet disappeared from the world, it is way too early to judge him and his performance or the performance of any other world leader. Pandemic has proven we human are prone to err and misjudge situation despite our best intents.

About six decades ago, US President John F. Kennedy in his inaugural address on 20 January 1961 reminded people of their civic duty and responsibility towards their country: 'Ask not what your country can do for you — ask what you can do for your country'. Not many people realise their responsibility towards their country, however. After all, a country is what people make it to be. People want everything — a job, freedom and a good lifestyle. But everything has a cost. Things don't happen by miracles; miracles have to be created, especially in times like the present.

People, especially the younger section of the population, must support their leaders and be prepared to temporarily sacrifice their comforts and freedoms — to go to the pub or public parks or beaches or just to roam around in the streets — when they are called upon to do so by their leaders. This will not only help to save their own lives but also help to save the lives of elderly people who are much more prone to die due to infection. It is a social contract, a social responsibility, which must be fulfilled and carried out by everyone. Nevertheless, it is a tricky balancing act between supporting economy and protecting people's lives. No one solution fits all economics and all communities, what may suit one country may not necessarily suit another country. On the one hand, we must support our leaders and do whatever we are told. But all things must be done carefully, without risking our life or the lives of others, whilst keep the economy going. We are indeed living a 'new' normal where things cannot be same as the 'old' normal. Our outdoor and social lives must be lived responsibly, with not much scope for complacency.

Deciphering the unusual human behaviour during the pandemic

Humans around the world have exhibited behaviour during the pandemic which at first may appear to be bizarre yet is no different from our normal behaviour. In situations where they feel threatened, most humans think and behave alike and the layers of sophistication come off one by one.

Humans have responded to the coronavirus in a more or less similar manner, across all countries, races, colours and socioeconomic classes, thereby proving that we belong to ONE and the same human race and are not very different to one another. Although the scientific field has already proved that humans share the same 99.9 percent of DNA, the human ego has continued to create divisions along the lines of religion, race, caste, gender, colour and class, proactively causing and nourishing strife in the human world. These deliberately created divisions benefit a minority of powerful and resourceful humans from the wealthy and privileged class, and are exploited for all material reasons, without any respite whatsoever for the significant majority of disadvantaged and underprivileged humans.

In the beginning of the pandemic, many people around the globe panicked and resorted to panic buying and hoarding of long-life food, basic medicines and other general household provisions, particularly toilet paper, as if the world was suddenly coming to an apocalyptic end. All this happened despite repeated assurances from their governments that there was enough for all people and that they should not panic. This behaviour disadvantaged many people who were left with nothing on the shelves. This panic behaviour was triggered by a heightened sense of insecurity and a total distrust in fellow humans and in government. Across Australia, shelves suddenly became empty where once there was toilet paper, flour, pasta and noodles, mincemeat, hand sanitiser, long-life milk and many other items. Many people bought deep freezers to store perishable food items.

Australia — panic buying, mass hoarding and xenophobia
Right at the beginning of the pandemic, in April 2020, as reports of anti-Chinese (and anti-Asian) racism made news across the world, ABC News reported that 'foreigners in China are also increasingly reporting incidents of hostility and discrimination'. Reportedly, a comic from China depicted a dark-skinned man in a rubbish bin. In the comic, foreigners in China were targeted for 'disposal' for 'publicly praising

China but secretly posting anti-China opinions online, scamming Chinese women into providing sex and money, and attacking health workers after testing positive for coronavirus'.

In May 2020, ABC News reported that, since the start of the pandemic, Asian-Australians had been 'verbally and physically assaulted, refused service, received death threats and had their properties damaged'. The Australian government had urged Australians to report and call out racist attacks when they see them. On 7 June, *The Sydney Morning Herald* reported on a survey showing that, since 2 April 2020, almost 400 racist attacks in Australia against Asian-Australians had occurred. The survey also revealed that about 90 percent of racist incidents 'were not being reported to police and the vast majority were perpetrated by strangers in public places'.

In early April, I was a witness to one such incident in a Perth store, in which an Anglo-Australian woman, in her late sixties or early seventies, was heard admonishing a younger woman wearing a face mask, seemingly of South-East Asian or Chinese background, against buying long-life milk. Speaking in a mild but firm tone, the elderly lady said: 'At least leave it for us retirees; we can't afford the fresh milk'. The younger woman responded politely, 'But I have my children to feed'. I walked quickly past them and did not hear the rest of the exchange, but a moment later the younger woman defiantly end the conversation in a louder voice, saying 'None of your business'.

In May, the United Nations Secretary-General, Antonio Guterres, summed up the issue and called for an 'all-out effort' to end the 'tsunami of hate and xenophobia' sparked by the coronavirus pandemic. As reported on SBS News on 8 May, Guterres said: 'The pandemic continues to unleash a tsunami of hate and xenophobia, scapegoating and scare-mongering. Anti-foreigner sentiment has surged online and in the streets. Anti-Semitic conspiracy theories have spread and COVID-19-related anti-Muslim attacks have occurred.' He claimed migrants and refugees had been 'vilified as a source of the virus and then denied access to medical treatment' and that 'journalists, whistle-blowers, health professionals, aid workers and human rights defenders are being targeted simply for doing their jobs'. He also condemned 'contemptible memes' that suggested older people, some of the most vulnerable to the virus, 'are also the most expendable'. He appealed for 'an all-out effort to end hate speech globally' and singled out educational institutions to help teach 'digital literacy' to young people, whom he called 'captive and potentially despairing audiences', and called on 'the media, especially social media companies, to do much more to flag and remove racist, misogynist and other harmful content'.

The *South China Morning Post* reported on 30 May that two white Australian teenagers, one carrying a knife, had spewed racial abuse on two young Vietnamese-Australian sisters in an unprovoked attack, calling them 'Asian whores', 'Asian dogs' and 'Asian sluts', before 'spitting' on their face at a pedestrian road-crossing in the suburb of Marrickville in New South Wales.

SBS Punjabi news reported at the end of June that a 35-year-old, turban-wearing international student from India had allegedly been targeted in a 'racially-motivated' incident at an Adelaide train station. He had been approached by an aggressive-looking woman who asked him about his nationality. Initially, he had ignored her but when she again asked him in a louder voice, he had said he was from India. Thereafter, she kept on swearing and making racial comments against his community and nationality before ordering him: 'Go back to your f**king country, you brought coronavirus here'.

While panic buying and hoarding alongside xenophobia was seen in Australia, India witnessed issues of its own kind.

Some disturbing stories from India during COVID-19 pandemic

The following sections illustrate some ugly shades of life and strange human behaviours in India that one would not normally expect in this country of nearly 1.4 billion humans who are fighting to survive the pandemic.

The crisis of migrant workers in India

In an unprecedented move, Indian Railways announced the suspension of all its passenger services across the nation from midnight of 22 March to midnight of 31 March 2020, allowing only goods trains to move during that period. Described as the 'transport lifeline of the nation', the 175-year-old, government-owned Indian Railways is the world's fourth-largest railway network, with a route length of 68,155 kilometres. In the fiscal year ending March 2019, it carried 8.44 billion passengers and transported 1.23 billion tonnes of freight, on more than 70,000 passenger coaches and more than 11,000 locomotives. It runs 13,523 passenger trains daily, covering 7321 stations across India.

The nationwide lockdown imposed huge economic costs on the country, throwing millions of people out of work, especially migrant workers with meagrely paid jobs, and putting food supply chains at risk. The countrywide suspension of train services came after hundreds of migrant workers across India had started leaving metro cities in hordes to go back to their hometowns via trains, as reported by *India Today*. But as the lockdown continued for about two months, millions of people, especially migrant workers – from mostly rural and regional areas – were stranded and had to make their own way home, which involved walking on foot for hundreds of kilometres, or cycling, or hitchhiking on two-wheeled scooters, bullock carts or crowded vans and trucks. Fathers carried their children on their shoulders and women carried their meagre belongings on their heads, all determined to reach home. There are stories of mothers and daughters driving their two-wheeled scooters for thousands of kilometres to bring back their children or parents.

Many people walked along railway tracks to return home, as the railway tracks provide the shortest distances over ground. Many people, young and old, died due to hunger, thirst and exhaustion while walking long distances in the hot sun. Many pregnant women delivered babies while travelling.

On 8 May, sixteen exhausted migrant workers who were sleeping on the tracks in the state of Maharashtra were run over. Perhaps they had not been aware that freight trains were still moving. They had walked thirty-six kilometres before falling asleep on the tracks. A week later in Auraiya in Uttar Pradesh, twenty-seven returning migrant workers were killed when two trucks carrying workers collided.

National Geographic has reported that the coronavirus pandemic has left many of India's poor without jobs, food or a way to get home, and many migrant workers fleeing India's cities complained: 'They treat us like stray dogs'. The following excerpts from *National Geographic*'s article illustrate these stories as well as the overall condition of the poor in India:

- Five men had left Jaipur on bicycles to try to reach Gopalganj in Bihar, about 960 kilometres away. The men brought with them only what they could fit on their bicycles. They had cycled 600 kilometres over five days, often through the night, until they were too exhausted to continue. 'We slept for just two nights,' said one of them, 'We carried dry snacks and bought and ate cucumbers on the way.'

- A 23-year-old migrant worker paid a truck driver almost four days' worth of wages to stand with 108 others in the back of a truck travelling from Aligarh in Uttar Pradesh to Patna, the capital of Bihar. The police intercepted the truck and placed its human cargo in quarantine at an isolation centre in Lucknow.

- Of the estimated 139 million internal migrants working for daily wages, many farmers who become daily wage workers to pay off debts or earn money for seeds and farming equipment. They work in the informal economy, unprotected by unions, with their wages and benefits up to their employers' discretion.

- Nearly two-thirds of India's 1.4 billion people live in rural areas, where the economy has struggled. Back-to-back droughts in 2014 and 2015 were followed by the 2016 cash crisis when the government suddenly banned 80 percent of bills in circulation in an effort to crack down on corruption.
- Suicide rates in rural areas are high: according to the National Crime Records Bureau, 10,349 farmers committed suicide in 2018 — an average of more than twenty-eight deaths a day. The return of migrant workers during the pandemic could push 400 million informal workers in India into deeper poverty, heightening the risk for suicide.
- As of 6 May 2020, the unemployment rate in rural India was at 24.3 percent, up from around 16 percent in April.

Jean Dreze, a Belgian-born Indian developmental economist and an expert on food security and hunger, told *National Geographic*, 'The lockdown and return of the migrant workers are going to create a huge pool of unemployed workers in rural areas … If the government doesn't extend the Public Distribution System and generate more work under the Mahatma Gandhi National Rural Employment Act soon, we are looking at a wave of extreme poverty in rural areas … The rural crisis has not yet unfolded, it is due in the next few weeks, and it might be catastrophic.'

India had partially reopened its rail network by 12 May to enable migrant workers to return home, just a day after recording its second-highest daily infection rate at that time. On 25 June 2020, however, regular train services were suspended again, till 12 August.

At the beginning of April, Indian Railways had announced plans to convert some 20,000 coaches into isolation wards for COVID-19 patients, to bring relief to the country's healthcare system. Each coach would accommodate sixteen patients, with space for a doctor and nurse's station and storage of medical supplies. In mid-June the BBC reported that India was converting 'another 500 railway carriages to create 8000 more beds for coronavirus patients in Delhi'.

As per an ABC report, dated 31 August 2020, as city-based employers in India are struggling to find workers, migrant workers are known to have said that they would like to 'starve' rather than face 'humiliation' of returning to cities, as they 'will not forget being branded COVID-19 carriers'.

Islamophobia

India has also been in the news because of Islamophobia in the country.

A Muslim congregation in Delhi in mid-March reportedly sparked a new wave of coronavirus infections. More than 300 positive cases were traced to an event of Tablighi Jamaat, a 100-year old Islamic missionary movement, which was attended by over 3000 people from India and abroad, including Indonesia, Malaysia, Bangladesh and Kyrgyzstan. Indian police evacuated 2300 people from the Delhi venue and sent 1800 of them to various quarantine centres. Islamophobic memes circulated on social media, one showing China as the 'producer' and Muslims as the 'distributors' of the virus. Though there were restrictions on gatherings, the Indian government had declared at the time of the event that COVID-19 was 'not a health emergency'. The lockdown came into force ten days after the event.

The Islamophobia unnerved Indian Muslims as it had come soon after weeks-long religious riots in Delhi following the controversial Citizenship Amendment Act (CAA), which was championed by Prime Minister Modi's BJP government. Many people in India and internationally deemed the CAA to be discriminatory. Protests against the proposed legislation had erupted at the end of 2019 when the CAA was passed by the Parliament of India on 11 December 2019 after amending Citizenship Act of 1955. The CAA allowed Indian citizenship for those illegal immigrants from Pakistan, Bangladesh and Afghanistan who had entered India before December 2014 and belonged only to Hindu, Sikh, Buddhist, Jain, Parsi and Christian faiths, thereby excluding illegal immigrants belonging to the Muslim faith.

In February 2020, Delhi was gripped with anti-Muslim mob violence after supporters of the ruling party attacked protesters against the CAA. Sections of Indian news media remained embroiled in divisive debates even while the world was coming to terms with the pandemic. The day before the lockdown, police cleared out the last vestiges of the anti-CAA protests in New Delhi led by Muslims.

After a government spokesperson publicly linked a spike in coronavirus cases to the Tablighi Jamaat event, a large section of the Indian media accused Indian Muslims of spreading coronavirus, leading to further vilification of Indian Muslims. Kavita Krishnan, an activist, told Al Jazeera: 'The media chose not to ask the government why foreign participants were not tested at airports, [and] why Delhi and the central government and police agencies gave permission for the gathering, which was denied by the Maharashtra government'. Shahid Siddiqui, a political analyst, said: 'The media are distorting facts to suggest that every Muslim belongs to Tablighi Jamaat, every Muslim is responsible for the coronavirus and coronavirus is a synonym for Muslim'. In addition, he termed the participants of the Islamic conference as 'irresponsible, callous and foolish'.

On 19 April, the Organisation of Islamic Cooperation expressed concern about anti-Muslim sentiment and Islamophobia in India, following which Indian government authorities repeatedly advised against stigmatisation of Muslims as coronavirus spreaders. Al Jazeera quoted a senior health journalist who said that, in everyday media briefings, the health and home ministries actively blamed the Muslim community for the spread of coronavirus in India, seemingly following a pattern of blaming those who get infected instead of taking humane and scientific remedial measures. Yet police and other government agencies had reportedly been countering or correcting tweets by news organisations and their representatives that stoked anti-Muslim sentiment on social media and in the mainstream media.

The Organisation for World Peace has reported that Islamophobia in India, which had surged since the outbreak of coronavirus, is threatening religious cohesion in Nepal. Muslims make up about 4 percent of the population in Nepal and have been living peacefully for centuries with the majority Hindu population, 'but India's right-wingers are trying hard to change that', according to a *Foreign Policy* article.

Stigmatisation of medical and airline professionals
The pandemic days have witnessed the stigmatisation of doctors and other health professionals, and airline professionals. Incidents of attacks and abuse across India have been reported by *Al Jazeera*. In one case, police were accused of beating a delivery driver carrying medicines. The BBC has also reported that many healthcare workers in India have been attacked, with doctors being spat at and chased away from their homes, and patients directing abusive and vulgar language towards female nurses. Physicians and their families have been ostracised by their neighbours because of their exposure to patients infected with coronavirus. In one video, a mob was shown throwing stones at two female doctors wearing personal protective equipment.

A doctor in the western city of Surat said her neighbours had blocked her at the entrance to her apartment building and threatened 'consequences' if she continued to work. Doctors at the All India Institute of Medical Sciences sent a letter to the government appealing for help after health workers were forced out of their homes by panicked landlords and housing societies: 'Many doctors are stranded on the roads with all their luggage, nowhere to go, across the country.'

Many airline and airport staff, required to work to evacuate Indians stuck overseas and to manage key cargo deliveries, reportedly have also been threatened. An Air India flight attendant said her neighbours had threatened to evict her from her apartment, saying she would 'infect everyone'. A colleague of hers had been forced out of her home and was now living with her parents. The Indian Commercial Pilots'

Association told *AFP* that the organisation had received more than fifty complaints from airline crew: 'Airline staffers are being stopped from entering their own residential premises by security guards.'

Indian doctors have complained of being reprimanded and intimidated by authorities for reporting shortages of safety kits. Doctors fear an inadequate supply of PPE makes them vulnerable to getting infected. In Indian-administered Kashmir, doctors were also threatened with 'strict action' and up to six months in jail for speaking out about the government's alleged failures. With 1.2 million doctors, the doctor–population ratio in India is 1:1456, whereas the WHO recommends 1:1000.

Many stories continue to come out of India, though not necessarily reported in the media. For fear of being stigmatised, many families choose to hide and quietly quarantine an infected member of the family till the patient does not need hospitalisation, which means the reported infection cases are possibly much less than the actual number of cases.

A delayed cremation cost several lives

In a sad case, on 18 June 2020 two men, aged thirty-five and forty, wearing PPE died of dehydration and fatigue on the bank of the River Tawi in Sidhra area of Jammu district. Reportedly, the men collapsed in the river while waiting for the cremation of their 65-year-old relative, who had died of COVID-19.

The family of the victims accused the administration of refusing their request to immediately perform the last rites for the COVID-19 victim at Shakti Nagar crematorium, which is a preferred cremation ground for the community at Jammu. The administrative delay reportedly resulted in the men becoming dehydrated after they carried the victim from the hospital where he died, wearing the PPE under the scorching sun of Jammu on that day. For religious reasons, Indian Hindus prefer to cremate a dead body before sunset on the day of the death itself.

Bizarre acts of criminals and police

In early July, eight policemen were allegedly gunned down by a notorious killer, Vikas Dubey (fifty), in the state of Uttar Pradesh, ruled by BJP, India's ruling party. After a frantic countrywide hunt, during which five of Dubey's associates, including his bodyguard, were killed, the alleged killer reportedly turned himself in to the police in a temple in the adjacent state of Madhya Pradesh. However, a day later, as per the police account, he was gunned down by police in equally dramatic circumstances when the police vehicle in which he was being transported back to Uttar Pradesh overturned on a wet road and he had tried to escape.

Dubey was accused of more than sixty killings, attempted murders and a number of other crimes, such as extortion and robbery. In 2001, he is alleged to have chased Santosh Shukla, Minister of State and a member of BJP, into a police station and shot him dead, but got out on bail. Obviously, he had strong political patronage. All twenty-five cops who were witnesses to the murder turned hostile, as reported by *NewsBytes.*

The entire episode involving first the killing of the eight policemen and then the death of the alleged killer himself, without any trial, is extremely intriguing but not uncommon. One question is, had he not allegedly killed those policemen, would he still be free? How did he operate freely if he had allegedly killed so many people? Was it a revenge killing by the police, possibly staged? Did he name his political masters?

As stated in the *Guardian*'s report, within hours of Indian television channels showing the images of Dubey's dead body, 'human rights lawyers and activists alleged that police had killed Dubey to prevent him revealing his connections with powerful people'. Priyanka Gandhi, a senior opposition Congress party leader, called for a judicial inquiry into the killing and alleged that the people 'protecting' him were still free.

This case illustrates how the police in India typically operate and how they deal with alleged criminals.

Despite his notoriety as a ruthless killer, Dubey reportedly had built considerable local political links over the past two decades. The Chief Minister of Uttar Pradesh, Yogi Adityanath, who belongs to the BJP, has publicly endorsed police killings as a 'deterrent' to crime and pledged to root out crime from the state. His tenure has been characterised with a rise in the number of deaths of criminals in police shootouts. *The Guardian* sums it up: '"Encounter killings" have a long history in India. For decades they were staged to bypass India's judicial system when police battled armed separatist movements in West Bengal, Punjab, Kashmir and elsewhere.'

Political horse-trading

The Indian political circus has continued to be defined and characterised by horse-trading even during the pandemic. Politicians, especially the younger generation, have been seen to look after their personal political interests and power ambitions much more than their loyalty to the people who voted them in or the party that nourished them and gave them the ticket to stand in the elections.

Two such seemingly identical cases, defining a kind of pattern, came to the fore during the last few months, in which the old guards of India's Congress party were challenged by younger challengers, first in Madhya Pradesh and then in Rajasthan (in July 2020).

The two younger challengers, Jyotiraditya Scindia and Sachin Pilot — both erstwhile deputy chief ministers in the two states, which are ruled by the Congress party, are sons of two close associates of Rajiv Gandhi (1944–1991) who were also senior ministers in his government in the eighties. As India's youngest prime minister at the age of forty, Rajiv Gandhi took office in 1984 after the assassination of his mother, Prime Minister Indira Gandhi.

Madhavrao Scindia came from a royal family and was railways

minister in the Rajiv Gandhi ministry. He died in a plane crash at the age of fifty-six in 2001. Squadron Leader Rajesh Pilot, was a former Indian Air Force officer who joined politics in 1979 under the influence of Rajiv Gandhi, his friend. He died in a car accident at the age of fifty-five in 2000.

As reported by *India Today* on 20 March 2020, the Congress party lost another state when Madhya Pradesh Chief Minister Kamal Nath resigned ahead of a floor test in the state assembly because he did not have the required numbers, accusing the BJP of 'conspiring against his government'. At that time, a few other Indian states — Punjab, Rajasthan, Maharashtra, Jharkhand, Chhattisgarh and the Union Territory of Puducherry — were also ruled by the Congress party. Raising a finger towards the BJP, Nath said that the people of Madhya Pradesh would not forgive these 'greedy and rebellious' people and that, 'My government was able to prove majority in the house on three occasions. The BJP could not tolerate it. So, it conspired with a maharaj (Jyotiraditya Scindia) and 22 greedy MLAs and planned to topple my government.' Jyotiraditya Scindia joined the BJP and was given the ticket to the upper house of India's parliament. He is expected to get a ministerial post in the Modi government later in the term.

About four months later, the Congress government in Rajasthan was also shaken by a similar challenge from its deputy chief minister, Sachin Pilot. On 14 July, *The Hindu* reported that the Congress party had accused Pilot of colluding with the BJP in its conspiracy to topple the state government. In addition, two other ministers affiliated with him in the 'rebel camp' were dropped from the state cabinet. Reportedly, the BJP was going for the kill now. *Firstpost* reported that former Rajasthan Chief Minister Vasundhara Raje was meeting the BJP MLAs in the day. Congress alleged that 'there is nothing in Sachin's hands; it is the BJP which is running the show'.

So the power saga continues in India, a country of 1.4 billion souls, while the majority poor as well as the many not-so-poor people continue to fight coronavirus and the common challenges of life. The politicians live in a power world of their own, remote from the lives of common people.

In a nutshell

India is the seventh-largest country by land area in the world and second-largest country by population, with nearly 1.4 billion people, which cannot be, and does not seem to be, easy to manage. India is undoubtedly suffering from serious issues caused by humans alone, and exacerbated by the ever-growing population, which has grown fourfold since independence from the British seventy-three years ago.

Religion continues to play a significant role, much more than ever before — in all fields of life, including Indian politics.

The Indian democratic system, in its most misused, abused and flawed form, on the back of a majority vote system, enables politicians to taste disproportionate power and, once they taste it, they know how to exploit the system itself. The country remains as it was before, albeit with a few breadcrumbs being thrown every now and then to the voters to entice them to keep casting their votes.

The wealthy and professionals know how to lead their lives, with or without a government. In most matters of life and living, they don't practically need any government except to the extent of providing some manageable protection against opportunistic criminals, and other internal and external threats. It is only the significantly poorer who need benevolent politicians to turn their fate around, but that is a dream for most. The poorer lot are the sacrificial pawns direly needed for vote gathering, beyond which they are perceived and treated as commodities by politicians and as 'others' by the wealthy. The poorer lot pray to different gods than the wealthy and powerful.

One can only wonder, amid so much political idolatry, chicanery and adultery in the great Indian political circus, how politicians would actually find the time or the will to help the poor. It is common

knowledge that most of the eligible voters from the upper socioeconomic class don't actually bother to queue at the polling booths to cast
their vote at the ballot box. In essence, therefore, Indian democracy
depends on the poor but, ironically, they are the ones who struggle with
life every day and are not looked after well other than being fed with
breadcrumbs. The wealthy and the influential know how to manage
the politicians and, in turn, the politicians know how to exploit the
poor who vote them in.

Voting is not compulsory in India. In the last two general elections,
the voter turnout was reported to be in the order of 67 percent, meaning
that about one-third of eligible voters don't bother to vote. A majority
of the votes cast are from the people belonging to the lower economic
class who strive at the ballot box to aspire, dream and pray for a change
that may one day turn their lives around. How long will the goose that
lays the golden eggs survive? The goose is underfed, hungry and being
fleeced continuously. It is only a matter of time till the goose either dies
or wakes up.

The current government is in its second term. The last few months
have reflected its work over the last five years in very bold and clear
terms. The current government seems to be in a hurry to redefine India
and fast-track the fulfilment of the dreams of some influential and
visionary leaders of the past to regain the lost glory and culture of the
land, believed to be lost more than half a millennium ago.

India is a multicultural, multi-religious and multi-ethnic country, in
which Dalits (scheduled caste), scheduled tribes and other disadvantaged classes comprise around 30 percent of the population and minorities (Muslims, Sikhs, Christians and Buddhists) around 20 percent.
Hindus belonging to the upper four castes comprise about 50 percent.

The effects of demonetisation in 2016 — introduced for the explicit
reason of crushing corruption and militancy in the country — and,
more recently, decisions in which politico-religious thought has
clearly played a significant role, have been clearly visible in the last few

months. Such decisions include the clearance by the Supreme Count of India to rebuild Ram Minder in Ayodhya (2019); removal of the semi-autonomous status of the erstwhile State of Jammu and Kashmir, followed by its division and downgrading to a union territory (2019); and the introduction of the Citizenship Amendment Act (2019).

About five decades ago, India and China had comparable economies. Since then, the Chinese economy and defence funding have grown five times as much as India. While China is marching on in 2020 as strongly as it has been over the past decades, with a unified vision and purpose, India is still in a process of discovering itself and seemingly embroiled in correcting perceived historical lapses about its identity, glory and culture.

The following excerpts from a report by SOS Children's villages, retrieved on 11 July 2020, sums up the condition of a significant majority of Indians from across all social and religious divisions:

- Two-thirds of Indians live in poverty and a third of the total Indian population lives in extreme poverty, which makes the Indian subcontinent one of the poorest in the world.
- India has one of the highest child mortality rates in the world, with about 1.4 million children dying each year in India before reaching their fifth birthday. Most deaths are caused due to pneumonia, malaria, diarrheal diseases and chronic malnutrition.
- Child labour is prohibited by law. However, 12.5 million children between the ages of five and fourteen are reported to be working. Aid agencies estimate about 65 million children between six and fourteen years do not go to school but work in the field, in factories, in quarries, in private households and in prostitution to support their families.
- According to UNICEF, about a quarter of children in India have no access to education. The number of children excluded from school is higher among girls than boys. Although women

and men are treated equally under Indian law, girls and women, especially in the lower social caste, are considered inferior and are oppressed by their fathers, brothers and husbands. Without education, the chance of finding a living wage from employment in India is virtually hopeless.

Some strange and typical human behaviours

The good, the bad and the ugly are inherent to all humans, labelling some aspects as 'strange' or 'bizarre' suggests some exceptional behaviours that are not common.

The following five vignettes are true but the names have been changed or concealed to protect the identity of the main characters of these stories. The purpose of including these stories is to support my assertion that no one human can be called solely a good person or bad or ugly. Humans exhibit all shades from time to time, in varying proportions. Their situations and circumstances bring out dormant shades of their general character, which not only surprises and embarrasses them in hindsight, but also those who know them closely.

Humans are bundles of everything. They can be angels as well as demons; the difference is marked only by the space they are thrown into by the vagaries of life. Different humans react differently to threats and challenges and opportunities. It is best to forgive them for their bad and ugly behaviours during their testing times. Forgiveness brings healing to both victims and the accused. Without forgiveness, the guilt in the accused and the hurt in the victims consume them in a perpetual struggle and no one gets liberated. The fortunate ones ask for forgiveness and also forgive in return.

A case of divide and rule

A few years ago, Rachel was (falsely) accused of making a 'sinister remark' against a close relative. The serious accusation, which was made without her knowledge, surfaced a couple of years after she was alleged to have said it. During those years, many of their common relatives remained cold and distanced themselves from her, while she kept wondering about the sudden negative change in their behaviour.

By sheer luck, one day Rachel came to know about the accusation. Initially, she was stunned and then, after gathering herself but still in utter disbelief, she pleaded innocence. However, whatever she said fell on deaf ears and the relationships remained strained to some extent, as the accusing party chose to stick to their belief. She was alleged to have made the remark during an informal, cursory conversation with a common relative. Yet that relative flatly denied having any knowledge about it when she asked for clarification.

Obviously, one of the three individuals had lied and continued to lie. At the time, Rachel was actively helping one of the two parties involved. She had never been able to understand why it all happened. Who lied and why? Was it a deliberate act of 'divide and rule' by one person or just an exhibition of another shade of the enigmatic human character that illustrates human fallibility?

Sadistic social slander

Bill was a victim of a vicious, well-coordinated, social slander. About three years ago, Blossom, a close relative, suddenly started sending him messages with abusive language, threatening to take him to court for defamation. Bill was accused of including some factual information about Blossom's family in his book, which had reportedly offended the extended family members.

For Bill, as the author of a memoir, inclusion of that information was necessary in the context of an extremely difficult phase of his childhood, which had introduced him to many harsh realities of life. What had happened was common knowledge among all their common relatives and fell well within the range of ordinary habits, behaviours and mindsets of people from their social background. More seriously, however, he was also accused of not glorifying the role played by

Blossom's family in his life in the same way as he had highlighted the role of some of their other relatives.

Out of sheer rage, the accusing family tried to sabotage Bill's book launch. They visited the publisher's office a day before the scheduled launch at an important public event. By sheer chance, Bill was there at the time. They threatened him and the publisher with dire consequences, which the latter handled with a cool and mature head, dismissing the first accusation as insubstantial or trivial. As for the second accusation, the family failed to produce any evidence. When asked if they had really read the book, they replied in the negative. When politely challenged about the basis of their accusation, they said their other relatives, who had apparently read the book, had urged them to trash it and punish Bill for defaming them. At that point, the faces of several relatives came to Bill's mind; most of them had immensely benefited from his family and, for years, had (in hindsight, undeservingly) enjoyed extremely warm hospitality at his parents' home.

After failing to defend their allegations and losing face in the publisher's office, Blossom and her three family members looked defeated, stunned and jittery. Despite that, before leaving, they still had the audacity to ask the publisher for a formal invitation to attend the book launch the next day. Being apprehensive of any further drama at the high-profile public event, the publisher decided against inviting them. Bill felt sorry for them and deeply sad, as he had always considered them as his flesh and blood.

On the whole, it was a sad situation. Bill cut a sorry figure in his publisher's office. He felt highly embarrassed at such unimaginable behaviour of his relatives. From that moment, he distanced himself from them and all their extended family. When analysed carefully, it looked like a third party had influenced them against him. Or, perhaps, they themselves had given that third party some feelers against him. In any case, it seemed the accusing party on the whole had acted with reckless disregard for Bill's sensitivities.

A sacrificial commodity

About three decades ago, when Boy was an inexperienced young man in his early twenties, on a Sunday afternoon a couple of elderly relatives visited his home to get his opinion about the suitability of a certain individual for their daughter in marriage. Incidentally, a few days earlier, at an interstate wedding party, a close relative from his wife's side, who happened to be a well-respected gentleman of good standing, had cursorily discussed this individual in confidence with Boy, which had not left a very good impression about the person in Boy's mind. Before that moment, however, Boy had never heard of or interacted with him.

On the basis of what had been fed to him, Boy did not approve of the soliciting prospective groom's offer to marry the daughter. Sadly, Boy was not mature enough or aware of the worldly ways of showing political correctness in such matters. He narrated the whole story to them, i.e. when and where he had seen this person first, albeit from a distance and without interaction, and how the other gentleman had described him.

Boy was extremely naïve at that time. He had no clue that the two visiting relatives were there only to tick a box, out of mere formality and political correctness, and that a decision had perhaps already been taken to accept the offer of the soliciting prospective groom. Interestingly, the relative who had earlier described the individual at the wedding party, and was himself about seven years older than Boy, had approved the engagement. As if that was not surprising enough, Boy was flabbergasted to learn that his disapproval had become the talk of the town. A few days later, an elderly colleague asked him at his workplace about the reasons underlying his committal of the 'sin of disapproval'.

Not surprisingly, the language and behaviour of the prospective groom was cold and abrasive towards Boy on the day of the engagement. Subsequently, all the family members and relatives reflected similar behaviour towards Boy on the wedding day. They never became friends. In hindsight, Boy was compromised by his own relatives and he never understood why. Why did they give in and appease the person, sacrificing Boy in the process? During the past three decades, no one ever took responsibility for what happened then. No one ever apologised or even bothered to explain to him why his opinions, provided on trust and in confidence, were aired to the public? Boy was left to reconcile with another dark shade of the human character.

A new life

Early morning on that day, Patience came out of bed and started combing her hair, half-intoxicated by the feeling of love. She just had stepped into the next phase of her life — a new life for her with the prince of her life who was still lying in the bed, with his eyes closed or perhaps sleeping. Birds chirping outside were adding to the music of her life. She felt nothing but love inside and outside — love is in the air, as they say. Patience even stole looks at her own reflection in the mirror; maybe, she was shy or afraid of losing the treasure of her love. She had her prince, who was the first and the only love of her life, with whom she was going to live through the rest of her life, a new life. She had everything that she had wished for in her new life! She wondered at how her parents had named her Patience.

As Patience imagined herself rocking in the air with her prince, he got up and gave her a tight hug from behind, which further elated her. The next moment, he showed her a picture of his ex-girlfriend, seemingly still in love with her. Patience crashed and her dreams of making her prince the king of her life and her aspirations of having a happy family too crashed. As she crashed, the boarding wedding guests started knocking at her bedroom door to greet her. She asked herself, 'What are you going to do, Patience? Is your name only a name or is it a virtue? You have just signed in for a lifetime of test, where your virtue will be tested.' She started preparing once again for a new life.

During the day, Patience interacted with the relatives of her beau, who was not her prince anymore, with civil and polite manners, controlling her emotions. Not a single tear rolled down her face but she tactfully redirected her tears inwards, as she was getting drowned in a storm of emotions. On their very first meeting, she recalled having told him very clearly that he should make an independent decision and not come under any family pressure to marry her. He categorically told her that there was no other woman in his life. She wondered how this new person had come into the picture now and why had the prince announced it at a time when they were about to start their new lives together?

Prince had proved his wisdom, though conniving, by not giving out a whiff of his earlier life to Patience till Patience formally, legally and socially, joined him. Prince had also been clever by lying to her, which transformed into ugliness by breaking the faith of an innocent trusting heart, giving Patience a lifetime of unhealable wound that she could never show to anyone but which would potentially kill her in time. It didn't matter whether she continued her life with him or is she left him; it didn't matter whether he apologised and abandoned the second woman, Patience was transformed at the onset of her new life, her real world had turned out to be different to what she had imagined to be.

A selfish and callous woman

Jemima was the apple of her parents' eyes. She was their first surviving child after they had lost four male children, one after the other, before any of the children had reached twelve years of age. Her heartbroken mother, Dorothy, had penanced before a deity for six months and begged for the survival of her children, after which Jemima was born. Seemingly, her mother's penance and her father's prayers had paid off.

Her father, Sherman — an upright, dedicated and passionate teacher of repute — remained busy mostly with teaching work at school, part-time tutoring and other regular household chores on the weekend when he would be at home. He had no time for socialising or gossip.

Due to his transferable government job, at times he would be away from the family for weeks or sometimes months. Normally, he worked eighteen hours a day, seven days a week.

After Jemima's birth, her parents bore three more children, a son and two daughters. Pretty and witty, Jemima grew to be a wise child, though a little pampered. She was loved and adored by everyone — her parents and all their relatives. She did well in her studies and graduated to be a teacher, following the footsteps of her illustrious father.

Sherman had great faith in his daughter and respected her worldly wisdom and street smarts. Her first transferable government teaching job took her to a hill station, about six to seven hours drive from home. She took up a makeshift residence at the place of her first posting. Soon she met a handsome engineer who was also posted at the same place. They fell in love but there was a problem. Their marriage was unthinkable between their two communities.

The relationship had potentially damaging consequences for her family, which she knew very well. But she was resolute in getting married. She decided to be careful and hide her love from the public eye, but could not. Her parents started hearing reports about her relationship. Many respected members of her community expressed extreme displeasure with her father but he refused to listen to them, as he had faith in his daughter whom he had raised with such love and care and whose wisdom he deeply respected.

Jemima knew very well that her marriage, if made public before the marriage of her younger siblings, would affect her family significantly. She knew the entire community would shun her family and they would be a laughing stock and virtual outcasts. But she pressed on, determined, as if she was possessed by her love. She tactfully hatched a plan to get by.

First, she encouraged her brilliant younger brother, Jay, to move interstate for further studies after he completed his first undergraduate degree with high distinction, being in the top three in the whole state.

Jay wished to be a statistician as he had heard statisticians earned well. But Jemima, perhaps influenced by her engineer boyfriend, strongly encouraged him to make engineering his career, for which he would have to move interstate. But Jay did not want to leave Dorothy, his ailing mother, on her own. He loved her and deeply cared for her. At this time Sherman, their hardworking father, was stationed at a remote location, high up in the Himalayas, on a teaching assignment for two years.

This is the early sixties. Jay was the man of the house at just eighteen. On days when Dorothy would be too unwell, Jay would cook and clean the house before leaving for college. His two younger sisters, Blossom (ten) and Patricia (fourteen), were school students. Once, when bad weather conditions meant their father's money order did not arrive for two months during winter, Jay went out to earn money to support the family. He tutored at Year 10 student. At that time, Jemima was working and living away.

Despite all odds and his own internal resistance to go interstate, Jay secured admission at a prestigious engineering school. As soon as that happened, Jemima got him engaged to a beautiful young lass, Rachel (seventeen), who lived not far from their home. As the date of moving drew nearer, Jay grew increasingly sad and unhappy. The very thought of leaving his ailing mother behind, with his two school-going younger sisters, made him anxious and worried. He felt sick and was bedridden for two weeks. Somehow, he recovered and travelled to reach his new institution where he was granted provisional admission for reporting late by a few weeks and missing the initial classes. He took up the challenge and qualified admirably in his first semester examinations a few months later. But very soon thereafter, he was asked to return home for his wedding, which he did not want to, as he thought he was too young to marry, particularly as his professional career had not yet begun. But somehow, he dragged himself home solely for the sake of his mother.

He thought his refusal to marry at the last moment would be a shock for his mother but another thought, that his wife would be his mother's companion, inspired him. A few days after the wedding, Jay returned to his hostel. Nine months later, Rachel delivered a baby boy, Bryan, through a difficult caesarean procedure. She was attended mainly by her relatives from her mother's side. Jay was not there, nor was Jemima or Sherman.

In the following years, the news of Jemima's mysterious blossoming relationship — given that it was with a man from a different community —trickled out and reached her parents but they continued to be in total denial because they trusted their daughter too much.

Rachel knew it too, which Jemima did not like. Jemima felt threatened by her and did not want her brother Jay to trust his wife, fearing she would tell him. When challenged by her parents or any other relative, Jemima would completely deny the relationship. She was painfully waiting to see her two younger sisters complete their undergraduate studies and be married off before announcing her own marriage to the public. She had to do something; she had to create a distraction.

Her softest target was Rachel, her young sister-in-law, who was clear-hearted, intelligent and sharp but also had a tendency to verbally react if provoked. So Jemima took her under her wing in Jay's absence, who was still interstate. By coercion, Jemima got an anti-pregnancy device installed medically in Rachel so that she would not deliver another baby when Jay returned. Then, in her subtle and devious manner, to malign Rachel's image and credibility at home and especially with Jay, she started poking and provoking her, knowing she would react. By the time Jay returned home, his relationship with Rachel was already straining, as scripted, staged, instigated and directed by Jemima and her influence on other members of the family. Eventually, Jemima's vicious verbal attacks escalated into physical beating of Rachel every now and then. She would even pull her long locks of curly brown hair.

Pretty soon, inspired by his scheming sister, who had poisoned everyone at home against Rachel, Jay also started beating his wife, at times pissing on her. Young Bryan witnessed everything, with his two little eyes, stunned. He never cried on seeing his mother get physically beaten by his aunt and father. No one from Jay's side helped Rachel, except their neighbours, who knew everything, and her own family. For days, Rachel would go without food. She felt that she was extremely alone, physically and internally, not even allowed to touch her baby, nor was Jay allowed to touch Bryan. Jemima controlled everything in their home, every decision and every action. No one had the freedom or guts to oppose her. As such, Bryan has no recollection of being with his biological parents in the first nine years of his life.

Over a period of eight long years, Jemima successfully disturbed her home and distracted the attention of all her family members away from her own self and towards Rachel. She was biding time for her sisters' marriages. In these eight years, her two younger sisters completed their undergraduate studies. Jemima wanted them married off quickly but Patricia was very picky about the prospects for about a year, which delayed her marriage. In the meantime, Jemma was running out of time and could wait no longer. One day, she eloped. A few days later, she married. The news travelled across the state like wildfire. Her whole community was stunned beyond belief. Her father passed dark stools (with blood) motion and her mother went into shock. The family members had to disperse and hide in the homes of various relatives. Their community was up in arms against them. Sherman was showered with insults by people on the street and even spat upon. Dorothy hid away from her relatives for a long time. Jay was humiliated by relatives and colleagues. Even young Bryan was not spared from humiliation and insults at his primary school.

A year passed by. Blossom and Patricia were married off. Blossom went interstate and the picky Patricia was married to a gentleman she should not have been married to in normal circumstances. Both sisters paid a heavy price for their sister's act and the family's notoriety. Her love was blind, selfish and corrupted. It is also true that Jemima had married a gentleman of a high order, a fine human being.

A question arises: why did Jemima, who had been known to be a nice and helpful person to all and sundry, target and oppress Rachel to the extent of sacrificing her altogether?

The answer could be that, at some stage of being ill-treated by her in-laws in her husband's absence, Rachel may have threatened to spill the beans with Jay and other close relatives, given that it had the potential to become a big community issue. Jemima could not afford that to happen as it would have an adverse impact on her and on her sisters, though it eventually did happen. Anecdotally, Dorothy was heard telling people that it was her daughter-in-law, Rachel, and not Jemima, who was involved with the man from the other community, because Jay was away. Possibly, Jemima had successfully convinced Dorothy that it was actually Rachel and not she who was involved, after sniffing out that Rachel may have informed the other members of the family about her relationship.

Rachel undoubtedly paid a very heavy price for Jemima's love and so did Jay, but for a different reason. He had been a good son and a good brother, but a bad husband and an extremely negligent father. Bryan's childhood was, thus, made a virtual hell and stolen away.

In the following years, Jemima became very cordial and friendly, even to Rachel. But it was always too late, too little. She had caused immense damage to her family and wreaked significant havoc with all her family members. At different times of her life, she had shown all three shades of her character – the good, the bad and the ugly – in accordance with her requirements from life. She was tactful but largely ruthless in her treatment of her family members. She compromised and sacrificed various members of her family in different ways and at different times, just to achieve her intended targets. And, at other times, she appeared as an angel to the same very family members in their need of the hour. All shades of her complex personality defined and characterised her.

A Plea to Death

This poem illustrates an eternal connection between life and death and how they are interwoven as the two essential shades of the Truth. It aims to rid a person of the intrinsic fear of death, which is the one and only certainty of life, and why it is more useful to live fearlessly till your final breath, after which death meets and greets us, and perhaps leads us into another mysterious phase of cosmic existence.

*****

Sometimes life torments one to such an extent that one wishes for death and sometimes the fear of death forces one to remain alive; how strange are these happenings; what a saga of life and death, the two essential faces of the Truth — the inevitable; what a connection!

Some of those who desire life, spend their life in the fear of death and some of those who wish to die are compelled to remain alive and die by inches; those who pray for death remain alive in the intense pain of life, and those who desire life compulsively spend their life in the fear of death.

Death is not always sudden, sometimes one has to die slowly over ages; when life suffocates and becomes a prison, death may provide freedom; sometimes, when living becomes a necessity, it becomes obligatory for one to live.

Death does not have to become an open exhibition, tell death not to make any noise; rocks don't make any noise when they die and merge with soil.

Somewhere someone is pleading to both life and death; either let his tears bring relief to a desolate place or bring him some relief by putting a healing balm on his painful heart.

Oh Death, arrive slowly and silently when you arrive, lest life gets even a sniff of your arrival, otherwise she may wake me up; life should be distracted with seeing a dream in my sleep when you arrive.

*****

Dua Maut Se'

Zindaghi tadpa kar maare' kabi, maut tadpa kar zinda rakhe' kabi, aisa be hota hai is duniya mai;
Kya ajab majra hai, kya ajeeb dastan hai, zindaghi aur maut do aham pehlu hai asliyat ke'; kya ajab silsala hai.

Kuchh log mur mur ke' zinda rehte' hai, kuchh log zinda rehte' hain mur mur ke' be yahan;
Woh jo murne' ki dua karte' hai, shiddat-e-dard main zinda rehte' hai aur woh jo zinda rehna chahte' hain, maut kee dahshat se jabran zinda rehte' hai yahan.

Achanak aati nahi hai maut hamesha, murna padta hai mudhat tuk kabi kabi;
Qaid jab ban jatee hai zindaghi, azadi deitee hai tubh maut; majboori bun jaati hai jub zindaghi; lazim hota hai jeena kabi kabi.

Maut woh nahi jo duniya dekhe', maut se keh do na kare' koi shore;
Chattanne' karti nahi koi shore, khamoshee se mittee mai gal jaatee hai woh aatee hai jub unkee maut.

Kahin koi khamosh dua karta hai dono zindaghi aur maut se';
Ya toh uske' aanso barsaat bankar aabad kar virani ko, ya uske' dil par marham rakh kar sukoon de usse'.

Ae maut, aana dheree se aaye jab tu, chupke' se' aana aaye' jab tu;
Zindaghi ko pata be na chale', kahin jaga na de woh; zindaghi neend main khwab deekh rahi ho aaye' jab tu

Chapter 4

VALUE OF A HUMAN LIFE IN KASHMIR

This chapter discuses general life and overall situation in Kashmir during the COVID-19 pandemic lockdown, general fear amongst Kashmiris about a demographic shift in Kashmir, and two painful case histories that illustrate the value of a human life in Kashmir.

The chapter ends with a poem, *Face Off with You, My Lord*.

The situation in Kashmir

As the COVID-19 pandemic continues to impact general life in India and the rest of the world, with India recording a total of around 3.46 million infections and around 62,700 deaths by 29 August 2020, Kashmir valley continues to lose young people who don't believe in the present political situation in the valley whom Indian security forces call 'terrorists', accusing neighbouring Pakistan of creating and backing. As per CNN, dated 28 August 2020, India recorded 85,687 and 77,266 new cases of COVID-19 infection on 26 and 27 August, respectively. However, Worldometer indicates that, for five consecutive days between 26 and 30 August 2020, India recorded more than 75,000 new cases. On 29 and 30 August, the numbers were 78,472 and 79,457, which surpassed an earlier daily infection record of 77,255 day set by the US on 16 July 2020.

Kashmiri people, especially the youth, are not happy with Indian administration after their state was stripped of its 72-year old semi-autonomous status, in August 2019, and then downgraded to Union Territory and administrated by representatives of the central government of India. The question is, how has the valley landed in such a situation? The ultimate responsibility lies with the government of India, both past and the present.

The incidence of militant activities in the Kashmir valley, including bloody encounters between Kashmiri militants and Indian security forces, are reported to have increased after the abrogation of Article 370 of the Indian Constitution in August 2019 by the Indian government. The subsequent division of the erstwhile State of Jammu and Kashmir in October, which included Ladakh, has led to the tense stand-off now taking place between Indian and Chinese troops at the Line of Actual Control (the LAC), which is the de facto border between the two countries.

The semi-autonomous status of the State of Jammu and Kashmir was unilaterally scrapped by the Indian government on 5 August 2019, without any notice, consent, consensus or discussion, in a sudden and shocking move for the entire world, especially Kashmiris. This put the valley in a complete lockdown, snapping all modes of communication in a months-long mobile phone blackout following the move. Kashmiri people lived without any telephone – fixed and mobile – and internet connectivity for a continuous period of 213 day (about 7 months), which is the longest shutdown in a democracy, before it was restored in a limited capacity on 4 March 2020, with only a 2G internet connectivity. On 17 August 2020, Aljazeera reported high speed 4G internet services were being restored, after a gap of more than a year, but only in two of the 22 districts in the union territory and that too on a trial basis till 8 September 2020.

Fear of a demographic shift in Kashmir

Kashmiris fear that India's ruling political party, BJP, may be planning to shift the demographic makeup of Kashmir.

Amid the COVID-19 lockdown, in April 2020, the Indian government notified the modified domicile laws for Jammu and Kashmir, making numerous people from outside the former state eligible for residency and jobs in the now union territory. As per the new law, any person who has lived in Jammu and Kashmir for at least fifteen years, or has studied there for at least seven years and passed their Year 10 or 12 examination is eligible for a domicile certificate. In addition, children of Indian government employees who have served in the state for ten years are also eligible to settle and claim local residency rights, including those children who have never lived in Kashmir.

In a thought-provoking article, on 28 June 2020, *Al Jazeera* reported up to 25,000 people had been granted domicile certificates. Domicile certificates had been granted since 18 May, in a move seen by Kashmiris as drawing parallels with the occupied West Bank.

The domicile certificate entitles its holders to residency and government jobs in the region, which had previously been reserved only for state subjects of Jammu and Kashmir, as guaranteed by Article 35(A) of the Indian Constitution, which did not allow outsiders, including Indian nationals from other states, to purchase land and immovable property or claim government jobs in Jammu and Kashmir. As per the 2011 census, Kashmir has a total population of 12.5 million, with Muslims comprising 68 percent and Hindus 28 percent.

At the end of June 2020, US Democrat presidential hopeful and former vice-president Joe Biden reportedly said: 'India should take all necessary steps to restore the rights of all the people of Kashmir'. A policy paper posted on his website says, 'Restrictions on dissent, such as peaceful protests or shutting or slowing down the internet weakens democracy'.

Around the same time a picture of the domicile certificate issued to an Indian bureaucrat, originally from the Indian state of Bihar, went viral on social media. Reportedly, out of a total of sixty-six top bureaucrats working in the union territory of Jammu and Kashmir, thirty-eight belong to other Indian states and many in centralised institutions, such as banks, post offices, telecommunication facilities, security institutions and universities.

The *Al Jazeera* report also noted that, 'Kashmiri politicians across the divide have said the revocation of special citizenship rights was aimed at reversing the Muslim majority character of the region, which is now directly ruled from New Delhi', and 'The Indian government says the move to change the status of Kashmir was done to integrate the Muslim-majority region with the rest of the country in order to bring development'.

Questions have been raised about the urgency shown by government in the issuance of the domicile certificates, with the government apparently threatening to penalise officials Rs50,000 (A$660) if a domicile certificate is not issued within the stipulated period of fourteen days. Human rights activists say this is not enough time to assess the veracity of an application.

Death of Bashir Ahmad Khan

In a heart-rending incident on 1 July 2020, a 65-year-old Kashmiri civilian, Bashir Ahmad Khan, was killed during a shootout in Sopore, Kashmir. A Kashmiri militant and an Indian soldier were also reportedly killed and three other Indian soldiers were injured.

By that time, around 230 people, including 33 civilians, 54 Indian security personnel and more than 143 Kashmiri youth fighting for Kashmir's independence had been killed in the conflict over the previous six months in more than 100 military operations.

The next day, *Al Jazeera* published a photograph of a three-year-old toddler sitting on the dead body of his grandfather, Bashir Ahmad Khan. This picture had sparked outrage in Kashmir, with the victim's brother saying, 'My brother was not a militant. He did not carry a gun. Why was he killed?'

The inspector-general of police in Kashmir is reported to have said that rebels had opened fire at security forces, which had set off a gun battle in which one security official was killed and three were injured, adding 'The family is being pressurised by the militants to blame it on the security forces'. But the victim's family refuses to accept the police claim, accusing the security forces of putting the toddler on his grandfather's dead body to take pictures.

The victim's son told *Al Jazeera* another version of events: 'We received a call that my father had met with an accident. When we reached Sopore, we were told he was killed in crossfire. If it was crossfire, his body should've been inside the car, but it was found on the road'. The victim's nephew said his dead uncle's car was without a scratch and claimed he had been taken out from his car and shot by the armed forces. One of the family's relatives claimed: 'They dragged the body out and put the child on top. The child's clothes were drenched in his grandfather's blood'.

Hundreds of people in Kashmir staged protests the day the picture was published and hundreds of mourners at the victim's funeral shouted, 'We want freedom [from Indian rule]'.

Indian security forces have reportedly intensified operations in Kashmir against rebels since a coronavirus lockdown was imposed in March 2020.

As per *Al Jazeera*, a spokesperson for BJP has drawn huge criticism for tweeting the photo of the toddler and commenting 'Pulitzer Lovers??' BJP leaders are reported to have criticised the awarding of the Pulitzer Prize to three Kashmiri journalists in May 2020, claiming the award-winning photographs and commentary on them were 'anti-India'.

This latest incident reflects some of the ugliest aspects of humans. The question is not who shot the 65-year-old grandfather but why did this all happen? The ultimate responsibility for a home or a country always lies with its head. Obviously, the situation in Kashmir is far from normal and deeply concerning.

Another question arises: why did the spokesperson try to be sarcastic in his tweet instead of being empathetic? Why did his nationalistic emotion take the better of his humane side, albeit temporarily? Does he see Kashmiris as India's enemies? Is this why his government abrogated Article 370 of India's Constitution?

And, alarmingly, all this happens during the pandemic! Humanity, where are you?

Value of life of Ajay Pandita

Is it possible to put a cost to a human life? The answer is yes and no, both. In terms of monetary value, it may be possible to do so, but solely for compensation purposes, and the cost will logically depend on the background of the person — age, social and professional standing, level of education, income and so on. In terms of the 'natural gift of life' itself, however, every life is invaluable, because no matter how rich one may be or how much medical effort one makes to revive a life, the loss is permanent once a person dies. Also, how can one quantify the suffering of and, therefore, the value of true compensation for the family members of a person who dies naturally or is killed, particularly if the deceased is a person like Ajay Pandita, who was killed on 8 June 2020 in Kashmir, by unidentified killers? He was the *sarpanch* (the village head) of Lukbawan village in Larkipora, located in Anantnag district. He is survived by his wife, two daughters and parents.

Undoubtedly, life means freedom; and without freedom, a life may not be worth living. An article that appeared in *The Economic Times*, dated 31 January 2019, attempted to quantity the cost of freedom, as an analogy with the cost of life:

As a continuum, let us look at the price of liberty. What is the price of liberty in India? For a rich man, it could be as much as Rs 200 crores as prognosticated by the Supreme Court in Subrata

Roy's [the head of Sahara Group] case. For a poor man wrongly accused, languishing in jail for years with no one to fight his case, the price of liberty is zero. And out of mind is out of sight in India.

So what should be the monetary value of Ajay's life? Can one quantify the monetary value of his dreams and aspirations? He was in his forties and had everything to look forward to.

A week after his death it was reported that Ajay's family received ex-gratia relief from the Lt Governor, who paid homage to Ajay, acknowledging his supreme sacrifice and 'hoping' the perpetrator of the dastardly act desisted from committing such crimes against humanity in the future.

The payment amounted to Rs 20 lakh (2 million Indian rupees), which is equivalent to US$26,300, or about US$63 per month, assuming Ajay would have lived for at least another thirty-five good years. Does that compensation reflect the true value of Ajay's life? Certainly not!

Regardless of the petty compensation, humanity owes Ajay an explanation as to why his life was suddenly cut short. A number of important questions must be answered:

- Why was Ajay killed?
- Who is responsible for his death?
- Who must be held accountable?
- In his death, who has lost?
- In his death, who may have possibly gained?
- Will he ever receive justice?

Half-hearted commentaries don't produce meaningful results. In fairness to Ajay, and considering the sensitive issue of Kashmir and the Kashmiri Pandits, this chapter provides a detailed commentary based on a number of newspaper reports, articles and interviews, with a number of important questions being raised. Nonetheless, it must be acknowledged that, in this polarised world of ours — where 'show me the person and I'll show you the rules' and 'might is right' are the order of the day — the answers to these questions will undoubtedly be subjective, as most answers are in the present day and age. One must not, however, ignore a useful saying: 'The loudest person in the room is the weakest'.

The greatest question of all, therefore, is if these questions can or will ever be answered honestly by various stakeholders, without bringing in a range of social and political prejudices and biases?

Why and when did Ajay return to the valley?

Ajay returned to Kashmir in 1996, six years after the mass exodus of Pandits. The family has a house in Jammu also. In the last twenty-four years, why was Ajay not targeted? Why was he targeted now? What has changed? Aren't there any other Pandits living in Kashmir? Will they also be targeted? Did the abrogation of Article 370 of the Indian Constitution contribute to his death? Did the abrogation of Article 370 further alienate Kashmiri Pandits from their Muslim brethren?

Ajay's father was quoted in the *Hindustan Times*, on 9 June 2020, as saying: 'In 1996, we returned to Kashmir and re-started our lives. At that time, Ajay was around 21 years old. He took bank loans and reconstructed our orchards and house … He used to say that it is our home …. Ajay had 'always rejected his suggestions that they should leave Kashmir because the situation was not normal'.

Let us first look at the number of Kashmiri Pandits who were killed in Kashmir three decades ago and those who are still living there. There is no consensus between different agencies on the actual numbers.

The numbers of Kashmiri Pandits displaced in 1990 is variously reported as 150,000–160,000, or 95 percent of those living in the valley, and between 250,000 and 300,000 from the state, according to the Internal Displacement Monitoring Centre of Norwegian Refugee Council and the CIA (both figures reported in *Quint*, 19 January 2020). The Srinagar-based Kashmiri Pandit Sangharsh Samiti (KPSS) organisation, estimates this is even higher, at around 325,000 people (or 75,000 Kashmiri Pandit families), with 808 Pandit families still living in Kashmir (as quoted in *Huffpost*, 10 June 2020).

The reported numbers of Kashmiri Pandits killed are just as varied: in 2008 the KPSS indicated that 399 Kashmiri Pandits had been killed in Kashmir, mostly during the first year of the insurgency. The Jammu and Kashmir government stated that 219 members of the Pandit community, out of the 1400 Hindus, had been killed from 1989 to 2004, but none thereafter. Panun Kashmir, a political group of Pandits, claims 1341 Pandits have been killed since 1990 up to now.

Author and journalist Shivam Vij raised a number of important points about the situation in Kashmir in an interesting article published in *The Print* on 2 December 2019. His article must be read in full (see the online address provided in the references to this chapter). I reproduce here some excerpts from the article to provide the readers with some idea about the ground reality in Kashmir, and how politicians and diplomats describe it to the world:

> On 2 August this year, the government of Jammu and Kashmir (under President's rule) cancelled the annual *Amarnath Yatra* ... The security situation must have been really, really bad because this was the first time the *Amarnath Yatra* was cancelled altogether. Yet, the security situation was good enough for the Narendra Modi government to make Article 370 null and void, as also Article 35A, divide the state into two union territories and place hundreds of pro-India political actors in jail ... Yet no Hindu — absolutely no one — seems to have cried hoarse about the hurt to Hindu sentiments ... Similarly, the political discourse around the issue of Kashmiri Pandits is replete with political hypocrisy.

> *Author*: In his article, Vij discusses comments made by Sandeep Chakravorty, India's consul general in New York, in addressing a private gathering of Kashmiri Pandits wherein he has allegedly made a number of assertions that may either be factually wrong or show a

lack of understanding of the history and culture of Kashmir. When challenged, Chakravorty claimed his remarks had been taken out of context. It seems Mr Chakravorty could have (wrongly) been referring to how a considerable number of exiled Pandits had lived in poor living conditions, at both Jammu and Delhi, in months immediately after their exodus in 1990.

Vij discusses one claim made by Chakravorty, that Pandits are not returning to the Kashmir valley because of fear. Yet there remain 808 Kashmiri Pandit families (or around 3000 to 4000 people) in the valley across 292 different locations, according to the KPSS. In addition, as Vij points out, thousands of Kashmiri Pandits visit the valley every year as tourists or for pilgrimages such as the annual Kheer Bhawani festival in Tulmulla or to visit many other traditional shrines and places of worship.

Vij continues:

Cruel and inhuman as the exodus of Kashmiri Pandits was, being a refugee is a complicated matter ... A resilient, educated, well-connected community, the Pandit refugees have got education and jobs and are now spread across India and the world. Would a Kashmiri Pandit refugee's son or daughter working in a corporate job want to return to the family home in the old city of Srinagar?

Author: The exodus of Kashmir Pandits happened three decades ago. Since then, barring those 30,000 to 35,000 people living in the government-provided camp accommodations in Jammu, they seem to have reasonably settled across the globe. There was no other option for them except to strive hard and reclaim their lives. It is not prudent, therefore, for any settled family to uproot itself and move back to its home, especially if the home continues to be disturbed. Such unrea-sonable expectations from any Kashmiri Pandit family are totally unrealistic and quite unfair. They have immensely suffered in the past — which is beyond words — and they can't be expected to keep suffering for the same loss, which is practically irreparable. They have lost one complete generation since their exodus. Yes, if their home is back in order and peaceful, some of them may consider moving back to the valley, albeit still with an element of risk and apprehension.

Vij goes on to discuss Chakravorty's comments about an Israel model that drew applause from his audience.

This model basically implies creating a special enclave for Pandits. So, there could be a Hindu Kashmir and a Muslim Kashmir, physically demarcated … The idea is an old one; it used to be known as 'Panun Kashmir'. Interestingly, the BJP never endorsed it, though one doesn't know what the BJP of Modi-Shah thinks. The removal of Article 35A has so far not been followed up with any reassurance that the Modi government will not settle Indians in the Kashmir Valley. So, if the plan is to bring about a demographic change in the Valley … then the Israel model is not what we are looking at. Instead, we are looking at the China model.

Author: The valley must not be divided in the similar way as the erstwhile state of Jammu and Kashmir was divided in late 2019. The two Kashmiri communities are interwoven in terms of their common history, identity and culture. As such, they must not be separated — physically or spiritually — if Kashmir has to become peaceful and prosperous. Such divisions potentially push India back to its past several decades ago.

Vij goes on:

And yet, there is an Indian model we have forgotten. This model died in Kashmir the day Jawaharlal Nehru had Sheikh Abdullah arrested, and maybe it's too late to revive it. The Indian model is one of 'integration'. The only meaningful way Kashmiri Pandits could 'return' to Kashmir is if the wall of suspicion and mistrust between Pandits and Muslims was brought down. This could be done through a South Africa-style truth and reconciliation exercise ...

Kashmiri, Hindu, and Indian are not the same thing. They could co-exist ...

Why was Ajay pleading for his security?

Ajay had been seeking security from the government for quite some time but, unfortunately, his request had been seemingly ignored. Why? It seems he did not feel safe particularly after Article 370 was abrogated in August 2019. Why was he not feeling safe? Despite that and his father's repeated suggestions to leave, why had he decided not to leave the valley? Was he 'hoping' nothing would happen to him? If yes, was his hope based on the trust that he had earned with his fellow Kashmiri people living in his Muslim-dominated village?

The Hindu, on 9 June 2020, reported on a December 2019 interview Ajay had done with a Jammu-based news channel, in which he had said that, during the *panchayat* elections in 2018, the local people from his village, especially from the Muslim community, had taken a considerable risk in coming out and voting for him but the administration had failed him: 'The Central government makes tall claims about *panch* and *sarpanches* on TV; they shoot from our shoulders ... I am an elected person but I am helpless ... I want to ask Prime Minister Narendra Modi and Amit Shah ... can't they see this? The UT administration never met the *sarpanches*, do they know who Ajay Bharti is? When I am not safe, how I can say my people are safe ... The administration treats us untouchables.'

Reportedly, Ajay had also raised an alarm about the safety of *sarpanches* in Kashmir after the killing of another *sarpanch*, Syed Rafiq Ahmed, and a government employee, Sheikh Zahoor, both Muslims, on 28 November 2019.

When it was claimed on social media that Ajay belonged to the ruling BJP of India, there was quite a bit of emotional furore among those who belonged to the Kashmiri Pandit community. This noise quietened down when it was revealed that he belonged to the Indian National Congress. Could that be a reason why he was not provided any security cover by the government despite his repeated requests, even after his emotional request on television about six months before he was killed?

The *Kashmir Walla's* report, dated 10 June 2020, quoted Sanjay Tickoo, president of the KPSS, who said, 'Militants are not lenient towards anyone participating in the political process'.

Who has claimed responsibility for Ajay's killing?

On 9 June 2020, *The Hindu* reported that a newly formed militant organisation, The Resistance Front (TRF), had taken the responsibility for the killing: 'TRF is promoted by Pakistan and was created in August last after the revocation of Article 370 in J&K'.

Ajay was targeted 'because he was part of the government machinery and democratic process and a member of the minority community ...', according to the director-general of police, who also said, 'The TRF is nothing but a front of the Pakistan backed Lashkar-e-Taiba (LeT). They only want to mislead. We have identified the terrorists who carried out the attack; they are from the Hizb.' Surprisingly, the DGP claimed that he was not aware of Ajay's requests for police protection.

The earliest mentions about the TRF appear in articles published in April 2020. *Outlook* claimed the TRF was floated three months earlier, sometime in February. *The Economic Times* reported that the 'Newly formed "The Resistance Front" is ... actively supported by Pakistan and consists of existing terror groups Hizbul Mujahidin, Jaish-e-Mohammad, LeT and Al-Badr, informed sources in the security establishment believe ...'. In June, *OpIndia* reported that, 'LeT's new proxy group TRF takes responsibility ... says no "political stooges" will be spared. The TRF had reportedly also threatened that "No one will be spared who is hand in glove with the occupational regime and strengthen their illegal occupation. Innocents won't be touched, so don't drag this with religion."'

Some important questions arise. It seems the TRF was born sometime in February 2020, about six months after the abrogation of Article 370. Who is its face? Is it a real organisation? Is it really a secular organisation? Is it likely to target other Kashmiri Pandits living in the valley or only those people, regardless of their religious background, whom they see speaking on behalf of the Indian government and acting for the Indian interest in the valley? Who funds it apart from the usual suspects? What was the need for its creation if there are already a number of such organisations operating in the valley?

What was the reaction to Ajay's death?

In Ajay's absence, the reaction of family members can be considered to provide vital clues for understanding (1) Ajay as a person; (2) the overall ground situation in Kashmir and, in particular, the situation that he may have possibly created for himself; and (3) the possible reasons why he could have been killed.

Did his pseudonym, Bharti (which means 'Indian'), contribute to his death? Was he known to be (publicly) using a language similar to that used by his family members after his death? If yes, could he have possibly been irking the Kashmiri separatists? In that case, should the Indian intelligence agencies not have known his vulnerability and provided him with necessary security — as they do to other prominent separatist leaders — especially when he had been himself pleading for it for several months? Did his patriotism (towards India) lead to his death? Did his valour and bravery eventually get the better of him? Was he like an unarmed solider, without any security personnel to protect him? Did the security agencies deliberately wait for him to be targeted? Was he seen as bait?

The 9 June *Hindustan Times* article quoted Ajay's father as saying,

My son was a lion … a true patriot … He used to say that it is our home. He used 'Bharti' in his name to show his love for the country. Some anti-nationals are behind his killing. They shot him in his back. He was a lion. My son has sacrificed his life for the country … There are forces who don't want Pandits to return and my son fell to the bullets of such ideology. We are not afraid, but will return and fulfil my son's mission.

Ajay's brother, who reportedly lit his pyre at Jammu, said:

We won't leave Kashmir but I have a demand that the government should first create a regiment of Kashmiri Pandits in the valley … He was helpful to all. He loved his roots and always extended a helping hand to the needy. After becoming *sarpanch*, he had decided to work for the welfare of Muslim villagers.

The next day *Huffington* (HuffPost India) published words that Ajay's father had spoken to them over the phone. Reportedly, Mr Pandita had heard the shots ring out at five in the evening.

I heard my daughter screaming … I ran outside and I spotted my son in a pool of blood … We were living happily. The villagers used to treat him like their own brother. It was just due to militancy, he was killed … He always wanted to develop his village. He wanted to uplift this area that has remained under-developed for decades … God knows why they didn't provide him security … I cannot explain to you the pain … What worse can be for a father who was carrying his dead son's body for cremation? … I kept looking at his face and thinking what was his fault?

While describing himself (Ajay) as a foot soldier of the Congress Party, Mr Pandita is also reported to have said that Ajay's political career was tragically cut short for no apparent reason. Two years after his family had returned to Kashmir, Ajay had contested the Urban Local Bodies polls as a Congress Party candidate and was elected the *sarpanch* of three villages — Lukhbhawan, Lirkipora and Mugalpora of Doru constituency, in Anantnag. After winning the 2018 election, Ajay had requested the deputy commissioner of Anantnag for security but received no response. The new deputy commissioner reportedly told *Huffpost* that no such request for security had come to his attention.

Ajay's daughter was reported in *Outlook* on 12 June as saying that she will follow in the footsteps of her brave father who was not dependent on any political party but a true patriot, one who loved his country and worked for the upliftment of the people. She also called the killers cowards, for they had shot Ajay from behind and did not have the courage to face him, adding that the family would soon move from Jammu back to Kashmir. The following excerpt is from her interview: 'Whatever the government deems right regarding giving security to *sarpanchs*, it must do that, I don't want a similar tragedy repeated in Kashmir.'

Ajay's daughter is also reported to have said that her father had contested the election on the insistence of the local people, who had then elected him as the *sarpanch*. She reiterated that, after a *sarpanch* was killed in Kashmir in November 2019, her father had demanded security cover from the government. She reminded the government that 'people's concerns must not be taken lightly otherwise the results could be very bad'.

On 9 June, *The Hindu* reported that Kashmiri Pandit organisations had described the 'planned murder of sarpanch as an attempt to trigger fear psychosis among the minorities in the valley' and urged the Central government to provide security to Kashmiri Pandits and other minority community members living in Kashmir. While Kashmiri Pandit organisations condemned the killing, their words were standard and nothing new. Such expressions of shock and con-dolences are routinely conveyed by these organisations and by many other prominent individuals when a person is killed in similar situations. But do they really matter? What does change, except a token payment of meagre compensation to the family of the deceased?

A life is gone. Did these Kashmiri Pandit organisations ever support

Ajay and ask for his security from the government as well as the security for other Kashmiri Pandit *sarpanches* in the valley? Do they have one voice? Are they united and fighting for the same cause? If not, why not?

Lip-service doesn't ever bring people back from dead. Lip-service doesn't matter to anyone except to the sympathisers themselves, who do it mainly for their individual political ambitions.

Upon Ajay's death, various prominent Kashmir and Indian politicians started their political tweeting. All the messages marked just standard formalities and no meaningful follow-up, meaning little to anyone except to the politicians themselves, for their political purposes.

Will these politicians now work and help to provide the necessary security cover to other *sarpanches* in the valley, regardless of whether they are affiliated to the Congress party or the BJP?

A *sarpanch* is elected by the village-level constitutional body of local self-government, called *Gram Sabha*, which retains decision-making power for five years. The *sarpanch*, along with other elected members (called commissioners or *panch*), constitute the *gram panchayat*, which the *sarpanch* heads. There are about 250,000 *gram panchayats* in India, of which about 4500 are in Jammu and Kashmir. It is understood that *gram panchayat* (village level) elections are not contested between political parties; nevertheless, candidates do receive support from political parties.

Was Ajay killed because he was a Kashmiri Pandit?
Two articles provide important clues for answering this question (the web addresses to read the articles in full are provided in the references for this chapter). The first, by Aliza Noor, published in *The Quint* on 19 January 2020, squarely blames Mohammad Abdullah Sheikh, the first prime minister of Jammu and Kashmir after the state's accession to India in 1947, for initiating the Islamisation of Kashmir. In 1980 his government renamed about 2500 villages from their original Kashmiri (possibly Sanskrit) names to new, Islamic names. Allegedly, Sheikh

was pushed by the then prime minister of India, Indira Gandhi, to take necessary measures to integrate the state with India (via the 1975 Accord), which did not sit well with the separatists, who subsequently started their insurgency in the state after 1987.

Noor talks about the alleged rigging of the 1987 state elections, which gave birth to the Muslim United Front, which propagated their idea of the Islamic resistance movement, assisted by Pakistan's Inter-Services Intelligence, which created and sponsored another terrorist group, Hizbul-Mujahideen. The militants from both groups allegedly spread anti-Pandit sentiment, convincing many Kashmiris of the need to cleanse the Kashmir valley of its Pandit population. Lawyer and BJP leader Tika Lal Tapoo was murdered outside his home on 14 September 1989, and three weeks later retired judge Nikalanth Ganjoo was killed in broad daylight, which instilled fear in the Pandit community.

In newspapers, on posters and in mosques in Kashmir were issued ultimatums to Pandits giving them three options to consider: *Ralive, Tsaliv ya Galive* (convert to Islam, quit Kashmir or perish). A note published in *Aftab*, a local Urdu daily, had issued a warning to Pandits who did not leave: 'If you do not obey, we will start with your children. Kashmir Liberation, Zindabad.'

The article recalls how, around 9 pm on 19 January 1990, the Kashmir valley had reverberated with war cries and pro-Pakistan slogans through loudspeakers. Reportedly, tens of thousands of Kashmiri Muslims, including the young, old and women, had come out on the streets and shouted slogans like 'death to India' and 'death to kafirs', which continued till morning. The Pandits were left to defend themselves when the police deserted their posts. The Gawkadal massacre took place on 21 January, in which Indian security forces fired at protesters, killing at least fifty people.

The station director of broadcaster Doordarshan Srinagar was shot dead in his office chair on 13 February. Pandit Sarwanand Koul Premi, a renowned Kashmiri poet, and his son were killed near their house. In the same month, a young social worker, Satish Tikkoo, was also killed. Reportedly, many Kashmiri Pandit women were kidnapped, raped and murdered through this period.

The outcome was that, as the article says:

Fear-stricken, the hapless Pandits had no option but to leave … They engaged in whatever means of transport they could manage … ending up in refugee camps … To the radical forces, it was perceived as the fruition of the Valley's ethnic cleansing. The sentiment was that Pandits had now been banished from their birthplace — not just for the future few decades, but for all times to come … Thousands of Kashmiri Pandit refugees settled into small rooms and abject conditions in refugee camps in Jammu and Delhi provided to them by the state government. Many of them hoped to return to their ancestral land but failed to do so.

The responses of the Kashmiri Pandit community to the abrogation of Article 370 and the Citizenship Amendment Act 2019 (CAA) were contrasting. Noor claims that sixty-four Kashmiri Pandits 'unequivocally condemned' the abrogation of Article 370 on the grounds that it was done without any consultation with the people of the state. However, the political group Panun Kashmir supported the CAA and the National Registrar of Citizens at a time when the nation was witnessing widespread protests against them between December 2019 and January 2020. Noor concludes that, 'Several Pandits feel the CAA is yet another tool using their plight for political gains, pandering to the majoritarian forces in the country. Their trauma is often used to engage in whataboutery, even as efforts to create effective political discourse and debate around their rehabilitation policies are nowhere in sight. Kashmiri Pandits may have been able to physically relocate, but they cannot go back in time.'

The second article, by Dr Simrit Kahlon, was published in *News Intervention* on 10 June 2020.

Pakistan's involvement in the decision to carry out the killing comes across quite clearly ... The situation for terrorists in Kashmir is so bad that Pakistan was forced to send a desperate request to China to create an issue along the Line of Actual Control (LAC) to divert attention from Kashmir. China, on its part, is so badly compromised by the non-starter China-Pakistan Economic Corridor (CPEC) and its own vulnerabilities in the post-COVID environment that it actually went ahead with the misadventure ... The terrorists, now under extreme pressure, needed to strike urgently and thus killed mercilessly the innocent Ajay Pandita and Danish Najar.

With great conviction, Kahlon has claimed the killing was designed and carried out by 'foreign' powers, curiously linking the incident with China, LAC and the CPEC. Yet has a criminal investigation been undertaken and its report made public? Kahlon goes on to say:

While the apprehensions of Kashmiri Pandit community are absolutely justified, one needs to keep in mind the fact that terrorists are indiscriminate in their choice of targets ... Terrorists have killed Hindus, Muslims, Sikhs and others without remorse all through the period of terrorism. Kashmiri Muslims have lost as much to terrorism, if not more, as have the Kashmiri Pandits. The need, therefore, is to fight the enemy together without giving it an opportunity to cause division on religious and community lines ... A vast majority of Kashmiri Muslims are eager to see the return of their Pandit brothers. The security forces have the security situation in the Valley well under control. This is the best time for Kashmiri Pandit community to move in and reclaim what is theirs.

Though attempting to cool tempers on all sides, these last words do not seem to be realistic. The majority of the Pandit population is scattered and has settled across India and around the globe. If anyone would be willing to return to settle back in the valley, it will be from that 5 to 10 percent of Kashmiri Pandits who currently live in the government-provided migrant flats at Jammu. Furthermore, had the security forces brought the situation in the valley 'well under control', the Kashmiris living in the valley would have been enjoying all the rights and privileges that are enjoyed by Indian citizens living in the rest of the country.

The situation in Kashmir is far from stable. The valley has been under a continued lockdown since the abrogation of Article 370 in the first week of August 2019, imposed initially for preventing unrest in the valley and later due to the COVID-19 pandemic.

In mid-June the director general of Jammu and Kashmir Police (DGP) said security forces had killed twenty-seven terrorists in the previous seventeen days in the valley, 'causing frustration among militants who are now targeting innocent people'. When asked about the lack of security for Ajay, the DGP reportedly said, 'Individual security is subject to the review of the security review committee of the union territory'.

India and China are currently in the midst of serious border issues in Ladakh (part of the erstwhile state of Jammu and Kashmir), where violent clashes between the forces of two nuclear-armed neighbours — the world's two most populated countries — have resulted in the deaths of scores of soldiers on either side. As reported in *The Guardian* on 17 June, the most recent clash was: the first fatal confrontation since 1975 and the most serious since 1967 ... Thus far at least, both Indian and Chinese forces have stuck to an agreement not to carry firearms on patrol near the LAC ... Over the decades, China has been more assertive than India in building infrastructure around the LAC, with roads and bunkers. In recent years, India has been trying to catch up ... Neither government wants this to escalate but the fact that there has been significant loss of life, at least on the Indian side, makes the situation much harder to defuse.

In light of this, the living conditions in the Kashmir valley cannot be considered as normal and stable enough to lure Kashmiri Pandits back to their home. They left the valley three decades ago as individual families and it is their right to choose if, when and how to return. They are not cattle who can be loaded on trucks, transported to the valley and lodged in designated secured areas, surrounded by armed security personnel, barbed wire and security towers. Being educated and dignified citizens, they are expected to judge the living conditions in the valley before taking any decision. It is not unreasonable to expect that their return to the valley will be possible only when their Muslim brethren in the valley start living in peaceful conditions — as other Indian citizens do in the rest of India — without the fear of guns or sudden lockdowns or loss of freedom of expression.

Kahlon continues:

The concept of a separate area being earmarked for them would, in military terms, be reflective of a siege mentality that would prove to be counterproductive in the long run. The community should aim at accessing the whole of Kashmir as it did earlier and not get constricted into a ghetto ... New Delhi can help by remaining sensitive to the vulnerabilities of the minority community in Kashmir ... Once the vulnerability is addressed and the ghetto mentality discarded, innovative solutions for enhancing security will present themselves ... One hundred percent security is not assured to anybody anywhere in the world and should not be expected in this case too. Let the sacrifice of Ajay Pandita not go in vain; if more people take a courageous step like him and his family, the terrorists will be defeated in their own game.

Note that the 'majority community' in the valley is also the 'minority community' in India as a whole. In addition, can politicians be defined as 'terrorists' if they indulge in similar activities or exhibit similar behaviours even though they may not actually wield a gun? What may appear as an act of terrorism to one side may be seen as an act of freedom-fighting by the other side.

Will Ajay ever receive justice?

Was Ajay like an unarmed solider, without any security to protect him when he needed it the most? Will he ever receive justice?

Ajay's life mirrors our times; it marks the life of any other human in Kashmir or the subcontinent, or in the wider world. He was just forty-four, full of dreams and aspirations, as any one of us is, seemingly with a noble vision and a determined mind to make a visible difference in the lives of people in Kashmir. But who really cares for a human life? Who cares for Kashmir? Who cares for justice? Where is the truth? Where is fairness? Where is honesty? All these terms seem to be idealistic and hypothetical.

How many members of his Kashmiri Pandit community had ever heard about him or knew him personally? Was he acting like a lone ranger? Did his community — standing under a common umbrella — ever support him in his call for security when he was still alive? After his emotional television interview in December 2019, did the Kashmiri Pandit leadership ever lend its voice in support of his plea? Going by the events, after a person is gone, all these political and social organisations which have sent condolences and offered their sympathies are nothing but hypocritical.

It is noteworthy that, within a couple of days of Ajay's killing, definitive conclusions had been made and announced to the world, about the possible killers and their sponsors, at the local police and the government level. If security intelligence was so sharp, shouldn't the local police have known that Ajay was vulnerable, especially after the revoking of Article 370? In particular, as Ajay had been openly demanding his security, it is extremely surprising, and rather disappointing, to hear the authorities say that they did not know anything about his request for security. Amazingly, without completing an investigation, how did the director general of the local police know who was behind Ajay's killing? Was it based purely on his guesswork about the usual suspect? Why is every security failure in Kashmir, or India, blamed on the usual suspect? The killers were understood to be on the run at the time of writing this chapter.

There must be absolutely no doubt that Ajay was extremely brave and courageous. But it is also commonly advised, 'discretion is the better part of valour', which literally means, 'it is wise to be careful and avoid unnecessary risks and dangerous situations'. This is the mantra that most Kashmiri Pandits follow, as demonstrated by them when they exiled themselves three decades ago and, thereafter, in their general reluctance to return home to the valley. It is another thing that many Kashmiris and Indians have called them cowards. In Shakespeare's *Henry IV* (Part I), when Prince Hal sees the cowardly Falstaff fallen on the battlefield as if he were dead, he assumes Falstaff has been killed. But after Prince Hal departs the scene, Falstaff rationalises his act: 'The better part of Valour, is Discretion; in the which better part, I have saved my life'. Kashmiri Pandits, a literary community, would have understood Shakespeare.

This chapter ends with a short write-up on Bhagat Singh, the iconic Indian freedom fighter and social revolutionary who was tried by the British in a conspiracy case and hanged to death on 23 March 1931, in a Lahore jail, at the age of twenty-three. Bhagat Singh never received justice. The Indian Supreme Court described his trial as 'contrary to the fundamental doctrine of criminal jurisprudence', in which the judgment was passed ex-parte, as he was kept away from the court through the trial and given absolutely no opportunity to defend himself. Reportedly, an honorary judge had supervised his execution, as no magistrate was willing to supervise the hanging. After the hanging, the body was quietly removed by the jail authorities, after making a hole in the rear wall of the jail. His body was secretly cremated and ashes thrown into the Sutlej River under the cover of darkness. Like, Bhagat Singh, will Ajay or the likes of him ever receive justice?

Face Off with You, My Lord

This poem tries to establish a one-to-one relationship between God and man — as parts of the One and the same One Being, perceiving them essentially as reflections of each other. The poem also illustrates man's desire for God to appear on the Earth so that he could question Him and make Him behold Himself through his (man's) eyes. The man's intention is to make God appreciate and address human struggles and helplessness, especially of the poor, downtrodden and the unprivileged. Interestingly, the man sets an audacious condition for their face-to-face meeting, which requires God to ensure his (man's) eyes do not close — after blushing in God's splendorous presence — or become moist due to emotions on getting overwhelmed by God's glory when they meet each other face to face. While making God responsible for everything, including his own self, pride and the ego, the man cleverly exonerates himself of his trespasses, reminding both to show full respect to each other when they meet face to face.

*****

I am ashamed of myself, You must also be ashamed of Yourself; when we'll face off each other day, my Lord, I'll question You!

My request to you, my Lord, sometime demonstrate Your Divinity; anyhow, I know every picture out there reflects Your image; Your wonder is everywhere.

When You arrive, appear in Your radiant grandness, in Your complete splendour; however, appear only on the condition, my Lord, that my eyes do not close due to my abashment nor become tearful.

The sun, the moon and stars are all your playing toys; your splendour immerses everything; come and appear sometime on the earth also, my Lord, and behold Yourself with my eyes.

I am ashamed of Yourself, of your silence, as well as I am ashamed of myself; if you are God, You are a part of my existence too, as my spirit; Your Divinity is intertwined with my ego and pride.

This complaint of mine is also my ardent appeal to You; but whatever it is, it is as per Your will and acquiescence; I have committed this crime in my bewilderment and out of my amazement of your splendour and my love for You.

Come sometime and behold Yourself with my eyes, my Lord; You will also blush on seeing Yourself; You will also wonder at Yourself; You will also have complaints against Yourself.

Your Divinity is embedded within my pride and ego and mine in Yours; in Your will and acquiescence lie my will and acquiescence; I may be weak and helpless, You too are burdened; in my impatience lies your helplessness, my Lord.

Now come once, my Lord, and behold Yourself with my desperate eyes; don't humiliate and dishonour me, my Lord; my disappointment will make You feel disappointed with Yourself; You will also become embarrassed of Yourself; You will also develop resentment against Yourself.

Undoubtedly, my appeal to you may appear to be smeared with infidelity but, undoubtedly, I am not an infidel; as you are not a human, my Lord, I don't fear You; you are neither arrogant nor cruel as humans.

I know, my Lord, You are brighter than the brightest sun; thus, I wish my impatient eyes don't close due my abashment or become tearful when I am face to face with You, so that neither You are disrespected nor I am dishonoured.

My Lord, my Guide, never forget that my Self, my pride and ego are all intertwined with Your Divinity and Your Divinity is embedded very much into my Self and my pride and ego.

*****

Ruu-ba-ruu tujse, mere Khuda

Sharaminda hun main khud se', sharamindaghi tuje' bhi hogi khud se';
Jab honge' tumse hum ruu-ba-ruu, mere Khuda, karenghe' tum se' hum kuchh sawalat.

Guzarish hai tujse', dikha de kabi khudai apni, mere Khuda;
Yun toh malum hai muje' be ki har tasveer mein hai tera deedar, sub taraf hai teri karamat.

Jab aaoge, aana apni shaan ke saath aur dikha jaana apna jalwa;
Shart magar hai meri, mere Khuda, aankh meri bandh na ho sharam se, na ho namnaak jab ho tera deedar.

Chand sitare' aur suraj, yeh sab hai tere khilone', tera he jalwa hai har taraf;
Ab kabi meri zameen par be aa, mere Khuda, aur khud ko dekh meri aankh se' be.

Sharamandaghi hai muje' tuj se, teri khamoshi se, sharamandaghi hai meje khud se' be;
Agar tu Khuda hai, hai tu mere wajood mein be, meri ruh mein; hai meri khudi teri Khudai mein be.

Yeh shikwa be hai, fariyad be hai tujse, jo be hai teri he razamandi se hai;
Yeh jurm be kiya hai maine madhoshi mein, mere Khuda, teri noorani se, teri mohabbat mein.

Aa kabi dekh khud ko merei aankh se, mere Khuda;
Sharma jayega tu be khud ko dekh kar, hairat tuje be hogi khud ko dekh
kar, shikayat tuje be hogi khud se.

Meri khudi mein hai teri Khudai, teri Khudai mein hai meri khudi
Teri razamandi mein hai meri razamandi, bebass main be hun, majboor
tu be hai, meri besabri main hai teri bebassi, mere Khuda.

Aa ek baar ab, mere Khuda, aur dekh khud ko meri be-bas aankh se be;
Rusva na kar, mere Khuda, meri mayoosi se khud be hoga tu khud se
mayoos, tuje be sharam aayegi khud se, tuje be shikayat rahegi khud se.

Yekinan hai kufr meri guzaarish main, lekin kafir nahi hun main
yekinan;
Insaan nahi hai tu, mere Khuda, is wajeh se durr nahi hai muje' tujse',
insaanu jaisa garoor be nahi hai tujme, na hai tu un ke jaise bereham.

Maloom hai muje, mere Khuda, suraj se be zyada noor hain tuj mein;
Meri besabr aank nah ho band sharam se, nah ho namnaak jub ho jaon
ruu-ba-ruu tuj se; na ho teri shaan mein koi gustakhi, na ho meri koi
rusvai.

Itna na boolna kabi, mere Khuda, mere Rahbar;
Teri Khudai mein hai meri khudi aur meri khudi mein hain teri Khudai.

Chapter 5

GEOPOLITICAL CRISES

This chapter discusses geopolitics during COVID-19 pandemic and how the world is currently positioned precariously, all due to the ego and personal political ambitions of some powerful political leaders. It discusses the ongoing Hong Kong crisis, Middle-East conflicts, India's current tense relationship with its neighbours – Pakistan, China and Nepal; South-China Sea conflict and the stand-off between the US and China; the role of the Quad – Australia, India, Japan and the US in the Indo-Pacific region; and the importance of the November 2020 US presidential election for the stability of the world and, in particular, Asia.

The chapter ends with a short poem, *Life passed by, unnoticed.*

Various geopolitical issues

During the pandemic, when one would expect the least, the human ego has continued to take the better of us. Many geopolitical issues, including military confrontations, are taking place around the world, including:

- crises in the Middle East — in Libya, Yemen and Saudi Arabia
- border conflict between India and Nepal
- border conflict between India and China
- mistrust and cross-border firing between India and Pakistan
- South-China Sea conflict between China and the United States.

India has found itself in confrontational mode with three of its neighbours — China, Nepal and Pakistan. China, meanwhile, has come face to face with India and the US.

New alliances have been forged. China has aligned with Russia, in response to the recent wedding between the US and India, and its relationship with Pakistan continues to thrive. The Quadrilateral Security Dialogue, known as the Quad, is an informal strategic forum between Australia, India, Japan and the United States which is focused on China.

India and Pakistan have been exchanging fire across the Line of Control (LOC), with India blaming Pakistan for pushing militants across the LOC and also instigating 'terrorist' activities in Kashmir. It culminated in India expelling half the staff of the Pakistan High Commission in New Delhi, after accusing the staff of espionage. Pakistan quickly reciprocated.

[Readers must note that the de-facto border between India and China is termed as the Line of Actual Control (LAC), which is different than the LOC between India and Pakistan.]

The surprise confrontation has been with Nepal, the closest historical ally of India and a country that has depended on India. But their relationship has soured since 2015 when India imposed a two-month embargo on imports on Nepal. In May 2020, when India inaugurated a road of strategic, trade and religious importance at Kalpani, which passes through a territory claimed by Nepal, the latter protested and passed a new geopolitical map of Nepal in its parliament, claiming ownership of those areas, which did not sit well with India. People in Nepal protested against India.

Alarmingly, the two nuclear-armed neighbours, India and China, are in a tense diplomatic and military stand-off. On 15 June 2020, a deadly border clash between the two countries — at Galwan Valley in Ladakh — took the lives of at least twenty Indian soldiers, with many injured. The casualties on the Chinese side were not known at the time of writing. Given that India and China have fought their last three military conflicts during the period of September to November, the current conflict in eastern Ladakh looks quite ominous. Interestingly, during that period, the US will be occupied with the presidential election.

Of all the conflicts, the two most potentially dangerous stand-offs have been in the South China Sea and the Ladakh region of India. Both these conflicts involve nuclear powers. If one or both of them spiral out of control, the world may be headed to World War III.

The coming months, in particular, till the onset of winter in the northern hemisphere that also coincides with the November 2020 US election, are extremely delicate for the entire world from various angles, with the COVID-19 pandemic, military conflicts and the global economy all having the potential to unleash significant misery on the human race.

Soldiers

Soldiers are humans who dedicate their lives to the service of their country. They guard and defend their country's borders — in rain, snow or sunshine, in melting heat or freezing cold. They remain away from their homes and families for extended periods of time. They also undertake humanitarian rescue missions and risk their own lives to save people's lives during natural catastrophes, such as earthquakes, forest fires and floods. At times, when needed by civil administration, they also help to maintain law and order, alongside police, during times of civil unrest and even during epidemics and pandemics.

Soldiers are professionally groomed and expected to follow, unconditionally and unquestioningly, the orders from their superiors. The chain of command goes right up to the head of the government of the country. They are professionally trained, through the strictest discipline and toughest training, to survive through war and kill enemy soldiers while defending their own.

Howsoever hurtful or blasphemous or disrespectful it may be construed, soldiers are practically pawns in the hands of their government. Their patriotism becomes a cause of their death, as it is generally exploited by their government. Sadly, therefore, they are considered expendable. While the civilian leadership itself lives and operates mostly from secured, comfortable buildings, soldiers brave the elements in some of the most hostile and harshest environments on the planet and perform their most 'sacred duty' towards their country.

Soldiers kill or get killed on the behest of their superiors, carrying out the decisions made by their government which are, in many cases, influenced by the ego, pride and political ambitions of the leadership. As such, soldiers don't carry any personal animosity or grudge against soldiers of their clear or perceived enemy. In times of military conflict and war, they just follow the chain of command and it becomes a case of choosing between saving their own lives or taking the lives of enemy soldiers. In such situations, they kill or get killed. Many soldiers also get maimed and many suffer from debilitating mental illnesses, such as post-traumatic stress disorder, depression, anxiety, alcohol misuse and substance abuse. Many soldiers also commit suicide, whether during service or once retired, for varied reasons when they struggle with their mental health.

The bulk of an army, especially in Asia, Africa and South America, comprises non-commissioned officers, who usually come from lower-middle and relatively poorer families. Commissioned officers usually come from the middle class and upper-middle class, and many come from military backgrounds. During any military conflict or war, therefore, it is soldiers who come from relatively poorer socioeconomic strata of society who make up most of the casualties and pay the ultimate price with their own lives.

Because soldiers remain ever ready to sacrifice their own lives in the service and defence of their country, they may be construed as 'saint warriors'. As such, soldiers exemplify the highest form of altruism and spirituality wherein death, which inhibits most humans from living a full life, becomes a way of life and loses significance.

Australia plans to build a larger military

At the beginning of July, the Australian government announced it would spend A\$270 billion over the next decade on defence capabilities, building a larger military and accumulating powerful strike weapons, cyber capabilities and a high-tech underwater surveillance system, to prepare for a 'poorer, more dangerous' world and the rise of China.

Australian Prime Minister Scott Morrison warned that Australia faced regional challenges on a scale not seen since World War II. He argued that the Indo-Pacific is the 'epicentre' of rising strategic competition and 'the risk of miscalculation, and even conflict, is heightening'. Without referring to China or any other country, Morrison said, 'The Indo-Pacific is where we live — and we want an open, sovereign Indo-Pacific, free from coercion and hegemony'.

In a televised interview Morrison did make direct reference: 'The strategic competition between China and the United States means that there's a lot of tension in the cord and a lot of risk of miscalculation'. He has also reportedly said: 'The ADF now needs stronger deterrence capabilities … Capabilities that can hold potential adversaries' forces and critical infrastructure at risk from a distance, thereby deterring an attack on Australia and helping to prevent war'.

Peter Jennings from the Australian Strategic Policy Institute was reported to have said, 'the world had changed dramatically … particularly in the era of COVID-19', adding there was

> only one country with both the capacity and the desire to dominate the Indo-Pacific region in a way that works against Australia's interest … when they talk about the bad behaviour that's happening in the region, the annexation of territory, coercion, the influencing of domestic politics, the use of cyber-attacks — it's

really only one country which is doing that at industrial levels, and that's the People's Republic of China.

The timing is ominous, as China is under intense pressure to redeem itself after being widely criticised — by Australia, Brazil, the European Union, the UK, the US, India and many other countries — for its initial handling of the pandemic. In fact, Australia was among the first countries which demanded a probe into the creation and the spread of the coronavirus, backed by the US and EU countries. China also had to defend itself against a conspiracy theory, driven by anti-China powers, that the virus was created in a lab at Wuhan, despite evidence against that theory.

The timing is crucial due to the US presidential election on 3 November 2020. China is currently involved in a border stand-off with India, at eastern Ladakh, as well as facing a potential US threat in the South China Sea.

Australian economy and coronavirus

The International Monetary fund (IMF) reported in June that the Australian economy would contract by 4.5 percent in 2020. Two months earlier, the IMF had forecast a 6.7 percent contraction in Australia. Before COVID-19, Australia was ranked fourteenth in the world in terms of overall GDP and twelfth in terms of GDP per capita.

In a *Business Insider Australia* article dated 25 June 2020, Jack Derwin wrote: 'Australia's economy looks to be in surprisingly decent shape, according to the IMF, as it navigates a worsening global recession'. He does, however, warn that Australia won't emerge unscathed. The country's geography may have safeguarded it relative to other countries, in terms of the number of infections and their control, but the recent spike in infection rates in the Australian state of Victoria could threaten the recovery effort of the federal government, especially as other states are in the process of cautiously reopening.

Around mid-July 2020, infections had spread across the New South

Wales–Victoria border. For the first time in more than one hundred years, the NSW–Victoria border was closed indefinitely from 8 July 2020 and the country's coronavirus death toll had reached 106. But thereafter, due to a deadly second wave of the outbreak in Victoria, the total number of deaths in the country had reached 600 by 29 August 2020, with a death rate of 23 per million people and Australia had conducted 239,345 tests per million people. As per the Australian Government Department of Health's report, dated 29 August 2020, Australia has recorded a total of 25,547 cases, with 4,033 cases (52 deaths) in New South Wales ('NSW'), 18,903 in Victoria (513 deaths), 1,117 in Queensland (6 deaths), 463 in South Australia (4 deaths), 655 in Western Australia (9 deaths), 230 in Tasmania (13 deaths), 113 (with 3 deaths) in the Australian Capital Territory ('ACT') and 33 cases (with no deaths) in the Northern Territory ('NT').

Hong Kong crisis

Hong Kong was a British colony for 156 years. At the end of the First Opium War (1839–42), it became a colony of the British Empire after the Qing Empire ceded Hong Kong Island. In 1860, after the Second Opium War, the colony was expanded and included the Kowloon Peninsula. In 1898, Britain obtained a 99-year lease of the New Territories, which was to end in 1997. On 19 December 1984, the United Kingdom and China signed the Sino-British Joint Declaration on the Question of Hong Kong, according to which Hong Kong would see a transitional government over the thirteen years before the 99-year lease ended.

In 1997, at midnight of 1 July, the British handed over the entire territory of Hong Kong back to China on the condition that the Hong Kong special administrative region would enjoy a high degree of autonomy, except in matters of foreign relations and defence. Under a 'one country, two systems' framework, it was agreed that the social and economic systems, as well as the lifestyle, of Hong Kong would remain unchanged for the next fifty years, till 2047.

The total area of Hong Kong is 1104 square kilometres. With more than 7.5 million people of various nationalities, it is one of the most densely populated cities in the world. It is a highly developed area and ranks fourth on the UN Human Development Index, with the largest number of skyscrapers of any city in the world. Its residents have among the highest life expectancy in the world. It is ranked sixth in the Global Financial Centres Index and fourth in Asia after Tokyo, Shanghai and Singapore.

In June 2019, the Hong Kong government considered an extradition bill that would allow criminal suspects from Hong Kong to be extradited to mainland China for trial. On 12 June, tens of thousands of protesters surrounded the legislative building of Hong Kong, which had delayed the start of a debate on the extradition bill. In response, police used tear gas and rubber bullets to disperse the protesters. In the following months, regular violent clashes were witnessed in Hong Kong in which protesters demanded the scrapping of the extradition bill and greater democracy.

With the imposition of the coronavirus lockdown early in 2020, the protest movement quietened down. By the middle of the year, however, after the Hong Kong government agreed to enact a new national security law for Hong Kong — aimed at curbing secessionist and subversive behaviour and preventing foreign intervention in its internal affairs — protests had erupted again.

On 12 June, thousands of people sang protest songs and marched across Hong Kong to mark the one-year anniversary of the first demonstration against the extradition bill. More than one hundred people holding flags that read 'Hong Kong independence' and 'The people fear not death, why threaten them with it?' had joined a lunchtime protest in a luxury shopping mall. Later, in the evening, thousands of people across Hong Kong marched on, singing the protest anthem 'Glory to Hong Kong', while the riot police stood by and looked on. In Mong Kok unchanged for the next fifty years, till 2047.

The total area of Hong Kong is 1104 square kilometres. With more than 7.5 million people of various nationalities, it is one of the most densely populated cities in the world. It is a highly developed area and ranks fourth on the UN Human Development Index, with the largest number of skyscrapers of any city in the world. Its residents have among the highest life expectancy in the world. It is ranked sixth in the Global Financial Centres Index and fourth in Asia after Tokyo, Shanghai and Singapore.

In June 2019, the Hong Kong government considered an extradition bill that would allow criminal suspects from Hong Kong to be extradited to mainland China for trial. On 12 June, tens of thousands of protesters surrounded the legislative building of Hong Kong, which had delayed the start of a debate on the extradition bill. In response, police used tear gas and rubber bullets to disperse the protesters. In the following months, regular violent clashes were witnessed in Hong Kong in which protesters demanded the scrapping of the extradition bill and greater democracy.

With the imposition of the coronavirus lockdown early in 2020, the protest movement quietened down. By the middle of the year, however, after the Hong Kong government agreed to enact a new national security law for Hong Kong — aimed at curbing secessionist and subversive behaviour and preventing foreign intervention in its internal affairs — protests had erupted again.

On 12 June, thousands of people sang protest songs and marched across Hong Kong to mark the one-year anniversary of the first demonstration against the extradition bill. More than one hundred people holding flags that read 'Hong Kong independence' and 'The people fear not death, why threaten them with it?' had joined a lunchtime protest in a luxury shopping mall. Later, in the evening, thousands of people across Hong Kong marched on, singing the protest anthem 'Glory to Hong Kong', while the riot police stood by and looked on. In Mong Kok and Causeway Bay shopping districts, police raised a blue flag, which signalled the gatherings were deemed unlawful. Groups of protesters were subsequently detained in Mong Kok. Police used pepper spray in Causeway Bay and a number of protesters, including pro-democracy lawmaker Ted Hui, were arrested. The police reported that a total of thirty-five people had been arrested for unlawful assembly and possession of weapons.

As per a report in The Diplomat, dated 13 June 2020, China's foreign ministry lashed out at the UK on its issuing a regular six-month report on developments in Hong Kong: 'Hong Kong affairs are China's internal affairs. No foreign organisation or individual has the right to intervene. The British side has no sovereignty, governance, supervision or so-called responsibility over Hong Kong.' Defending the proposed new national security legislation, Hua sent a warning to the UK and asked that it 'face up to reality, respect China's sovereignty, security and integrity, and stop interfering in Hong Kong affairs in any way … The more external forces intervene in Hong Kong affairs, the more determined China is to advance the national security legislation in Hong Kong'.

Following the British government's offer, Australian Prime Minister Scott Morrison said Australia too would open a path to Australian citizenship for millions of Hong Kong residents. In response, the Chinese foreign ministry hit back, saying 'Stop interfering in China's internal affairs with Hong Kong as a pretext, and refrain from going further down the wrong path', urging Australia to look at the national security legislation in a 'correct and objective' light.

As reported in The Canberra Times, the Chinese foreign ministry also lashed out at the UK: 'This is a serious breach of its own commitment and grave violation of international law and basic norms of international relations. China strongly condemns this and reserves the right of further reactions, the consequences of which shall be borne by the British side.'

and Causeway Bay shopping districts, police raised a blue flag, which signalled the gatherings were deemed unlawful. Groups of protesters were subsequently detained in Mong Kok. Police used pepper spray in Causeway Bay and a number of protesters, including pro-democracy lawmaker Ted Hui, were arrested. The police reported that a total of thirty-five people had been arrested for unlawful assembly and possession of weapons.

As per a report in The Diplomat, dated 13 June 2020, China's foreign ministry lashed out at the UK on its issuing a regular six-month report on developments in Hong Kong: 'Hong Kong affairs are China's internal affairs. No foreign organisation or individual has the right to intervene. The British side has no sovereignty, governance, supervision or so-called responsibility over Hong Kong.' Defending the proposed new national security legislation, Hua sent a warning to the UK and asked that it 'face up to reality, respect China's sovereignty, security and integrity, and stop interfering in Hong Kong affairs in any way … The more external forces intervene in Hong Kong affairs, the more determined China is to advance the national security legislation in Hong Kong.'

Following the British government's offer, Australian Prime Minister Scott Morrison said Australia too would open a path to Australian citizenship for millions of Hong Kong residents. In response, the Chinese foreign ministry hit back, saying 'Stop interfering in China's internal affairs with Hong Kong as a pretext, and refrain from going further down the wrong path', urging Australia to look at the national security legislation in a 'correct and objective' light.

As reported in The Canberra Times, the Chinese foreign ministry also lashed out at the UK: 'This is a serious breach of its own commitment and grave violation of international law and basic norms of international relations. China strongly condemns this and reserves the right of further reactions, the consequences of which shall be borne by the British side.'

On 7 July 2020, it was reported that a 23-year-old man was the first person to be charged under the new security law, which was imposed the previous week. He had been charged with terrorism and inciting secession for allegedly driving a motorbike into a group of police.

As per the new law, any activity that the government interprets as secessionist, subversive or terrorist, including perceived foreign intervention in the internal affairs of Hong Kong, will be deemed illegal, carrying a maximum penalty of life imprisonment. As such, shouting slogans or holding up banners and flags calling for independence are illegal, regardless of whether violence is used. Accordingly, the popular protest slogan 'Liberate Hong Kong, revolution of our time' has been criminalised for its separatist connotations.

China censored Hong Kong internet on 7 July 2020 when the Chinese government released a 116-page plan for censoring internet and to access users' data in Hong Kong. The plans provide Hong Kong police with expanded powers, allowing allow them to conduct warrantless raids and surveillance.

Middle East conflicts

The Middle East has continued to witness a number of conflicts between various countries and regimes despite being affected by the COVID-19 pandemic. The civil war continues in Syria. Libya and Yemen are caught up in proxy wars resulting in significant humanitarian crises. Saudi Arabia too has been attacked. Iran has alleged cyber warfare against its nuclear installation.

On 12 June 2020, *Al Jazeera* report presented to the UN Security Council found that, on examination of debris, the weapons used in several attacks on facilities in Saudi Arabia in 2019 were of 'Iranian origin', despite Yemen's Houthi rebels previously claiming responsibility for attacks on the Saudi Aramco facilities. Iran has completely denied any involvement in the attacks.

The attacks had been carried out on a Saudi oil facility in Afif in

May 2019; Abha international airport in June and August 2019; and the Saudi Aramco oil facilities in Khurais and Abqaiq in September 2019.

Since 2015, a Saudi-led coalition has been fighting Yemen's Houthi rebels to restore the government of Yemeni President Abd Rabbuh Mansur Hadi. It is believed the Houthi rebels are being actively supported by Iran, in a continuation of the historical conflict between Sunni and Shia Muslims, which is also being fought in the ongoing Syrian civil war (since March 2011) and was behind the eight-year Iran–Iraq War (1980–1988).

On 23 June 2020, *Bloomberg* reported that the capital Riyadh and other cities, Najran and Jazan, of Saudi Arabia had come under a missile and drone attack from the Houthi rebels. Saudi air defences had intercepted at least four ballistic missiles and also destroyed eight explosives-laden drones. A Houthi spokesperson said that the attacks had targeted the Saudi defence ministry, military and intelligence bases, and other locations in the three Saudi cities. The next day it was reported that the weapons had been launched from an unidentified location, somewhere to the north of Saudi Arabia, but not Yemen.

In Iran on 2 July 2020, a fire reportedly damaged a building above the underground Natanz nuclear enrichment facility, located in central Isfahan province where enrichment activity has been ramped up in the past year. The site has previously been a target of cyberattacks and cyber sabotage was suspected to be behind this attack too. This was the third prominent industrial accident in Iran in a short space of time. While Iranian officials downplayed the incident, US satellite data has shown an explosion or fire large enough to be detected from space.

The Natanz site includes buildings buried to a depth of around 7.5 metres to protect them from aerial attacks. Since Iran's 2015 nuclear agreement with the US and other countries, the site is among those monitored by the International Atomic Energy Agency (IAEA). In 2007 and since, the facility has reportedly been targeted by a sophisticated, malicious computer virus, Stuxnet, widely thought to have been developed by the US and Israel and their allies. In May 2018, the US unilaterally pulled out of the Iran nuclear agreement. The IAEA claims that, since then, Iran has been using the Natanz facility to enrich uranium to about 4.5 percent purity, which is above the terms of the agreement but below weapons-grade threshold.

The Natanz fire incident follows a large explosion on 26 June 2020 in the eastern mountains in an area which is believed to hide an underground tunnel system and missile production facility.

An Iranian nuclear official is reported to have said that the Natanz fire had caused significant damage to the facility, which could slow down the development of advanced centrifuges used to enrich uranium. Iran has warned it would retaliate against any country that carried out the attack. The Revolutionary Guards Navy chief has said that Iran has built underground 'missile cities' along the Gulf coastline and warned of a 'nightmare for Iran's enemies'.

Ranj Alaaldin, visiting fellow at Brookings Doha Centre, published in April 2020 an exhaustive commentary on the Middle East conflicts. He said COVID-19 would prolong conflicts in the Middle East. Cross-border attacks would destabilise countries that had earlier managed to keep conflicts outside of their borders. In economically and militarily weakened countries, exacerbated by the pandemic, militias, terrorists and other armed sub-state actors would fill the role of governance, in some cases with brutal subjugation. Since the territorial defeat of ISIS three years ago, the region continues to struggle to achieve peace.

In conflict-stricken countries, such as Syria, Libya and Yemen, healthcare facilities have been targeted by warring factions and their external sponsors. In those countries, the impact of the pandemic is expected to be significant. Instead of pushing these conflicts towards peace, the pandemic will most likely act as a conflict-multiplier. The humanitarian cost of the ongoing conflicts is extreme. Hundreds of thousands of people are believed to have been killed and millions displaced and forced into a life of destitution.

- In Libya, hospitals are routinely targeted by rocket attacks. The pandemic has provided a boost to militias, providing them with an opportunity to channel medical supplies to their fighters.
- In Yemen, indiscriminate attacks have destroyed medical facilities and water supplies, contributing to what the international community has described as the world's greatest human-made humanitarian crisis, including the worst cholera outbreak in modern history.
- In Lebanon, Hezbollah has reinforced its status as an alternative to the Lebanese state by committing close to 5000 doctors, medics and nurses to fight the pandemic.
- In Iraq, ISIS has ramped up its attacks in northern Iraqi villages, aiming to exploit the escalation between the US and Iran, the decline in oil prices, and countrywide protests.
- In Syria, the civil war has shattered formal governing structures and infrastructure, including hospitals, from the outset of the nine-year conflict. Syria is effectively three countries: (1) Syrian government-controlled territories; (2) the Kurdish northeast; and (3) Idlib in the northwest.

Alaaldin says the Syrian civil war has displaced, internally and externally, more than 12 million people, which is half the Syrian population. In addition, about 6.5 million people have been displaced internally in Iraq and Yemen, and more than 435,000 people in Libya. About 11 million people need humanitarian aid in Syria, 24 million in Yemen, 2.4 million in Libya and 4.1 million in Iraq.

To conclude, even during the COVID-19 pandemic, it seems the historical conflict between the Sunni and Shia Muslims has continued to play a dominant part in the ongoing conflicts in the Middle East, including the ongoing Syrian civil war and the historical eight-year Iran–Iraq War and the current conflicts in Yemen, Libya and Iraq. The division between the two sects of Islam has possibly been exploited by many third parties from time to time, in one shape or another, with the division underlying most conflicts in the region. Political, economic and military alliances are forged along these lines.

The Middle East has undoubtedly paid a significant price in terms of peace and stability for containing some of the world's largest oil reserves. If not for a continued mutual distrust between humans following the two main branches of the same religion (Islam) and the differences due to their ethnicity (Arabs, Africans and Persians), exacerbated by intrinsic greed from both within the region and outside it, the entire Middle East would have been a vibrant, prosperous, happy and peaceful region of the world.

The Middle East has undoubtedly paid heavily for its natural resources in a similar way as many magnificent wild animals — lions, tigers, leopards, bears, deer and antelopes — used to be, or possibly still are, hunted for their trophy heads, skin and body parts. Elephants too are killed for their tusks and ivory. One's best asset becomes one's enemy, thanks to human greed and cunning.

India–Nepal border dispute

Nepal is a landlocked country, located mostly in the Himalayas, with parts of it in the Indo-Gangetic plains. It is, thus, characterised by a diverse geography, which includes fertile plains and subalpine forested hills. India surrounds it along its southern, eastern and western borders, and China borders it to the north. It boasts of containing eight of the world's ten tallest mountains, including Mount Everest. It has five climatic zones, broadly corresponding to the altitudes. Since the Vedic period of the Indian subcontinent, the name 'Nepal' is believed to exist in ancient Indian texts. Siddhartha Gautama (Gautama Buddha) is believed to have been born in Lumbini, in southern Nepal, circa 480 BCE.

Nepal has an area of 147,181 square kilometres and a population of 29 million. It ranks 93 in the world in terms of its land area and 49 in terms of its population. Its official language is Nepalese and Hinduism is its predominant religion.

Nepal is a multi-ethnic country, with parts of northern Nepal intertwined with the Tibetan culture and the centrally located Kathmandu Valley intertwined with the culture of Indo-Aryans.

Nepal shares a 1751-kilometre border with five Indian states — Uttarakhand (263 kilometres), Uttar Pradesh (560 kilometres), Bihar (729 kilometres), West Bengal (100 kilometres) and Sikkim (99 kilometres) — which influence the culture in the border areas. An estimated six million Nepalese are believed to be living and working in India.

As per the *Hindustan Times* on 12 December 2017, India and Nepal share an open and unfenced border, however, 'there are political issues over 2% of the border length and the length of the Indo-Nepal border could change after re-demarcation', as many areas left out during the previous mapping will be added after a re-demarcation process. The length of the boundary was calculated nearly two centuries ago, circa 1815. It was agreed that the earlier mapping had not been undertaken conspicuously and some areas were not included in the process of demarcation. There were supposed to be nearly 4000 pillars along the border, most of which were reported to have either been damaged or gone missing. The 98 per cent of the border length had been agreed and approved by the two countries; however, there were political issues over the remaining 2% of the border length, pending which the final agreement would be signed.

Major areas of dispute between India and Nepal are in Kalapani territory, Limpiyahura, Susta, Mechi, Tanakpur and Kuthi Valley. In November 2019, there was a protest in Kathmandu against a new political map of India that shows Kalapani as part of India.

On 8 May 2020, India inaugurated a new 80-kilometre road in Uttarakhand, which connects it with the LAC (with China) at the Lipulekh pass. The Nepali government immediately protested, claiming the road passes through Nepalese territory, and accused India of changing the status quo on the border, without even undertaking any diplomatic consultations.

In the following days, Nepal deployed its troops to the region and summoned the Indian ambassador in Kathmandu, and initiated a constitutional amendment to formalise its territorial claims over a contentious 400-square-kilometre area around the source of Kali River. In return, India offered to have a dialogue but only after the COVID-19 crisis. On 20 May 2020, Nepal published its own map showing Kalapani as part of Nepal. On 10 June 2020, the Nepalese parliament moved to approve its new map, which includes the disputed areas of Kalapani, Limpiyadhur and Lipulekh, which India claims to be within Uttarakhand.

On 15 June 2020, Indian border police reported that border pillars were missing along the India–Nepal border and Nepali border police had established five new border outposts near the disputed area. Since the 1962 Indo-China War, Kalapani has been controlled by India's Indo-Tibetan Border Police.

On 18 June, Nepal's National Assembly unanimously passed the Constitution Amendment Bill to update the country's map, incorporating Indian territories. India quickly rejected the map, saying that such 'artificial enlargement' of territorial claim was just untenable.

On 19 June, Nepal started deploying its troops near the Kalapani area and other disputed areas. The troops established camps and started working on building a helipad in the area. Nepali Army Chief, General Purna Chandra Thapa, after visiting the Kalapani border area, said that the Nepali army would start building army barracks and border outposts near the Kalapani area.

Nepal claims the ownership of the river flowing to the west of Kalapani, as the main Kali River. The river separates Darchula, in the Nepalese Sudurpashchim Pradesh, from Pithoragarh, in the Indian state of Uttarakhand. As per the Treaty of Sugauli, signed by Nepal and British India on 3 March 1815, Kali River marks the original Nepal's western border with India. However, subsequent maps drawn by British surveyors show the source of Kali River at different places, which has led to boundary disputes between the two countries, with each country producing a map that supports its claim. The exact size of the disputed area varies from source to source, but is considered to be in the order of 400 square kilometres.

Nepal claims to have conducted a census in Kalapani in the early 1950s and refers to the Treaty of Sugauli to legitimise its claims. However, India has effectively been in control of the area since the 1962 Indo-China War. In 2015, China agreed to expand trade between the two countries through the Lipulekh pass.

The newly inaugurated road provides an important route for thousands of Indian Hindu pilgrims who trek every year across the LAC with China to visit Mount Kailash. Given the strategic, trade and religious importance of the road, therefore, India is unlikely to relinquish civilian and military control of the territories through which it passes. As far as the timing of the inauguration of the road, 8 May 2020 would have suited the Indian government to score a domestic success during the coronavirus lockdown period. So it does not seem that India has been acting in any way against Nepal or Nepal's interest.

In an exhaustive article dated 11 June 2020, Dr Constantino Xavier, fellow of Brookings India, discusses some of the possible factors that would have escalated the dispute between the two countries.

- The Nepalese reaction to the road is surprising as the road would have taken some time to be constructed and was not built overnight. As such, the Nepal government would have been well aware about the situation in Kalapani. For beleaguered Nepalese Prime Minister Oli, whose government faced an internal crisis in late April 2020, the 8 May announcement would have been a God-send. It enabled him to swiftly mobilise public opinion, rake up nationalist sentiments, rally his opponents behind him and divert attention from his failed ordinances and challenges to contain the pandemic.

- Nepal has one of the youngest populations in the world. After India's implicit support for the 2015 blockade, anti-India sentiments have been running high in the country, which provide the new generation of Nepalese politicians with opportunities to mobilise the electorate. As a result, Nepal chose not to attend a multilateral counter-terrorism exercise in 2018 in India.

In conclusion, it is unreasonable to solely blame China for creating the border dispute between the two countries, as the border dispute between India and Nepal has been brewing for several months. However, Xavier does not discount that, due to China's growing political influence on Nepal, especially after the 2015 blockade, China may have influenced Nepal to adopt a more assertive position against India, especially against the backdrop of the China–India military stand-off in Ladakh, as that country is known to exploit every opportunity to put pressure on India, especially when its relations with India become tense, using India's neighbours as proxies.

Since the 2015 blockade, Nepalese politicians have also become used to adopting anti-India rhetoric for their internal political gain. On the external front, especially to achieve leverage against India, they have become adept at playing the China card in situations where India appears to ignore their requests and demands.

On 21 June 2020, Nepalese youth protested in Darchula, upset with China interfering in their country's internal matters and that Prime Minister Oli had become a 'puppet' at the hands of China. During the week before that, thousands of students were reported to have gathered in Kathmandu to protest against the Nepalese government's inability to deal with the coronavirus epidemic. *Zee News* reported that the Nepalese youth were very upset that Nepal was involved in a border dispute with India. It reported: 'The people have expressed their anger at the government's failure to deal with the growing corruption in the country and the rise in number of coronavirus infections. Citizens also showed their displeasure on the ongoing border dispute with India calling it a diversionary tactic to distract attention from the issue of corruption.'

South China Sea dispute

The islands in the South China Sea are variously claimed by six different nations, as per a CNN report dated 4 June 2020. China claims virtually the entire waterway in the South China Sea — one of the busiest in the world — on historical grounds despite an international tribunal in The Hague in 2016 that invalidated its claim based on the UN Convention on the Law of the Sea. China claims almost all of the South China Sea's 3.3 million square kilometres as its own, despite other regional coastal states having baselines that are far closer to the disputed waters. As such, China's unilateral claim over much of the South China Sea violates the Exclusive Economic Zones of several regional coastal states in the area.

There are over 250 islands, atolls, cays, shoals, reefs and sandbars in the South China Sea. The islands have few inhabitants and, collectively, have a total land surface area of less than 15 square kilometres at low tide. They are subject to overlapping territorial claims by the countries bordering the South China Sea. The main disputed island groups are:

- The Paracel Islands, disputed between China, Taiwan and Vietnam, occupied by China since 1974 following the Battle of the Paracel Islands.
- The Pratas Islands, disputed between China and Taiwan, occupied by China.
- The Spratly Islands, disputed between China, Taiwan and Vietnam, with Malaysia, the Philippines and, to a lesser degree, Brunei also claiming various parts of the archipelago.
- The Zhongsha Islands: Macclesfield Bank, with no land above sea level, is disputed between China, Taiwan and the Philippines; and Scarborough Shoal, with only rocks above sea level, is disputed between China, Taiwan and the Philippines.

As a part of its occupation of Indochina (1857–1954), France controlled the Spratly Islands until the 1930s, exchanging a few with the British. Japan occupied all South China Sea islands during World War II. Thereafter, since 1949, China has claimed the islands as part of the province of Canton (Guangdong), and later of the Hainan special administrative region.

Historically, in 1421, Zheng He — the legendary Chinese mariner, explorer, diplomat, fleet admiral and court eunuch during China's early Ming dynasty — is claimed to have prepared the Mao Kun map, referred to as Zheng He's Navigation Map by Chinese people, which included the South China Sea islands. Between 1405 and 1433, using large ships that were almost twice as long as any wooden ship ever recorded and carrying hundreds of sailors on four decks, he is understood to have commanded various expeditionary voyages to South-East Asia, the Indian subcontinent, western Asia and east Africa.

The Philippines has claimed the Chinese army has been staging military exercises off the Paracel Islands since 1 July 2020, and the Chinese navy has also prohibited all vessels from navigating within the area of the Chinese manoeuvres. It has warned China of 'the severest response, diplomatic and whatever else is appropriate' if its exercises encroach into Philippines territory.

The area where the Chinese exercises have been taking place is reportedly also claimed by Vietnam. Earlier, in April 2020, a Chinese coast guard ship reportedly sank a Vietnamese fishing boat, with eight fishermen, off the Paracel Islands. At that time, Vietnam's protest was backed strongly by the Philippines, as the area where it had happened is disputed and not unequivocally accepted by the regional countries as belonging to China.

During Australian Prime Minister Scott Morrison's first to Vietnam in 2019, the two countries had shown their commitment to maintain independence and sovereignty in the region, with an indirect reference to undertaking joint efforts to restrict Chinese expansion in the South China Sea.

At that time, Vietnamese and Chinese vessels were locked in a tense stand-off in Vietnam-controlled waters but Australia never explicitly condemned China for its posturing and military build-up in the area. When Morrison was asked why he did not name the perpetrator, he said: 'It isn't about picking sides'. Standing alongside Morrison, the statement of Vietnamese Prime Minister Nguyen Xuan Phuc at that time — his first on the conflict — was: 'We are deeply concerned about the recent complicated developments in the East Sea and agree to cooperate in maintaining peace, stability, security, safety and freedom of navigation and overflight', using the Vietnamese name for South China Sea.'

China has blamed the US for increased tensions in the region while rejecting criticism from all parties of its plan to conduct military exercises in the South China Sea. It maintains the military exercises are within the scope of its sovereignty and certain 'non-regional countries' conducting military exercises in the South China Sea were affecting the region's stability, hinting at the US but not naming it.

The US had accused China of conducting military exercises over the disputed territory, stating they were 'counter-productive to efforts at easing tensions and maintaining stability'. Making a direct reference to China, a Pentagon statement said: 'The military exercises are the latest in a long string of PRC [People's Republic of China] actions to assert unlawful maritime claims and disadvantage its Southeast Asian neighbours in the South China Sea'.

The US–China confrontation

The US has no territorial claims in the South China Sea. However, it claims to have been maintaining peace in the disputed waters for decades. While constantly chastising China for its increased militarisation of the waterway, the US has been firmly asserting its freedom of access to international waterways by sending its warships in the area every now and then, and conducting a number of navigation operations there.

As reported in *The New York Times* on 21 April 2020, a spokesperson for the US Indo-Pacific Command, has said: 'Through our continued operational presence in the South China Sea, we are working with our allies and partners to promote freedom of navigation and overflight, and the international principles that underpin security and prosperity for the Indo-Pacific … The US supports the efforts of our allies and partners to determine their own economic interests.'

In a move coming 'as a war of words between the United States and China over the coronavirus pandemic intensifies', US warships had entered the disputed waters of the South China Sea around 200 nautical miles off the coast of Malaysia. Three countries — Malaysia, China and Vietnam — claim rights to the natural resources in the area.

The US move reportedly heightened a stand-off in the waterway between the two countries. A US amphibious assault ship and a guided missile cruiser had entered the contested waters, accompanied by an Australian frigate. Defence experts have said that a Chinese destroyer was also operating off the coast of Malaysia at the same time.

Earlier, a Chinese government survey ship had been shadowing an oil drill ship operated by the Malaysian state oil company, Petronas. Before that, China was accused of ramming and sinking a Vietnamese fishing boat in the area. In March 2020, China had reportedly opened two new research stations on artificial reefs, which it had built on maritime turf and equipped with defence silos and military-grade runways. The reefs are claimed by the Philippines and others.

China accuses the US of destabilising the region by sending its warships into the area. The regional governments are also understood to have shown concern that the US has 'a habit of briefly showing up in hot spots only to depart, leaving them to contend with an increasingly muscular Beijing'.

Interestingly, an American aircraft carrier, the *Theodore Roosevelt*, which had been sailing in the South China Sea earlier in the year, had an outbreak of COVID-19. One US sailor died and hundreds of other sailors were infected. In contrast, not a single member of the Chinese army or navy are known to have come down with the coronavirus.

Ian Storey, a South China Sea expert at a Singapore-based think tank ISEAS-Yusof Ishak Institute, summed it up as follows: 'What is the intention of the US here? Is it just to say, "We're here?" Or are they going to shadow the Chinese survey ship to try to stop it from operating? ... The optics for the US Navy in the region don't look so good, even as the Trump administration is trying to reassure its allies ... China can say, "Look at our superior governance system, which has beaten back the epidemic. And then, look at the US."'

In an ominous news report on 3 July 2020, *The Wall Street Journal* reported that the US had sent two aircraft carriers to the South China Sea for exercises as China held drills nearby. The timing is ominous because the US presidential election was just four months away at the time.

To conclude, it is evident that the top two world economies are continually showing off their economic and military strength in one way or another, acting like two street bullies. While China is trying to assert its dominance mostly in its backyard, the US continues to operate miles away from its mainland and to treat the whole world as its backyard. Of late, China seems to be standing up to the US and resisting US posturing. Russia, Iran and North Korea also don't make the Americans very happy through their own acts of defiance. With its controversial and dismissive performance during the pandemic, it does not sit right that the US claims itself to be the champion of the world's people.

Return of the Cold War era?

Despite a tense relationship, the US and the USSR together fought as allies against the Axis powers during World War II. The US had long been wary of Soviet communism and concerned about the Russian leader Joseph Stalin. On the other side, the Soviets had grievances against the Americans for their delayed entry into World War II, which had resulted in the deaths of tens of millions of Russians, and their refusal to accept the Soviet Union as a legitimate part of the international community for decades. After the war ended, the Soviet grievances ripened into mutual distrust and enmity.

The post-war Soviet expansion in Eastern Europe made America fear a Russian plan to control the world. In return, the Soviets resented what they perceived as American officials' bellicose rhetoric, arms build-up and interventionist approach to international relations. As such, no single country was entirely to blame for a hostile atmosphere during the 44-year-long Cold War era.

After the dissolution of the USSR, on 26 December 1991, the US would have hoped for a free and uninhibited dominance over the entire world but that did not last very long. Although Russia has reclaimed its character to some extent under President Putin's reign, it is China that has been putting up a stiff resistance, much to the dislike of Americans.

It seems the US has adopted the same policy of 'containment' against China, which it had used in the past against the USSR in the Cold War era and perhaps against Russia now and other countries too. Otherwise, why should the US marshal its warships and aircraft carriers in China's backyard?

When the two US aircraft carriers entered the South China Sea, daily COVID-19 infections in the US were at 54,442.

In the wake of the new security law imposed by China in Hong Kong, Trump had, on the back of bipartisan support in Congress, ended Hong Kong's special status with the US and sanctioned China, targeting Chinese businesses and officials. China reacted by condemning the US move and vowing to retaliate with sanctions of its own. Trump is reported to have said that the US would now treat Hong Kong the same as mainland China, with 'no special privileges, no special economic treatment and no export of sensitive technologies', adding: 'Their freedom has been taken away; their rights have been taken away. And with it goes Hong Kong, in my opinion, because it will no longer be able to compete with free markets. A lot of people will be leaving Hong Kong.'

The UK's mobile phone providers have been banned from buying new Huawei 5G equipment from China after 31 December 2020 and they must remove all Huawei 5G kit from their networks by 2027. As reported by the BBC on 15 July, the UK's digital secretary told the House of Commons: 'This has not been an easy decision, but it is the right one for the UK telecoms networks, for our national security and our economy, both now and indeed in the long run'.

The geopolitical saga goes on, as the world continues to battle coronavirus.

India and Australia sign defence pacts

After a virtual summit between Australian Prime Minister Scott Morrison and Indian Prime Minister Narendra Modi, the two countries signed two bilateral military agreements on 4 June 2020 as the 'first step in deepening of the defence relationship' between Australia and India. The two pacts come in the wake of the rising military tensions in the Indo-Pacific region and commit the two countries to deepening military integration through more complex exercises, granting them access to each other's military bases for logistical support.

It is obvious that Australia and India have aligned themselves to the US in its confrontation — political, economic and now military — against China in the Indo-Pacific region. Reportedly, after India signed the first such agreement with the US in 2016, Australia intended to have its agreement with India signed during a planned visit of India's defence minister to Australia in 2019, though this was cancelled due to his domestic engagements. Thereafter, it was expected to be signed during the Modi–Morrison summit in January 2020, which was postponed due to the Australian bushfires, and deferred gain in May 2019 due to the COVID-19 pandemic.

Australia has maintained a long-time presence in the South China Sea. According to the Lowy Institute, it has been conducting airborne surveillance patrols in the area since 1980 and its warships visit the area regularly. In April 2020, it also participated in exercises with US warships in the area on the back of its long-standing security ties with the US. In 2019, Indian warships joined US, Japanese and Philippine naval vessels in a transit of the South China Sea.

As a marked shift away from its traditional ally, the USSR and then Russia, India has been coming closer to the US after 11 September 2001 and especially in the last four years during which Trump and Modi are known to have bonded well. The leaders of the world's two largest democracies share similar ideas and support each other unequivocally. Logically, therefore, India has been increasing its defence ties with the US.

During the annual Malabar naval exercises, the US and Indian militaries shall align themselves with the Japanese self-defence forces, as all three countries, together with Australia, share common concerns in regard to China.

On 3 June 2020, *The Hindu* reported that the Australian High Commissioner to India, Barry O'Farrell, had said that the bilateral defence cooperation between India and Australia had 'quadrupled in the last six years'. In regard to Malabar, it was a matter for the partners — India, US and Japan — to decide, with O'Farrell adding: 'We would be delighted to participate in Malabar, but I do think that at times the focus on Malabar gets in the way of the underappreciated growth and significance of defence ties between Australia and India'. The *Hindu* stated, 'The inclusion of Australia in the Malabar exercise would be a major shift from the past for India's Indo-Pacific plans'.

Malabar naval exercises started in 1992, between India and the US. In 2015, Japan was included. Since 2016, Australia too has been requesting to join in. The then Australian prime minister, Malcolm Turnbull, had said that the talks on Malabar were 'progressing well';

however, India decided otherwise and instead continued to participate in the bilateral AUSINDEX naval and other military exercises with Australia which started in 2014.

The *Hindu* provides the possible reason why India had earlier resisted inviting Australia: 'ostensibly over concerns that it would give the appearance of a "quadrilateral military alliance" aimed at China'.

Now that a new geopolitical picture is fast emerging, seemingly with less chance of finding diplomatic solutions with China, and in preparation for a possible showdown with China — along the LAC, at Ladakh, or elsewhere in India or the South China Sea — India had openly come out with its intention.

And the pandemic is on. As per www.worldmeters.info , by 1 pm (AWST) on 5 July 2020, India had recorded about 674,000 Corona-virus cases, of which about 409,000 people had recovered and 19,279 people had died. As per Business Standard, dated 5 July 2020, India had reported biggest spike of 24,850 new cases in the 24 hours. Globally, on that day, the deadly infection had reached about 11.4 million and the fatalities spiked to 532,856. Globally, in the last 24 hours, the world had seen about 200,000 new cases, and about 4,500 new deaths.

[Over the next 55 days, India's infection rate per day increased significantly and by 30 August 2020, India was the world leader in daily infection rates, setting global records for the number of infections per day. On 30 August 2020, at 7.25 am (AWST), India had recorded a total of 3,539,712 infections, with 78,472 new infections in a day, which were the highest in the world and around two times the number of infections in a day in the US on the same day. But the death rate per million people in India was only 46, which was less than 10 percent of the US and Brazil. The total number of deaths recorded in India was 63,657, with 944 new deaths in one day. India had conducted a total of around 40.4 million tests, but due to its significant population of more than 1.38 billion, the rate of tests was only 29,234 per million people.

On a global level, on 30 August 2020, the total number of infection had reached above 15.1 million, with 845,578 deaths (i.e. about 3.3% mortality). Around 17.48 million people had recovered. The US continued to be the world leader in terms of the total number of 6,135,904 infections, 186,792 deaths and a death rate of 564 per million people. Brazil was second on the list with a total number of 3,846,965 infections, 120,498 deaths and a death rate of 566 per million people. India was third on the list.]

An overall snapshot of the Quad and China – July 2020

It would be interesting to take a quick look at some current parameters of the four countries – Australia, China, India and United States, and Japan – who could be involved in a South China military conflict, if at all, unless the current posturing by these countries – in Ladakh or in South China Sea – is proved to be a mock show in the future and scripted deliberately for entirely different objectives. Logic completely defies the current military posturing of the countries involved, especially when the humanity is battling the COVID-19 pandemic.

Population

The following populations are approximate and as noted on 6 July 2020, at 2.30 pm AWST, (https://www.worldometers.info/world-population/). The world population was approx. 7.8 billion.

- Australia: 25.5 million (**Rank 55**)
- China: 1.44 billion (**Rank 1**)
- India: 1.38 billion (**Rank 2**)
- Japan: 126 million (**Rank 11**)
- US: 331 million (**Rank 3**)

Economy (Feb 2020)

The following were the projected GDP ranking on 20 February 2020, published by Statistics Times (http://statisticstimes.com/economy/projected-world-gdp-ranking.php) prior to the COVID-19 lockdown, but retrieved on 6 July 2020:

- Australia (Rank 14): GDP $1,375 billion, growth @ 2.26%, GDP / person $52,952 (Rank 12)
- China (Rank 2): GDP $15,269 billion, growth @ 6.0% , GDP / person $10,873 (Rank 69)
- India (Rank 5): GDP $3,202 billion, growth @ 5.8% , GDP / person $2,338 (Rank 144)
- Japan (Rank 3): GDP $5,413 billion, growth @ 0.7% , GDP / person $43.043 (Rank 69)
- US (Rank 1): GDP $22,321 billion, growth @ 2.0% , GDP / person $67,427 (Rank 7)

Military

The following rankings were published, for the top 138 militarily strong countries, by Global Firepower (https://www.globalfirepower.com/countries-listing.asp), retrieved on 6 July 2020:

- Australia (**Rank 19**): Total military personnel 79,000 (incl. 19,700 reserve personnel)
  Air force: 464 total strength, 82 fighters, 6 dedicated attack, 38 transports, 133 helicopters, 22 attack helicopters, 174 trainers and 31 special missions
  Land force: 59 tanks, 3,051 armoured vehicles, 0 self-propelled artillery, 54 towed artillery and 0 rocket projectors.
  Naval force: 48 assets, 2 aircraft carriers, 2 destroyers, 8 frigates, 6 submarines, 13 patrols, 6 mine warfare and 0 corvettes
- China (**Rank 3**): Total military personnel 2.69 million (incl. 0.51 million reserve personnel)
  Air force: 3,210 total strength, 1,232 fighters, 371 dedicated attack, 224 transports, 911 helicopters, 281 attack helicopters, 314 trainers and 111 special missions
  Land force: 3,500 tanks, 33,000 armoured vehicles, 3,800 self-propelled artillery, 3,600 towed artillery and 2,650 rocket projectors

Naval force: 777 assets, 2 aircraft carriers, 36 destroyers, 52 frigates, 74 submarines, 220 patrols, 29 mine warfare and 50 corvettes

- India (**Rank 4**): Total military personnel 3.54 million (incl. 2.1 million reserve personnel)

  Air force: 2,123 total strength, 538 fighters, 172 dedicated attack, 250 transports, 722 helicopters, 23 attack helicopters, 359 trainers and 77 special missions

  Land force: 4,292 tanks, 8,686 armoured vehicles, 235 self-propelled artillery, 4,060 towed artillery and 266 rocket projectors

  Naval force: 285 assets, 1 aircraft carrier, 10 destroyers, 13 frigates, 16 submarines, 139 patrols, 3 mine warfare and 19 corvettes

- Japan (**Rank 5**): Total military personnel 303,160 (incl. 56,000 reserve personnel)

  Air force: 1,561 total strength, 279 fighters, 12 dedicated attack, 60 transports, 637 helicopters, 119 attack helicopters, 427 trainers and 152 special missions

  Land force: 1,004 tanks, 3,130 armoured vehicles, 238 self-propelled artillery, 500 towed artillery and 99 rocket projectors

  Naval force: 155 assets, 4 aircraft carriers, 40 destroyers, 0 frigates, 20 submarines, 6 patrols, 25 mine warfare and 6 corvettes

- US (**Rank 1**): Total military personnel 2.26 million (incl. 0.86 million reserve personnel)

  Air force: 13,264 total strength, 2,085 fighters, 715 dedicated attack, 945 transports, 5,768 helicopters, 967 attack helicopters, 2,643 trainers and 742 special missions

  Land force: 6,289 tanks, 39,253 armoured vehicles, 1,465 self-propelled artillery, 2,740 towed artillery and 1,366 rocket projectors

  Naval force: 490 assets, 20 aircraft carriers, 91 destroyers, 0 frigates, 66 submarines, 13 patrols, 11 mine warfare and 19 corvettes

On the basis of population, economic and military data, the following conclusions can be logically drawn:

- The tussle seems to be mainly between the US and China, with India tagging along with the US.
- Based on its relatively low rankings in all aforementioned parameters, Australia seems to be an outsider and an unlikely player in the geopolitics between China and India, and between China and the US, but it seems it is pulled into the picture by its traditional ally, the US, , which puts it in the same league as India and Japan.
- There is a significant difference between the military strengths and economies of the US and China, with the US leading the world by a significant margin. Despite that, the US is wary of China's recent growth spurt.
- There is also a significant difference between the military strengths and economies of China and India, with China leading by a significant margin. Despite that, currently riding on a nationalistic wave and prompted mainly by the US, India is trying to stand up to China.
- Acting individually, China can't beat the US and India can't beat China in any full-blown conventional warfare.
- On paper, India may be able to tackle China, without American help, if Japan and Australia come to its rescue and distract China.
- India will need full backing from the US in a full-blown conventional military conflict with China.
- If India and China fight each other at the LAC, in Ladakh or on the east in Arunachal Pradesh, India will need the US to distract China in the South China Sea. In that case, China may also want to involve Pakistan to distract India on its west border. In such a case, it is doubtful if Russia will come to assist India, as it has done in the past, given that India has tilted towards the US

in recent years and also due to Russia's strategic alliance with China and, therefore, indirectly with Pakistan, both alliances forged by its traditional difficult relationship with the US.

Now that Russia and Pakistan have been mentioned, it would be logical to also explore the probability of their involvement, and the disastrous effects thereof, of a major military conflict in the region.

Russia

- Population (**Rank 9**): 145,936,323
- Economy (**Rank 11**): GDP $ 1,657 billion; growth @1.87%; GDP / person $11,305 (Rank 68)
- Defence (**Rank 2**): Total military personnel 3.0 million (incl. 2.0 million reserve personnel)
  Air force: 4,163 total strength, 873 fighters, 742 dedicated attack, 424 transports, 1,522 helicopters, 531 attack helicopters, 497 trainers and 127 special missions
  Land force: 12,950 tanks, 27,038 armoured vehicles, 6,083 self-propelled artillery, 4,465 towed artillery and 3,860 rocket projectors
  Naval force: 603 assets, 1 aircraft carriers, 16 destroyers, 10 frigates, 62 submarines, 41 patrols, 48 mine warfare and 79 corvettes

Pakistan

- Population (**Rank 5**): 220,978,917
- Economy (**Rank 48**): GDP $260 billion, growth @ 2.35%, GDP / person $162 (Rank 162)
- Defence (**Rank 15**): Total military personnel 1.2 million (incl. 0.55 million reserve personnel)
  Air force: 1,372 total strength, 356 fighters, 90 dedicated attack, 49 transports, 346 helicopters, 56 attack helicopters, 513 trainers and 29 special missions

Land force: 2,200 tanks, 7,730 armoured vehicles, 429 self-propelled artillery, 1,226 towed artillery and 100 rocket projectors
Naval force: 100 assets, 0 aircraft carriers, 0 destroyers, 9 frigates,
8 submarines, 12 patrols, 3 mine warfare and 2 corvettes

Russia is, thus, a formidable player and Pakistan is not a pushover.
One can only imagine the scenario if they both get involved in a
regional conflict between the US and China and/or between China
and India.

To conclude, some important questions that must be answered:

- For the US, could its top ranking in defence and economy have
  led to its top ranking in COVID-19 infections and deaths,
  purely due to complacency and then denial, or looking for
  something to blame and punish China with?
- Is the US trying to instigate and use India as a buffer against
  China to dent the latter's attack?
- Will the current global economic scenario, as summarised in
  the next section, lead to a war to generate work, known as 'destruction for construction'?
- Are the current global conflicts and fear being driven mainly
  for the sale of weapons, including fighter planes, and to improve
  the economies of the selling nations?

Economic outlook

According to a June 2020 report by the IMF, the economic crisis
triggered by the COVID-19 pandemic is 'a crisis like no other' with
'an uncertain recovery'. The report says that the current global growth,
after having fallen by 1.9 percentage points since the April 2020 World
Economic Outlook forecast, is now projected at −4.9 percent in 2020.
Seemingly, the pandemic has had a more negative impact in the first
half of 2020 than anticipated originally and, therefore, the recovery is
projected to be more gradual than initially thought. In 2021, however,
global growth is projected at 5.4 percent. As per the IMF report, the

pandemic and the economic scenario will adversely impact on low-income households and the countries that are struggling to control infection rates; a lengthier lockdown will inflict an additional toll on economic activity. The report provides the following important advice to the world:

> Strong multilateral cooperation remains essential on multiple fronts ... Beyond the pandemic, policymakers must cooperate to resolve trade and technology tensions that endanger an eventual recovery from the COVID-19 crisis.

> Furthermore, building on the record drop in greenhouse gas emissions during the pandemic, policymakers should both implement their climate change mitigation commitments and work together to scale up equitably designed carbon taxation or equivalent schemes.

> The global community must act now to avoid a repeat of this catastrophe by building global stockpiles of essential supplies and protective equipment, funding research and supporting public health systems, and putting in place effective modalities for delivering relief to the neediest.

The IMF has put the collective 2020 and 2021 losses from 'The Great Lockdown' at US$12 trillion (about A$17 trillion). Between Australia, China, India, Japan and the US, China is steady and seemingly outperforming the rest by far and the US is the worst performer, as illustrated by the published data. For the five countries discussed above, the following are the *projected annual percent changes* in terms of real GDP:

- Australia: - 4.5% in 2020; and 6.5% in 2021
- China: +1.0% in 2020; and 8.2% in 2021
- India: - 4.9% in 2020; and 6.0% in 2021
- Japan: - 5.8% in 2020; and 2.4% in 2021
- US: - 8.0% in 2020; and 4.5% in 2021

As per Trade Economics (https://tradingeconomics.com), these five countries compare as follows in terms of their latest unemployment rate (in May and June 2020):

- Australia: 7.1% (May 2020), after being 5.1 to 5.3 percent between July 2019 and March 2020
- China: 5.9% (June 2020), after being 5.1 to 5.3 percent between July 2019 and January 2020, peaking at 6.2% in February 2020
- India: 11% (June 2020) , after being 7.2 to 8.2 percent between July 2019 and February 2020, peaking at 23.5% in April and May 2020
- Japan: 2.9% (May 2020) after being 2.2 to 2.4 percent between July 2019 and February 2020
- US: 11.1% (June 2020), after being 3.5 to 3.7 percent between July 2019 and February 2020, peaking at 14.7% in April 2020

India –Pakistan conflict

India and Pakistan have been exchanging fire across the Line of Control (LOC), with India blaming Pakistan for pushing militants across the LOC and also instigating 'terrorist' activities in Kashmir. In the months of May and June 2020, India is reported to have killed dozens of pro-independence militants in Kashmir valley, which it calls 'terrorists' and claims they are supported — armed, trained, sponsored and directed from across the LOC — by Pakistan.

Al Jazeera reported on 1 June 2020 that India had expelled two staff members of the Pakistani High Commission in New Delhi on 31 May 2002, on charges of espionage, declaring them *persona non grata* and giving them twenty-four hours to leave. The two staff members returned to Pakistan via the Wagah border crossing on 1 June 2010.

Three weeks later, *Al Jazeera* reported: 'India has said it will expel half the staff in Pakistan's embassy in New Delhi over alleged spying by officials there, prompting Islamabad to say it would respond in kind'. The Indian foreign ministry had made a statement that, 'They [Pakistan] have been engaged in acts of espionage and maintained dealings with terrorist organisations'.

The Indians had accused Pakistan of 'recent abduction at gunpoint' of two Indian officials and their torture, following an alleged hit-and-run incident in Islamabad involving those two officials. As per the Indian foreign ministry, the two Indian officials had then returned to India where they had 'provided graphic details of the barbaric treatment that they experienced at the hands of Pakistani agencies'.

Pakistan dismissed the Indian allegations that its staff in New Delhi had violated the Vienna Convention, adding: 'Pakistan also rejects the insinuations of intimidation of Indian High Commission officials in Islamabad ... The Indian government's smear campaign against Pakistan cannot obfuscate the illegal activities in which the Indian High Commission officials were found involved in', apparently referring to a 16 June traffic incident in Islamabad in which that the two Indian officials were involved and had allegedly fled the scene.

Al Jazeera reported that, on 29 June 2020, there was a terrorist attack in Karachi, Pakistan, on the Pakistan Stock Exchange, carried out by four gunmen, armed with grenades, in which two Pakistani guards and a policeman were killed before security forces killed all four of them. *Al Jazeera* reported that Pakistani Prime Minister Imran Khan had told Parliament that he had no doubt India was behind the attack, though without offering any evidence in support of his allegation, but claiming intelligence reports had forewarned about the attacks and he had informed his cabinet about the threat. The charge had earlier been denied by India.

Khan reportedly said that the attackers had intended to take hostages to replicate the 2008 Mumbai attacks, and their failure to do so, due to a rapid response by security forces, was as a 'big victory'. He has also said that intelligence agencies had successfully pre-empted at least four such major terrorist attacks in Pakistan, two of which had targeted Islamabad, while conceding it was not possible to prevent all such attacks.

The Baloch Liberation Army (BLA), which is an armed separatist group from the southwestern province of Balochistan, had claimed responsibility for the attack on Twitter. In 2018, the BLA had also taken responsibility for an attack on the Chinese consulate in Karachi. The BLA, classified by the US as a global terrorist group, has officially been banned in Pakistan since 2006. Pakistan has regularly blamed India for supporting Baloch separatists, a charge Delhi has repeatedly denied.

Life passed by, unnoticed (a short poem)

I kept chasing mirages while many an oasis passed by, unnoticed.
I befriended ghosts while many an angel stood around, unnoticed.
I got lost, looking at stars, while the moon shone bright, unnoticed.
I lived my little hell while my heaven lay well before me, unnoticed.

Chapter 6

INDIA-CHINA CONFLICTS

This chapter provides a detailed account of the ongoing India-China conflict and a brief history of the relationship between the two Asian neigbouring giants over the past six decades. It emphasises why a military conflict between the world's two most populated countries, which contain about 36-percent of the total world population, with their defence forces and economies amongst the world's most powerful, can be disastrous for the entire region and the rest of the world. It also discusses the possible influence of the November 2020 US presidential election on the situation at the Line of Actual Control (LAC), which is the de-facto Himalyan border between the two countries.

This chapter ends with a short poem, *Life, Oh Life!*

A brief history

The two nuclear-armed neighbours, India and China, are in a tense diplomatic and military stand-off. The entire India–China border — including the western portion of the Line of Actual Control (LAC), the small undisputed section in the centre, and the McMahon Line in the east — is 4056 kilometres long. It traverses across Ladakh, part of the erstwhile state of Jammu and Kashmir till October 2019 and now a union territory, and runs along four Indian states, Uttarakhand, Himachal Pradesh, Sikkim and Arunachal Pradesh.

The LAC represents a de facto demarcation that separates the

Indian-controlled territory of Ladakh from the Chinese-controlled territory called Aksai Chin. India considers the LAC to be around 3488 kilometres long, while the Chinese consider it to be only about 2000 kilometres. It is divided into three sections:

- the western section in Ladakh, comprising the LAC, which is under constant dispute;
- the middle section, along Uttarakhand and Himachal Pradesh, which is the least controversial section; and
- the eastern section, spanning Arunachal Pradesh and Sikkim, along the 1914 McMahon Line, over which there are some minor disputes about positions on the ground.

The Himalayan border, thus, extends between Pakistan to the west and Burma to the east, divided into three sections by Nepal, Sikkim and Bhutan. To the west, the Aksai Chin region — claimed by India as part of Ladakh and Kashmir — sits between Xinjiang and Tibet, which China declared as an autonomous region in 1965. The Indian state of Arunachal Pradesh, which was formerly called the North-East Frontier Agency and is located between Burma and Bhutan, comprises the eastern end of the border.

Indo–China War, 1962

In 1962, the two countries fought a 31-day war — between 20 October and 20 November — called the Sino-Indian War or the Indo-China War or even the Sino-Indian Border Conflict, which was caused mainly by a dispute between the two countries over the sovereignty of the widely separated regions of Aksai Chin to the west and Arunachal Pradesh to the east. China claims Aksai Chin as part of Xinjiang. It contains a road link that connects Tibet and Xinjiang, making it important for China.

After the Tibetan uprising in 1959, when India granted asylum to the Dalai Lama, which irked China, a series of violent border skirmishes took place between the two countries and, as a result, in 1960, India adopted a defensive Forward Policy to discourage Chinese military patrols and logistics in the Ladakh border area. In the two years preceding the war, China kept proposing diplomatic settlements but India kept rejecting them, which frustrated the Chinese. As a result, on 30 April 1962, the Chinese military recommenced previously banned 'forward patrols' in Ladakh. Finally, on 20 October 1962, China invaded the disputed territory, in Ladakh, along the long Himalayan border and across the McMahon Line. Chinese troops captured Rezang La in Chushul to the west and Tawang to the east. The fighting mainly took place in harsh mountain areas, at altitudes of over 4000 metres, notably without the use of a navy or air force by either side. China eventually declared a ceasefire on 20 November, ending the war and announcing its withdrawal to a line it claimed as the Line of Actual Control. Since then, the LAC has become the de facto border between the two countries.

Clashes at Cho La and Nathu La, 1967

In 1967, a series of military clashes took place between the two countries, first at Nathu La, between 11 and 14 September, and then at Cho La on 1 October — also known as the Second Sino-Indian War or Second Indo-China War — alongside the border of the Himalayan Kingdom of Sikkim, which was then an Indian protectorate. It is understood that the Indian forces achieved some decisive tactical advantages during the clashes, especially at Nathu La, where the Indian troops drove back the attacking Chinese forces and destroyed many of their military fortifications.

As per an article in the *Economics Times* on 13 June 2020, China lost around 400 soldiers at Nathu La, while at Cho La eighty-eight Indian soldiers were killed and 163 wounded.

Chinese ambush at Tulung La, 1975

The clashes in 1967, where India got the better of China, were not the last time the two countries clashed on the contested boundary. Exactly eight years later, on 20 October 1975, four Indian soldiers lost their lives when their patrol was ambushed by Chinese troops at Tulung La, in Arunachal Pradesh. This incident marks the last time when shots were fired on the LAC.

The Indian government has maintained that the Chinese had crossed the LAC and ambushed the Indian patrol but the Chinese have denied this and blamed India for the incident. Subsequently, in 1975, after a referendum, Sikkim became an Indian state but without receiving any recognition from China. However, later in 2003, after India agreed to accept the Tibet Autonomous Region as part of China, China dropped its resistance to Sikkim's annexation with India, which seemingly led to some thaw in the relations between the two.

Sumdorong Chu standoff, 1986–87

The river Sumdorong Chu, flowing in a north–south direction, is located to the northeast of the confluence of the two rivers Namka Chu and Nyamjiang Chu in Arunachal Pradesh. In 1986, the Chinese army entered the Sumdorong Chu valley and started building helipads and permanent structures there. To resist their intrusion, several battalions of the Indian army were airlifted to the Indo–China border. In a bloodless war, the Indian troops stood at the border eyeball to eyeball with their Chinese counterparts for more than year until China agreed to retreat.

The stand-off could potentially have led to a major war between the two countries. However, Indian diplomacy, mixed with caution and aggression, not only avoided war but also brought the Chinese to the negotiating table. In 1988, Rajiv Gandhi visited China, becoming the second prime minister of India, after his illustrious grandfather, Jawaharlal Nehru, to do so. Indian experts believe that it was on this occasion that the two sides agreed to a border settlement and to maintain peace and tranquillity along the border.

The standoff will be remembered for military finesse of Indian army's General K Sunderji, who launched Operation Chequerboard in autumn 1987, which was a high-altitude military exercise along the border in Arunachal Pradesh and reportedly involved 10 divisions of the Indian Army and several squadrons of the IAF. The Indian Army moved three divisions to positions around Wangdung, where they were supplied and maintained solely by air. These troop reinforcements were over and above the 50,000 troops already present across Arunachal Pradesh. Reportedly, the Chinese were so impressed by General Sunderji's military genius that they invited him to visit China, which he did but only after his retirement.

Depsang valley incursion, 2013

On 15 April 2013, Chinese troops were reported to have intruded about 19 kilometres into India's territory in the Depsang Bulge area of the DBO (Daulat Beg Oldie) sector in eastern Ladakh, with a platoon of fifty Chinese troops establishing an encampment of four tents. Although both sides normally patrol the area, till then they had avoided establishing permanent bases and fortifications there.

The Indians responded quickly and established their own encampment about 300 metres away, which led to a 21-day face-off that saw the two armies pitching tents and indulging in banner drills. Negotiations between China and India lasted nearly three weeks, during which the Chinese reinforced their position by bringing in trucks and helicopters. The dispute was resolved finally on 5 May 2013, after which both sides agreed to withdraw.

As part of the resolution, the Indian army had agreed to dismantle some military infrastructure about 250 kilometres to the south in the disputed Chumar sector, which the Chinese had perceived as threatening.

Doklam valley standoff, 2017

In June 2017, a stand-off took place between the two sides in the Doklam valley when Chinese troops started constructing a road in the area. Doklam valley is located at the India–Bhutan–China tri-junction, making it an important strategic point for all three countries.

Chinese troops had attempted to construct a road near Doklam plateau, using construction vehicles and road-building equipment, in an area k claimed by both China and Bhutan, India's ally. The road was to be an extension of an existing road running southwards. China has apparently long tried to induce Bhutan to barter the Doklam valley area with some other territory, which Bhutan has refused.

About 270 Indian troops, armed with weapons and two bulldozers, crossed the Sikkim border on 18 June and skirmishes took place at Doklam during a 72-day period.

After six weeks of diplomatic talks, India and China reached an agreement to pull back their armies from the site. The Chinese troops removed equipment and tents by 150 metres into their own territory and the Indians returned to their original positions.

Then 15 June 2020 happened, when at least twenty Indian soldiers were killed and scores injured in scuffles between the two sides at Galwan Valley in eastern Ladakh — the first deaths in forty-five years from either side.

What about the LAC?

India had consistently rejected the concept of the LAC, both in 1959 at the time of the Tibetan uprising and again in 1962. Sushant Singh, in an article in *The Indian Express* on 18 June 2020, quotes Prime Minister Nehru, who said at the time: 'There is no sense or meaning in the Chinese offer to withdraw twenty kilometres from what they call "line of actual control". What is this "line of control"? Is this the line they have created by aggression since the beginning of September (1962)?' India's position was that the Chinese line 'was a disconnected series of points on a map that could be joined up in many ways; the line should omit gains from aggression in 1962 and, therefore, should be based on the actual position on September 8, 1962 before the Chinese attack; and the vagueness of the Chinese definition left it open for China to continue its creeping attempt to change facts on the ground by military force'.

The article refers to Shivshankar Menon's book, *Choices: Inside the Making of India's Foreign Policy*, according to which the LAC was 'described only in general terms on maps not to scale' by the Chinese. Menon served as national security adviser of India under Prime Minister Manmohan Singh after serving as the foreign secretary in the Ministry of External Affairs. Earlier, he had been Indian High Commissioner to Pakistan and to Sri Lanka, and ambassador to China and Israel.

In 1976, India formed a China Study Group, which reviewed and revised the patrolling limits, rules of engagement and pattern of Indian presence along the border. Despite that, Indian and Chinese patrols were coming in more frequent contact during the mid-1980s.

In 1991, Chinese Premier Li Peng visited India to meet Prime Minister PV Narsimha Rao and thaw the relations between the two countries. The leaders agreed to maintain peace and tranquillity along the LAC. In 1993, Rao paid a return visit to Beijing, during which the two sides signed the Agreement to Maintain Peace and Tranquillity at the LAC. The LAC that was discussed in that summit was not the LAC of 1959 or the LAC of 1962, but a line agreed upon at the time of signing. Reportedly, the two countries had also agreed that a joint working group on the border issue would work to clarify the alignment of the LAC and reconcile differences about some areas.

India–China clash, 15 June 2020

Despite no shots being fired, twenty Indian soldiers were killed and scores injured on 15 June 2020, in a medieval-style clash between the soldiers of the two countries at Galwan Valley, located at an altitude of about 4300 metres in the eastern part of Ladakh. Since early May 2020, Indian and Chinese troops had been engaged in number of stand-offs and skirmishes at several points along the LAC. In the nineties, the two countries had agreed that no shots would ever be fired by any side during a stand-off or while patrolling the LAC. That agreement seems to have been respected by both sides, till the time of writing this book.

The BBC reported that at least seventy-six Indian soldiers were injured in addition to the twenty dead, adding 'China has not released any information about Chinese casualties. The fighting took place without any firearms because of a 1996 agreement barring guns and explosives from the area.'

An article by Rahul Singh in Hindustan Times, dated 17 June 2020, provides a timeline of the June 2020 clash.

- On 5 and 6 May, scores of soldiers were injured at Pangong Tso in Ladakh, involving around 250 soldiers from either side. Soldiers exchanged blows and threw stones at each other. Chinese soldiers attacked Indian soldiers with nail-studded clubs.
- On 9 May, four Indian and seven Chinese soldiers were injured at north Sikkim in a skirmish involving 150 soldiers.
- On 19 May, China accused Indian soldiers of trespassing across the LAC and declared it had to take 'necessary countermeasures' after the Indians allegedly obstructed normal Chinese patrols.
- On 25 May, China reportedly mobilised about 5000 soldiers on its side of the LAC in Ladakh, prompting India to reciprocate.
- On 6 June, India's Lieutenant General Harinder Singh and China's Major General Liu Lin met and discussed a de-escalation plan.
- On 9 June, the Indian army said limited military disengagement had begun at three spots, including Galwan Valley.

- On 10 June, Major General ranked army officers from the two countries met at the Galwan Valley area, in the fourth round of talks.
- On 13 June, the Indian army said the situation was under control.
- On 15 June, Brigadier-ranked officers from the two countries met in Galwan Valley and colonel-ranked officers met in Hot Springs during the day. On the same evening, a violent clash occurred at Galwan Valley, killing scores of soldiers from both sides without a shot being fired.

Reportedly, fist-fighting had broken out, triggered by a disagreement between the two sides over two tents and observation towers erected by the Chinese, which the Indian army demolished, claiming they had been erected on its side of the LAC. Thereafter, a large group of Chinese soldiers had suddenly arrived on the scene, carrying iron rods and batons wrapped with barbed wire and spikes, and the two sides clashed. Going by the reports, the Chinese may have been waiting for the unsuspecting Indians, possibly booby-trapping them.

China has not officially declared its casualties but the Indian media has claimed that up to forty Chinese soldiers were killed, which China has denied, calling it 'fake news'.

As per *Al Jazeera*, dated 22 June 2020, in analysis of satellite pictures taken in the days leading up to the clash, Jeffrey Lewis, director of the East Asia Non-proliferation Program at California's Middlebury Institute of International Studies, is reported to have told Reuters: 'It looks like China is constructing roads in the valley and possibly damming the river ... There are a tonne of vehicles on both sides [of the LAC] — although they appear to be vastly more on the Chinese side. I count 30–40 Indian vehicles and well over 100 vehicles on the Chinese side.'

Why did the clash happen?

According to the experts, there are two reasons:

1. India's unilateral and sudden move, on 5 August 2019, to abrogate Article 370 of the Indian Constitution, thereby revoking the semi-autonomous status of the erstwhile state of Jammu and Kashmir, which included Ladakh. China and Pakistan strongly denounced the move at the UN Security Council in 2019. Later, in another sudden move in October 2019, India also divided the state into two union territories, governed from the Central Indian government.

2. India's recently increased construction activities along border areas, including the completion of the Darbuk-Shyok-Daulat Beg Oldie (DSDBO) road along the LAC, which potentially threatens the China–Pakistan Economic Corridor (CPEC) from China to Pakistan and central Asia, which passes through Karakoram, which India had objected to.

The CPEC is a collection of infrastructure projects, under construction since 2013, in Pakistan, valued o at US$62 billion in 2017. The DSBDO road is located close to the Galwan River valley, not far from the Aksai Chin plateau, which is claimed by India but has been under Chinese occupation. India claims China occupies an area of around 38,000 square kilometres of its territory in the plateau. It is a 255-kilometre, all-weather road at altitudes of 4,000 to 4,900 metres. The road has taken nearly twenty years (2000 to 2019) to complete. It comprises thirty-seven prefabricated military truss bridges, including a 500-metre-long Bailey bridge at an altitude of about 4,465 metres, believed to be the world's highest bridge of its type.

Due to its bridges, the DSBDO has traffic during the summer months when various areas through which the road passes become inundated due to the snow-fed Shyok River, also called the River of Death, and its tributaries. It replaces a previous fair-weather road, mostly comprising a track, which was practically impassable during summer.

An interesting article written by Nirupama Subramanian of *The Indian Express*, dated 16 June 2010, explains the strategic importance of the DSDBO road for India and why China wants to control it:

- The Chinese build-up along the Galwan Valley overlooks and potentially poses a direct threat to the DSDBO road.
- The DSDBO road, running almost parallel to the LAC at Aksai Chin, provides the Indian army with access to the section of the Tibet-Xinjiang highway that passes through Aksai Chin, which is the eastern ear of the erstwhile state of Jammu and Kashmir that China is understood to have occupied clandestinely in the 1950s, leading to the 1962 India–China war.
- It connects Leh, the capital town of Ladakh, with the Daulat Beg Oldie (DBO), which is the northernmost corner of the Indian territory in Ladakh and located virtually at the base of the Karakoram Pass that separates China's Xinjiang from India's Ladakh.
- Its emergence has seemingly threatened China, as evidenced by the intrusion of the Chinese troops in 2013, into the nearby Depsang Plains, which lasted for nearly three weeks.
- The DBO is located at a distance of less than 10 kilometres to the west of the LAC at Aksai Chin. In reaction to China's occupation of Aksai Chin in 1962, India constructed a military outpost there.
- To the west of the DBO is the Pakistan-occupied Gilgit-Baltistan area, a part of the erstwhile Kashmir principality, where China meets Pakistan. This is the region where, in 1963, Pakistan is reported to have ceded over 5,180 square kilometres of Pakistan-occupied Kashmir to China under a Sino–Pakistan Boundary Agreement, which India has contested.
- DBO has the world's highest airstrip, which was built originally by India during the 1962 India–China war but left abandoned. In August 2013, an Indian Air Force transport aircraft landed

there, thereby ceasing the use of helicopters for para-dropping supplies to the army deployments along the LAC.

An alternative route exists from Leh to the DBO but that passes through the Sasser Pass (also called Saser Pass or Saser La) at an altitude of about 5,335 metres. For most of the year, the pass remains snow-bound and inaccessible. This route was part of the ancient Silk Route that connected Leh with Yarkand.

India is reported to be currently building a glaciated road, linking Sasoma, located to the north of Leh (near the Nubra River) with the Sasser Pass. This could take several years to complete, emphasising the importance of the DSDBO for India's strategic interests.

Indian prime minister's statement

On the night of 19 June 2020, Indian Prime Minister Modi, addressing an all-party meeting through video conferencing, which was attended by most political parties, including the Congress, said: 'Neither have they intruded into our border, nor has any post been taken over by them', without naming China. His statement stirred controversy across the country, while raising a few eyebrows around the world. Rahul Gandhi, the leader of the opposition said the Indian prime minister had surrendered to Chinese aggression.

An article in *Gulf News*, dated 20 June 2020, claims that Mr Modi's statement was in stark contrast to the press note that was issued earlier by the Government of India. The article quotes a former colonel with the Indian Army, journalist and defence analyst Ajai Shukla: 'Given the Indian prime minister's image as a strongman, he is under pressure to downplay the incursions and to make out as if the situation is completely under control'. By saying there has been no Chinese incursions, the prime minister in a way 'is relinquishing Indian claim to that territory and this is extremely detrimental to India's position on border negotiations'. The article also quotes Professor Bharat Karnad, a security expert from the Centre for Policy Research, New Delhi: 'The blame has to be shared by the government and the army because the Indian government has been historically accommodationist where China is concerned. And the army influenced the government's caution in being unwilling to retaliate with harsh actions against the PLA.'

Mobile app protest wave across India

The Indian public has angrily demonstrated against the Chinese intrusion. Prominent Indian citizens, politicians and trade associations have been calling for punitive action by India against China, including boycotting Chinese goods, deleting Chinese mobile phone apps and cancelling contracts with Chinese firms. Protesters across the country have been seen burning Chinese flags and products on the streets, while videos on social media have shown teenagers destroying their Chinese-made mobile phones.

China is India's biggest trading partner, with annual bilateral trade worth US$92 billion; however, the trade imbalance is significant and heavily favours China. It seems the Indian public is committed to hurting China economically while their troops are busy doing what they are trained to do and directed to do at the LAC. Interestingly, all this is happening despite the COVID-19 pandemic sweeping around the globe and, reportedly, taking a huge toll on general life across this second-most populated country in the world. It seems the nationalistic people of India are much more concerned and bothered about their country's pride and honour than the pandemic that affects each and every aspect and hour of their life at present.

Al Jazeera reported on 30 June 2020 that India had banned fifty-nine Chinese mobile apps, including Bytedance's TikTok and Tencent's WeChat. Reportedly, Bytedance had plans to invest US$1 billion in India. They had opened a local data centre there and even started recruitment. As per *Al Jazeera*:

- The Chinese foreign ministry spokesperson reminded India about its responsibility to uphold the rights of Chinese businesses, saying 'We want to stress that the Chinese government always asks Chinese businesses to abide by international and local laws and regulations'.

- In response, the Indian technology ministry claimed the apps were 'prejudicial to the sovereignty and integrity of India, defence of India, security of state and public order'.
- An Indian government minister has demanded a ban on Chinese food.
- A prominent trading union announced a boycott of a range of commodities imported from China.
- A hotel union in New Delhi announced it would not allow Chinese guests to stay in their properties.
- Millions of Indians downloaded 'Remove China Apps', which helps users to detect and delete Chinese software, before it was removed by Google from its Play store.

Prime Minister Modi also deleted his account on Chinese social media platform WeiboAl Jazeera, joining his followers and proving my theory that a leader is created by the people, who then make the leader follow them and do what they want them to do. Reportedly, he had more than 200,000 followers and had made 100 posts before deleting the account on 1 July. He was among a handful of foreign leaders with a Weibo account.

An Indian government source told Reuters that it took them time to close down Modi's account: 'For VIP accounts, Weibo has a more complex procedure to quit which is why the official process was initiated. For reasons best known to the Chinese, there was great delay in granting this basic permission'. All of Modi's posts on Weibo had been deleted except two pictures of him with President Xi: 'On Weibo, it is difficult to remove posts with the photo of their president'. Notably, Modi had revealed the birth dates of both President Xi and Premier Li Keqiang by wishing them a happy birthday on Weibo. The birth dates of senior leaders in China are usually not revealed publicly.

US Secretary of State Mike Pompeo, as per *Al Jazeera* on 2 July 2020, applauded India's sweeping ban on Chinese apps, saying 'We welcome India's ban on certain mobile apps that can serve as appendages of the CCP [Chinese Communist Party] surveillance state. India's clean app approach will boost India's sovereignty and will also boost India's integrity and national security, as the Indian government cell itself has stated.'

On 4 July 2020, tensions were high along the LAC, with reports of additional troop and military hardware deployment by both sides. Reportedly, the Chinese army had engaged martial arts experts for assistance prior to the 15 June clash and they continue to be a part of the increased Chinese contingent at the LAC.

Is another Indo–China war inevitable?

Does Prime Minister Modi's controversial statement provide an indi-cation that India does not want a military confrontation with China? If yes, it makes sense. Notably, in 1975, when four Indian soldiers were ambushed and killed by Chinese forces in Arunachal Pradesh, the economies of the two countries were relatively comparable. Since then, however, China's economy has grown nearly five times the Indian economy in size, with its defence spending matching that multiplier.

The two countries don't match each other in economic power or military strength, despite many Indians believing that Indian soldiers are relatively more battle-hardened, thanks to continued friction with Pakistan, unending strife in Kashmir and growing nationalism in some parts of the country. In a major military conflict, therefore, although China is logically expected to prevail and emerge victorious, it would be nonetheless expected to pay a significant price for that victory. India is also a nuclear country and not to be pushed over, unlike what happened six decades ago, in 1962.

Now what are the chances of that major military conflict? The answer is 'significant'. And why? The answer is Indian nationalism on the one side and China's global ambitions and expansionism on the other side. The leaders of both countries have an image to keep and are not expected to make any concessions or take any backwards step for fear of losing their respective domestic and global images. Fear and strength practically run the world — psychology matters, not only in the economy but also in the political world. Perception is everything.

The 67-year-old Chinese president, Xi Jinping, with an illustrious background, has a global vision. In March 2018, China removed the two-term limit on the presidency, effectively allowing him to remain in power for life. On the other hand, 69-year-old Indian Prime Minister Narendra Damodardas Modi, also with a strong nationalist background, has a 1.4 billion population to keep engaged and impressed. People are whimsical, especially in democracies; they go away and elect other people. For example, the gentle and quiet demeanour of Dr Manmohan Singh, who was India's prime minister for nearly eleven years (2004 to 2014) and the third-longest serving prime minister after Jawaharlal Nehru and his daughter, Indira Gandhi, may have possibly created a vacuum among the people of India — who are usually driven by loud emotions and pomp — which may have then been filled by a vociferous Mr Modi on the back of his gift of the gab and roaring speeches. Indian people follow and respect people who are assertive and expressive. Bollywood plays a great part in Indian culture; people idolise actors and like their melodramatic personalities, especially those who openly indulge in jingoism and the glorification of the past Indian culture and civilisation.

So, despite Modi's effort to underplay the Chinese incursion, the two countries may still go to war because Indian people may be in a punishing mood. At the same time, because of strict control on the media in their country, the Chinese public is mainly reliant on the Indian media, which is loudly beaming jingoistic messages. The public outcry in India and jingoism could potentially annoy the Chinese public, who would then expect their own leadership to take decisive action and punish India.

Modi's controversial statement may paradoxically cast doubt in the minds of the Chinese people, which its leadership will try to dispel as hard and as quickly as possible. Is another India–China war inevitable, despite none of the countries really wanting it but maybe being compelled to for reasons of political pressure and expectations from their respective publics? When a leader feeds nationalism, in turn, the nationalists expect the leader to meet their expectations.

For China, among its grand global plan, the CPEC is the most important for its economy. The country is fully committed to it and has invested heavily in it in the past few years. But the CPEC may be seen by Indians to be a potential threat to their strategic interests. If the two interests collide, economic and military clashes are inevitable, perhaps tomorrow if not today. The only question is, when that military clash happens, what are the chances it will not spiral out of control and engulf the whole world?

India is neighboured by Pakistan, China and Nepal. These three neighbouring countries seem to be aligned currently in so far as challenging India strategic interests is concerned. India, on the other hand, is backed by the US, with Australia and Japan in reserve, if needed. The United States has its own conflict with China in the South China Sea as well as an ongoing trade war plus has levelled spying accusations against China, so things may escalate.

Hindustan Times reported on 24 August 2020 that India's Chief of Defence Staff Bipin Rawat had warned 'the military option is on the table if talks between New Delhi and Beijing to deescalate the tension along the border fail', adding:

'Transgressions along the LAC occur due to differing perceptions about its alignment ... Defence services always remain prepared for military actions should all efforts to restore status quo along the LAC do not succeed ... Defence minister Rajnath Singh, National Security Advisor Ajit Doval and all those responsible for national security are reviewing all options with the objective that PLA restores status quo ante in Ladakh.'

As per Hindustan Times, dated 27 August 2020, Indian government emphasised 'the need for a diplomatic solution to the stand-off with China based on agreements on the border issue, saying the disengagement of troops can move forward only if both sides implement actions they have agreed on in several rounds of diplomatic and military talks.' The Indian position was in response to the Chinese defence ministry asking New Delhi to look at the 'big picture' of bilateral ties and 'work with Beijing to bring the relationship back on track while avoiding misjudgements'.

On 30 August 2020, India Today and NDTV reported that Indian Navy has deployed warship in South China Sea, two months after the Galwan clash, which is maintaining a close contact with their American counterparts that are known to be operating on the other edge of the South China Sea. The deployment of the Indian warship has reportedly infuriated the Chinese government. India Today quoted top Indian government sources:

'We have deployed a frontline warship in the South China Sea region where the Chinese have been opposing and complaining against the presence of Indian warships.'

NDTV also reported that, in addition to the frontline warship, India has also deployed its frontline vessels along the Malacca Straits, near the Andaman and Nicobar Islands, to keep an eye on Chinese naval ships that use the route to enter the Indian Ocean region.

On 31 August 2020, as per *Al Jazeera* and BBC, the two countries have again traded accusations of provocative military movements at the LAC. India has claimed that its troops 'pre-empted Chinese army's activity on the Pangong Tso Lake in Ladakh' and thwarted 'the Chinese attempt to *unilaterally change* facts on the ground'. In return, China has rejected the Indian accusations, whilst making counter allegations that India was 'seriously violating China's territorial sovereignty'. China has demanded that Indian troops to withdraw.

As per The Print, dated 31 August 2020, China is also building heliports and missile launching infrastructure close to its borders with India and that there has been 'no movement in disengagement talks since July 2020'.

So, the game seems to be on.

The challenges of high-altitude warfare

High-altitude warfare is extremely challenging for any country due to narrow weather windows and harsh environment; the physiological requirements of acclimatisation in low-pressure environments; the physical limitations of the human body; and logistics.

A detailed commentary by Aidan Miliff, dated 8 June 2020, on the logistical and physiological constraints on the Indo–Chinse border, notes: 'Though the situation on China and India's Himalayan border facilitates frequent disputes and small land grabs, any individual conflict has relatively low potential to escalate into a conventional war. Difficulties of fighting in the high altitude and harsh terrain make large changes to the territorial status quo very costly. Reversing an adversary's small land grabs is not worth the prize.'

Miliff does not believe that either side would logically be interested in allowing things to escalate beyond control and ending up in war. Yet, as history shows, wars have been fought and are being fought seemingly for trivial and frivolous reasons. If wisdom would have prevailed in the past, history would not have seen such bled shed as it has. In the past century alone, the world has seen two world wars and a number of drawn-out conflicts in different parts of the world, which makes one think that wars are thrust upon nations from which they can't back out because of their alliances — political, strategic and economic — and, of course, the national and personal pride of their leaders.

Will the 2020 US election play a role in the India–China conflict?

Seventy-four-year-old Donald Trump is campaigning for the forth-coming US presidential election, scheduled for 3 November 2020. With his dwindling popularity among white voters, mainly due to his questionable performance during the COVID-19 pandemic, and his rival Democrat candidate, Joe Biden, the 78-year-old former vice-president, currently leading in the opinion polls, a victory in a military conflict with China may be all he needs to be re-elected. Otherwise, his chances of re-election look dampened.

On 27 June 2020, the BBC quoted US infectious disease chief Dr Anthony Fauci as saying that the nation had a 'serious problem', as sixteen states were reeling from a spike in COVID-19 cases. The BBC report also says health officials in the US estimate the true number of cases could be as high as ten times the reported figure.

On the contrary, Vice-president Mike Pence praised the US handling of the pandemic, noting 'extraordinary progress' in former virus hotspots, like New York and New Jersey. He is reported to have said, 'We slowed the spread, we flattened the curve, we saved lives', while denying any link between states reopening and the increase in cases, instead attributing the increase to positive test results from asymptomatic young people. The BBC report says the number of cases had shot up in those states where the state governors had reinforced President Trump's message that the nation was returning to normal.

Fauci warned the US Congress that new coronavirus cases in the US could rise to 100,000 a day. Stressing the importance of wearing masks 'for everyone' when outdoors, especially by millennials and the Generation Zs, and avoiding congregating in crowds, he warned: 'We are now having 40-plus thousand new cases a day. I would not be surprised if we go up to 100,000 a day if this does not turn around and so I am very concerned.'

All this is not going to help Trump in his re-election. He needs to act, and act fast, and be seen as the saviour of the American people. To start with, the US has reportedly bought nearly all the next three months of projected production of remdesivir, as reported by BBC News on 1 July 2020. The anti-viral treatment was originally found to be effective against Ebola. The news report quoted an expert as saying that the move 'so clearly signals an unwillingness to cooperate with other countries and the chilling effect this has on international agreements about intellectual property rights'.

What will President Trump do?

Trump's approval rating is constantly dwindling. Furthermore, his own Republicans are joining hands with Democrat presidential candidate Joe Biden. In an exclusive article, dated 23 June 2020, Tim Reid of Reuters reported that 'Dozens of Republican former US national security officials to back Biden'. As per the article:

'A group has been formed by some influential Republicans ... who will publicly endorse Joe Biden in the coming weeks. The group includes those officials who had served under Presidents Ronald Reagan, George HW Bush and George W. Bush. The group is expected to could go public before the Democratic National Convention ... when Biden formally becomes Democratic Party nominee. The group will argue that, if re-elected, the next four years of a Trump presidency would endanger the American national security. Speaking on condition of anonymity, a person from the group has said: 'Trump pals around with dictators. He's a real danger.'

All this is not going to make President Trump happy. On the basis of his personality, as witnessed by the world in the last four years, one can expect many a surprise from him in the lead-up to the election. No one knows what is going to happen but one thing is sure, that he will try his utmost to get re-elected and for that, he must win the confidence and support of American voters — both white and black voters. There are no two thoughts about the common ground on which Americans of all races stand, and that is under the US flag. If they are made to feel their country is under threat or at war, they will come together and stand behind their leader.

Post-Galwan situation on the Indo–China border

On 24 June 2020, Indian jets reportedly took off from a military base in Leh, at an altitude of 3500 metres, and headed towards the mountainous border 240 kilometres away. The residents of Leh had seen a frenzy of military activity around the main town, with long lines of military trucks and artillery, and checkpoints on main roads outside Leh.

On condition of anonymity, an official of the Indian army told AFP news agency: 'We now have a good strength present in the area'. A retired army officer based in Leh has said: 'I haven't seen this kind of military movement before'.

On its social media account, China's defence ministry maintains that India was responsible for the border clash, with the foreign ministry adding that the clash had occurred on 'China's side of the Line of Actual Control … and that Indian forces had illegally entered Chinese territory'.

On 25 June 2020, Reuters reported on satellite images that show China has built new structures near Galwan valley, comprising bunkers, tents and storage units for military hardware, which were not visible the previous month. British Prime Minister Boris Johnson expressed concern at the Indo–China stand-off.

NDTV reported that 'Indian and Chinese armies are engaged in the standoff in Pangong Tso, Galwan Valley, Demchok and the DBO in eastern Ladakh'. It also said that 'a sizable number of Chinese Army personnel even transgressed into the Indian side of the Line of Actual Control in several areas including Pangong Tso'.

A few days later Associated Press reported that satellite imagery appeared to show new construction activity underway on both the Indian and Chinese sides of the LAC along the Galwan River valley. It appeared that the Indians had built a wall on their side and the Chinese had expanded an outpost camp at the end of a long road connected to Chinese military bases further from the LAC.

The Chinese ambassador to India said that the two sides had agreed to build observation posts on either side of the mouth of the Galwan River. The satellite imagery, however, shows that, since 22 May, 'convoy after convoy of heavy trucks, diggers, bulldozers and some military armoured equipment' had been rolling down the Galwan valley towards the LAC in the weeks before and after the clash.

The stone wall India has built facing the new Chinese post is at the junction where the Galwan River turns west, an important supply route for a key Indian airfield. The wall has a layered set of barriers draped in camouflage netting and tarps that 'could also function as fighting positions'.

On 30 June 2020, India Today TV reported from Leh, Ladakh: 'China occupies hills near Pangong Tso, obstructs patrols. Locals say they are living in fear', adding 'Movement of locals in forward areas has been restricted and phone networks are down amid the ongoing tension at the LAC'. Reportedly, the Chinese army continues to obstruct Indian patrols, as its troops have occupied high mountains at Pangong Tso Lake. The Indian army has also not stopped infrastructure development even though this was one of the reasons that triggered the stand-off.

Local councillor Tashi Namgiyal, who represents the Tangste constituency, told India Today TV that people were frightened as they had not seen such large-scale military build-up in decades: 'Some people have shared details. Based on accounts of porters in the forward areas, the Chinese army has deployed troops. Indian army has not stopped construction work on bridges and roads despite the Chinese aggression.'

Prime Minister Modi visits the LAC

In the middle of the heightened tension between India and China, following no clear signs of any de-escalation, Prime Minister Modi paid a sudden and surprise visit to Ladakh on 3 July 2020, affirming India's current position about the border dispute with China, where he is reported to have met Indian army personnel at a forward post. Originally, India's defence minister was scheduled to arrive for this visit.

Modi's visit signals that India is in no mood to back down and is possibly prepared for any escalation. The timing of the visit seems to have at least a twofold purpose: one of them is to send a bold message to the Indian public — especially Modi's critics and the Indian opposition parties — and the wider world, including China, that he is confidently in control of the situation and prepared to lead from the front to defend his country's border. The second more obvious purpose is to support his troops at the front, boost their morale and understand the ground situation at the site.

As per *India Today* on 3 July 2020, the visit hints at India's intent to escalate China's cost of construction and maintenance of its infrastructure along the LAC by showing its own preparedness and intent to improve Indian infrastructure along the LAC. The article also tries to explore if India is acting alone or if there is a US connection to India's current stand and behind Modi's visit:

It is not yet clear if there has been diplomatic exchange between India and the US leading to some kind of agreement with regard to China. But it is significant that the US said it is pulling out its troops from Europe to deploy on China's eastern front, that is, in the South China Sea region. The US said its decision is influenced by the military tension between India and China along the LAC. The US has also linked it with a Chinese pattern that's commonly referred to as salami slicing. This means the US sees through the latest Chinese expansionist move. China has been pushing aggressively for expanding its territories on land

and water ever since it envisaged the Belt and Road Initiative, which many observers view as Chinese network of new-age imperialism.

According to *Al Jazeera*, while addressing Indian troops Modi reportedly said: 'Age of expansionism is over, this is the age of development. History is witness that expansionist forces have either lost or were forced to turn back.' To inspire the troops, he also said: 'Your courage is higher than the heights where you are posted today. The bravery that you and your compatriots showed, a message has gone to the world about India's strength.'

As per an ABC news report, dated 4 July 2020, Mr Modi praised the valour of Indian troops and said: 'Enemies of India have seen your fire and fury.'

In response, China's foreign ministry spokesperson criticised Indian officials for making 'irresponsible remarks' and warned 'India should not make a strategic miscalculation on China'. He also called on India to 'work with China to safeguard the overall situation of bilateral relations'.

Reacting to Modi's use of the term 'expansionist', the Chinese Embassy spokesperson in New Delhi, tweeted: 'China has demarcated boundaries with 12 of its 14 neighbouring countries through peaceful negotiations, turning land borders into bonds of friendly cooperation. It's groundless to view China as "expansionist", exaggerate & fabricate its disputes with neighbours.'

As per the *Al Jazeera* report, India has approved the purchase of twenty-one Russian MiG-29 and twelve Sukhoi Su-30MKI fighter aircraft, costing US$2.43 billion. India is also awaiting the arrival of the first batch of thirty-six Rafale fighter jets from France, as part of a US$8.78 billion deal signed in 2016.

The current world criticism of China, about its handling of coronavirus and Hong Kong, make its position significantly difficult. It seems the whole world is out to get China.

China's awkward position

'China was surprised in Doklam, never thought India would challenge it', reported *News Today* on 30 June 2020, quoting China expert Yun Sun, who is co-director of the East Asia Program at the Stimson Centre in the US. This article amply sums up the situation from the Chinese perspective and why things are as they are and what one can expect in the future.

Yun Sun said China had never expected India would challenge and stand up to it in 2017, when its soldiers stopped the Chinese from constructing a road at Doklam, in Bhutan, which led to the 72-day stand-off between the two countries. Seemingly, India's posturing had made China revisit its strategy about is engagement with India.

Understanding the Chinese motivation behind the recent moves was not very hard:

If you ask a Chinese government official, their reply would be that China was responding to what India had been doing along the Line of Actual Control ... So, when the Chinese identified that India is building roads and other infrastructural projects in their region, their concern was how should they (China) respond. They felt India is stabbing China on the back ... that India is putting China in an impossible position where either China responds aggressively and be seen as attacking India, or does nothing and actually end up losing territory.

In regard to the timing of the recent aggression, Yun Sun said although the border dispute between the two sides had been going on for years, China was currently under internal pressure due to perceived external attacks on it over the pandemic.

She also said: 'The power competition between India and China in Asia gives rise to conflicts and affects regional power balance'. Regardless of the power competition with India, Yun Sun said that China's main threat came from the US in the South China Sea and not from India, although many Indians may like to believe that China sees India as its main threat, perhaps because they see China as the threat to India. The US is identified as China's greatest military threat. Why would China then want to start a two-front war with India in the west and US in the east? That is not something in China's national interest in any sense ... China would like to have friendly relations with India, especially in context of the US trying to come closer to India and persuade it to get involved in the South China Sea. But if the Chinese perceive that India is trying to leverage its alliance with US to force China to abandon its territorial claims, then that is not something that it would ever entertain.

4 July 2020

On 4 July 2020, US Independence Day, the world media reported that two US aircraft carriers (USS *Ronald Reagan* and the USS *Nimitz*) had entered the South China Sea at the same time as China was conducting its own military exercises in the area (see Chapter 5). Earlier also, in April 2020, during the early days of the COVID-19 pandemic, an US amphibious assault ship (the *America*) and a guided missile cruiser (the *Bunker Hill*), along with an Australian frigate (the *Parramatta*), had entered the area at the same time when a Chinese destroyer (the *Wuhan*) was also operating there. The US posturing seems to be in line with its policy of 'containment', which it had used earlier against the Soviet Union between 1947 and 1991, and is now being used against a new threat, China.

Outwardly, it seems the US wants to be seen standing for all nations who feel threatened and trespassed by China — whether around the South China Sea or elsewhere in Asia, such as India. If the US is really behind India's position against China, the world may see something not seen ever before. Australia's recent defence pact with India and its warning of rising tension in the Indo-Pacific region and announce-ment of increased defence spending all seem to make sense. All these activities provide a hint about the coming weeks or months in the region, particularly about the South China Sea conflict between the US and China.

A day after Modi's surprise visit to the front at the LAC, the frontline Russian-made fighter aircraft (Sukoi-30MKI and the MiG-29) of the Indian Air Force (IAF) were reported to be flying consistently in and out of an airbase near the LAC, in a strong show of the air force's preparedness for a combat role in the area.

American transport aircraft (C-17 and the C-130J) and their Russian counterparts (Ilyushin-76 and the Antonov-32) have also reportedly been seen transporting troops and deploying equipment along the LAC since May 2020. American origin Apaches were also seen carrying out regular sorties, together with their heavy-lift counterpart Chinooks.

Emphasising the importance of the airbase, an IAF flight lieutenant reportedly said: 'This base plays a very important role in undertaking operations in this area. It is cleared for all contingencies and all combat and support operations to be undertaken in this area.'

A wing commander summed up the state of preparedness of the IAF:

> The Indian Air Force is fully prepared for operations and is ready to meet all challenges. Air power is a very powerful aspect of war-fighting and more relevant today ... Air power will play an important role in this area in both combat and support roles. We have all the resources in terms of men and equipment to meet all the challenges ... The Indian Air Force is ready in all aspects to undertake all operational tasks and providing the requisite support for all military operations.

The India–China conflict — what now?

Seemingly, India and China are caught up in such an awkward situation where it will be extremely difficult, if not impossible, for one or both to come out without losing face or conceding a strategic advantage to the other side. The question is which side will buckle first and concede. Even if the situation is defused in the next few months, the future is undoubtedly going to witness many a Doklam and Galwan stand-off, or even another like the Sumdorong Chu stand-off, between these two world's most populated, nuclear-armed neighbours sharing such a long unresolved Himalayan land border.

To conclude this chapter, given the history, most clashes between the two sides have taken place in the second half of the year, especially in and around the month of October. Weather plays a significant role in this high-altitude area of the planet. Therefore, if the situation has to escalate into something bigger, it may happen most likely in the months before winter sets in. It is to be seen if wisdom prevails on both sides and things de-escalate or if battle lines have already been drawn — by one or both sides to serve their respective strategic interests in the area, which seem to be on a collision path.

As for as the 1996 agreement between the two countries — that neither of them will use a firearm during a stand-off — there is no doubt that both countries have stuck to the agreement so far but the question is how long will they do it? In addition, one can't ignore the fact that, in the 15 June clash at Galwan valley, the Chinese had the intent, plan and preparedness to kill. Reportedly, they were armed with batons and steel rods, wrapped with barbed wire and spikes, and prepared to inflict fatal injuries on their opponents. Not only that, they wore special rubberised suits to protect themselves from hypothermia. It was a war indeed, well designed to kill the opponent, in medieval style.

The latest reports at the time of writing were that the two countries had agreed to disengage and pull back troops.

NDTV reported that India's defence minister had chaired a high-level meeting on 7 July to review the progress of various infrastructure projects under construction in border areas, including the Ladakh region. After the meeting, he had tweeted: 'The ongoing infrastructure projects of Border Road Organisation [BRO] were reviewed in a meeting today. BRO has been doing commendable work. The construction of strategic roads, bridges and tunnels in the border areas will be expedited. The BRO is working vigorously towards this goal.'

On 8 July 2020, *India Today* reported that, as per Indian government sources, the 'Indian Air Force is carrying out night time combat air patrols over the mountainous eastern Ladakh region as part of its decision to maintain a high-level of readiness notwithstanding disengagement of troops by China from a number of friction points in the area'. The sources had also said that 'the frequency of day and night operations by frontline fighter jets is a signal that India will continue to put pressure on China until the status quo ante is restored in all the areas in eastern Ladakh including Pangong Tso, Gogra and Hot Springs'. A senior official, on condition of anonymity, had said: 'There is no question of lowering our guard at this juncture'.

India Today also reported that in the last few days, in addition to significantly enhancing the deployment of its frontline jets, attack helicopters and transport fleet in all its key bases guarding the airspace along the LAC, the IAF had brought in C-17 Globemaster III transport aircraft and C-130J Super Hercules to transport heavy military equipment and weaponry to several forward bases.

At this stage, therefore, no one can certainly say what is going to happen in the next few weeks or months before winter sets in. Is the recent disengagement a sincere move towards de-escalation or a strategic move, on one or both sides, with the intent to suddenly escalate the situation?

Both sides are understood to have agreed to create a 3-kilometre-wide buffer zone between the two armies. Reportedly, the mountain mechanised divisions of the Chinese army have not moved from their last position. The topography in the area is such that it will be much easier for the Chinese troops to push ahead at short notice than their Indian counterparts.

Earlier, on 6 July, *Al Jazeera* published an opinion article by Tariq

Mir, a Srinagar-based Kashmiri journalist, in which he said: 'The face-off between Chinese and Indian troops in Ladakh might eventually turn out to be only a sideshow to what could become a much bigger military confrontation this year between India and Pakistan along their long border in Kashmir'.

Thinking about it, Mir's opinion has merit. In modern conventional warfare, which significantly depends on the airpower prowess of a country, it does not really matter where India deploys its troops and undertakes aerial exercises as long as they are within the region. Geographically, Ladakh is not far from resources-rich Baluchistan, which has been fighting for independence from Pakistan, and the Pakistan-administered Kashmir, which India has been eyeing to integrate with the Indian-administered Kashmir for the last few years. India's current battle preparedness in the high-altitude Ladakh area can work equally, or possibly better, for a potential military conflict with Pakistan later this year if that is really on the cards for the Indian government.

Interestingly, the last major Sino-Indian conflict military in 1962, and many other smaller skirmishes thereafter, have had taken place in the months of October and November. The significance of these two months remains in place in 2020.

So the game seems to be on during a difficult period in which the COVID-19 continues to cripple life and take precious human lives in the subcontinent and the rest of the world. The resources that are being used, perhaps wasted, could be used to uplift the lives of millions of people in the subcontinent. But that is another thing … humans don't always think logically.

Life, Oh Life (a short poem)

Life was much easier, simpler; I had the time to live.
I kept dreaming for a bit more, it was never enough.
My growing hunger was insatiable, for this and that.
I wanted all, I wanted everything, nothing was inedible.
The more I had, the more I wanted, greed blinded me.
My dreams consumed me, I consumed myself.
Time passed by, smiling; while I chased my greed.
Life was an illusion. I was silly, a disillusioned fool.

Chapter 7

OUR CHALLENGES

This chapter provides a philosophical commentary on the challenges that the world faces at the moment. It talks about the need to revolutionise the educational infrastructure and the general mind-set of people about the role and objectives of 'education', especially in the Indian subcontinent, so that 'education' inculcates human values and empathy in students and helps them to grow as responsible world citizens, with an aim to minimise unhappiness, social discords and strife between communities. It also talks about the importance of human endeavour and active citizenship in making this world a better place. A short discussion and about material effects of capitalism on human values is also included herein. A philosophical discussion about 'death', as a reminder to respect life and the importance of living life full, and with purpose, is also included in this chapter.

This chapter ends with a poem, *These Words*.

Educational Infrastructure and Mindset Needs a Revolution

This section reflects the author's independent thoughts, which are primarily based on his personal observations and experiences, both as a student and a teacher. Although, it is relevant more for a developing country like India, some aspects of the subject matter are relevant globally nevertheless. The objective is to challenge traditional thought and current practices in education in India, and elsewhere with similar educational infrastructure and practices, but with a sole aim to help produce happier and responsible human beings. The author does not claim to be an expert in the field of education.

What is education? What is it for? Who is educated? Does education mean only literacy? What are its core objectives? People from different backgrounds, at different socioeconomic levels, will come up with different answers to these seemingly innocent and simple questions. Educationists and planners will use jargon in answering these questions, which the average person may not be able to decipher readily. On superficial and relative levels, the answers may appear to be highly varied and subjective, yet not much variance in the answers is expected to occur logically at a deeper and absolute level. This section aims to provide an independent outsider's thoughts on the matter.

People who engage in scams and corruption of the highest order are all educated. Most schemers and devious individuals are educated. Not all educated people are crooks but most crooks are educated people.

One would argue why can't uneducated or illiterate individuals also be devious? Well, yes, it is possible but the sphere of their negative influence would not be as large as the sphere of negative-minded educated people. One can't argue about the significant extent of damage an educated but corrupt person can potentially cause to the world, especially if the person is influential and powerful in professional, social or political domains.

What matters, therefore, is the type of education that one has received and not whether a person is educated or not. An educated person lacking social responsibility and selfless empathetic care may be deemed more uneducated than an illiterate person.

In disappointment and disgust about current world affairs, I posted my thoughts on Twitter on 13 February 2020, without realising in that moment that my thoughts could potentially be misrepresented and grossly misinterpreted:

Fearful Ignorance and general naivety of the people are cleverly exploited by the wealthy and powerful amongst them. These are the prime reasons why and how deceptive individuals come to rule over them. Ignorance and illiteracy are curses and causes of doom and tears. — Bill Koul

Instead of 'illiteracy', I had actually meant 'lack of education'. Mere literacy is not good enough; education goes far beyond literacy.

As such, education is commonly claimed as a panacea for curing all societal ills and poverty. True, but what does 'education' really mean? When does it start and when does it end? How does education happen? Answers to these questions are practically person specific. As such, we may potentially have 7.8 billion answers to these questions, a different one from every person on the planet. 'Education' is one of the most loosely used everyday terms, other terms being 'love', 'respect' and 'human'. Don't blame the politicians and so-called uneducated people; not many so-called educated people, including many educationists, may really know what it is all about. For most, 'education' is just another job — a business, a source of income.

Educationists may attempt to use scholarly jargon in their answers to these questions — to keep things limited to their exclusive group — but if they can't explain things to a layperson, how do they expect to bring about a practical change for the better in the world through this panacea called 'education'? So, before we attempt to answer these questions here, let us first look at what education is not about. The whole process may appear to be rather reductive, but this is solely for the purpose of simplicity.

What is 'not' education?
The purpose of education is not to make parrots or monkeys. Education is not any of the following:
- cookie cutting;
- creating photocopies;
- making intellectual snobs and show-offs;

- transferring a load (or a burden) of knowledge — gained, created or borrowed — from a teacher to a student;
- rote learning and cramming knowledge; or
- assessments and scoring.

What is education?

Education is all of the following:

- discovering oneself and one's relationship with the world around us and beyond — the cosmos;
- becoming free and fearless — from one's inhibitions and fears, social stigmas and taboos, unfounded beliefs and slavery;
- becoming responsible global citizens;
- becoming humble, empathetic and caring;
- learning to think independently, uninhibited and critically, and being able to ask questions;
- inculcating common sense, which is fast becoming uncommon thanks to the mechanisation of life;
- researching and continuous learning from the open book of life;
- learning how and where to find the answers;
- enlightening the human mind and enhancing human wellbeing;
- knowing one's limitations and accepting what one does not know; and
- a never-ending process till one's last breath. Education doesn't end with formal education.

A school may not have a building or boastful fancy features; a school is not a school if it does not have a teacher. A school is not a good school if it does not have a good teacher. A good school can never become a world-class institution if it does not have a world-class teacher.

The author remembers, about 30 years ago, teaching a number of engineering subjects to three batches of displaced (migrant) civil engineering students — from Regional Engineering College, Srinagar,

Kashmir (now NIT Srinagar) — on the lawns of Jammu Polytechnic and sometimes, when lucky, using a concrete water tank or an old rusted school bus as a blackboard. All students passed the semester examination, conducted by Kashmir University, with flying colours. Adversity leads to innovation.

Pedagogical challenges

Academic education without research and experimentation to understand the practical relevance of what is being thought is useless and short-lived. A teacher is seen as someone who transfers knowledge to students, which is true to an extent but is that all?

How much content knowledge does the teacher truly have about the subject matter? Is the teacher continuously involved in personal professional development — in both teaching methods and the subject matter — and abreast with the related global research? Most importantly, is the teacher aware about his or her own limitations?

Teachers must remember that knowledge is ever growing and not stagnant. With each moment, the envelope of knowledge keeps pushing forward the boundaries of human imagination. This realisation must make teachers humble in their self-assessment and the assessment of students.

If a teacher can't explain the subject matter to students in their native language — using anecdotes, metaphors and examples from everyday life — the teacher has seemingly not understood the subject matter themselves. How can one expect real education to happen with such a teacher?

Honesty from teachers is a must. If a teacher can't explain the problem — because they have not fully understood the subject matter in the first place and/or are not able to converse fluently in the medium of instruction (e.g. English is generally a medium of instruction in a vastly Hindi-speaking India), the teacher must be honest in admitting, 'I don't know, let us work together on this' and then earnestly assist the student to find the answer. That is how the great philosopher Socrates learnt and taught.

Mentors and mentees can be likened to teachers and students, respectively. In many cases, the roles of mentors and mentees get exchanged after they have moved some distance in the journey of education — learning and teaching — guiding and facilitating. In many such cases, the mentee grows much more than the mentor's experience and capability and the mentor just can't keep up, causing the reversal of the process of mentoring. Such is the nature of education, it never stops and the direction is never constant.

Teachers try to penalise 'bad' students. But are there really bad students? Students are students; there can be difficult — stubborn and mischievous — students but not bad students. Young people are expected to be mischievous; it is their age to be defiant and left of the middle. Unfortunately, the system gives the teacher the implicit right to punish 'bad' students for whatever reason. Why should learning come with punishment? Where about the teacher's empathy, proactive care and respect for inherent human dignity?

If a teacher becomes angry when a student asks questions, and shows their anger by raising their voice, threatening to fail the student in exams or use old-school physical punishment, which is not allowed anymore by law, how can that teacher inculcate critical thinking?

If a student, immediately after taking the final examination, honestly tries to answer a question related to the subject matter which requires common sense and critical thinking — using logic, rationale and even a reductive process — and not come up with common excuses, such as this was not covered in the classroom or this was not in our syllabus, the student can be deemed to have met the objectives of education and to be treading the path of true learning.

Classroom environment

We talk about improving the 'classroom environment' for improving student performance. Do we know how much home and social environments — socio-political, socioeconomic, socio-religious— affect a student's learning? How many teachers in developing countries, or even in so-called developed countries, are aware of the baggage, mental and psychological, that a student may bring to the classroom?

A good shepherd is one who proactively cares for his flock or herd and is always humane. He bonds with them spiritually. He walks with them physically, in rain and shine, and never abandons them. If you don't know your flock or herd well enough, don't even think of leading it.

When evaluating a student's performance, how many teachers factor in what goes on in the student's life — physical, mental and/or sexual abuse at home by a family member, or by a street bully on the way between home and school, or by a bully on the school bus, or by a bully within the school premises, or by a classroom bully?

How many teachers try to understand why a student does not like them or their subject? How many teachers interact with their students with genuine respect and treat their so-called academically poor or difficult students with empathy and genuine care? History is full of anecdotes about how empathetic, caring teachers have turned around the lives of 'academically poor' students, especially from the economically disadvantaged strata of society, or 'difficult' students from the affluent and influential class.

Teachers who believe they have the right to be uncouth and treat students with scorn and disrespect, or punish them, or see them as inferior, or believe they oblige their students, don't deserve to be in the teaching profession.

Discussions and disagreements are necessary for the growth of knowledge in a vibrant classroom. Teachers — with temper — and lacking patience, prudence and empathetic care must not be in the teaching profession.

In addition to classrooms, learning and teaching can happen in out-of-classroom environments — in natural settings, such as playgrounds or in nature, on grass under trees. Literature, mathematics (arithmetic, geometry and trigonometry) and the sciences (natural and physics) can also be effectively studied and discussed in suitable open environments.

Unless the learning environment is made unregimented, informal and enjoyable, learning will not become easier or faster. Students must love their learning environment before their development can take place.

Teaching as profession

Do students attend school only to learn the subject matter? Should they not attend school also to become empathetic and responsible global citizens — as we all live in a global village — and learn the skills to think independently and critically, to use common sense and how to access the available literature to seek answers for their queries?

Unfortunately, in general and mostly in developing countries, the existing system places the lives of young students in the hands of so-called teachers and teaching institutions which may not be suited to even come close to dealing with students. How many top students go into the teaching profession after Year 12 or even after their Bachelor's degree?

As can be expected, some teachers may not be in the teaching profession by choice. They may have considered it a fall-back profession, to put food on the plate. They may have originally wanted to become scientists, engineers or doctors but, for lack of resources at the start of their tertiary education, or failure to secure admission due to high merit, reservations and/or competition, they may have been compelled to consider other, less-desired options.

On the other end of the spectrum, some people who naturally love to exercise control and power over other people eventually move in that direction — management and administration — even after getting their first degrees in engineering, commerce, economics, law or even medicine. They may never have had enough love for the area of their first degree. In the process, they waste a spot in their Bachelor's degree which could have gone to a more deserving student who would have loved that profession but could not get the seat in the first place for aforementioned reasons.

Empathy and proactive care are necessary for a teacher to connect with students. Those who lack these characteristics must not be teachers in the first place. Students should be taught by empathetic teachers to be empathetic (among other things) at school.

Develop a teacher to develop a country and the wider world. States must invest heavily in teacher education.

Going forward

Life is not only about survival. Life is for living — with a lifelong learning mindset — happily, truthfully and responsibly. Human development can't be measured by the wealth and assets of a very few but by the living standards of the most. Why do we do what we do and how we do it? These are the questions that we must keep asking ourselves. Becoming human machines is not human development.

Vocational training must be made necessary at all levels of schools and college education. Through a delicate and subtle screening process, the system must ensure that it does not install square pegs in round holes or the other way around. Just because a student wants to become a doctor does not mean that student deserves to be doctor. The student's temperament and aptitude must align with the student's enthusiasm. The student should be able to explain — not through coaching at coaching centres or coaching by parents, but by themselves — why they want to become a doctor. For such aptitude assessments, the screening process must be clever enough to screen out the impostors.

The school system should seamlessly provide separate pathways to students based on their individual aptitude — vocational or tertiary education — to pursue their natural interests, with each pathway providing equal respect, dignity and means of a decent livelihood. In the context of the Indian subcontinent, the students — under their parental or societal influence — should not be pushed to choose pathways for which they are not naturally cut out. Just because a certain profession can potentially bring one immense wealth and influence does not mean one should choose that profession, especially if one's temperament is not suited to it. This needs a significant shift in the societal paradigm. Some societies value some professions relatively much higher than the rest, solely based on the wealth and influence people earn in those professions. Not every student can become a civil servant, doctor or an engineer. For that matter not every student needs to go to university to pursue tertiary education.

A shift in the societal paradigm is possible only when a society recognises and embraces the dignity of labour and develops genuine respect for work — any work — irrespective of the type of work or the profession, whether manual or intellectual. Only by enabling such a positive shift in the mindset of society at large can the educational system produce right fits for right jobs, as it should be, without compulsion.

Currently, in the Indian subcontinent, many educational institutions and teachers seem to be functioning as cookie cutters. No wonder the mental health of the young is a growing issue. Ask any student why they go to school (school, college or university) and the answer will give you the reality. Thankfully, in developed countries, such as Australia, the situation is contrastingly different.

Education should be holistic — about the whole person — ethical, moral, physical and scholarly — to be able to develop an open mind, which is capable of thinking independently and seeking answers — and not follow blind — and challenge the existing knowledge.

Teaching is not a job like any other job and, therefore, must not be considered as one. It is supposed to be a delicate service, which must be rendered only by humans with the aptitude for learning and teaching towards their fellow humans, and the planet as a whole. It can't be done by any Tom, Dick or Harry. The challenge is to find them at a young age and then facilitate their development by gifted senior teachers. Practically, therefore, a complete shift in the paradigm is required.

Education should be constructivist — help to extract the student's own, original, independent understanding of the subject matter and develop it further.

To start with, the state must fully own and run the education system, allocate the largest chunk of funding towards education and for continuous teacher development, review the entire pedagogical structure and learning environment, invest in community and adult education, review and reform the assessment structure and give greater autonomy to the teacher in terms of how to teach the subject matter and how to assess student aptitude.

How to find future teachers who have an aptitude for teaching? The answer is: in the same way as we find soldiers, bureaucrats, engineers and doctors. Their selection process must include a multi-level assessment of physical and mental fitness; psychological, ethical and moral health; and attributes of empathy, self-control and patience, interpersonal communication skills, imagination, intelligence and wisdom.

Why do we need such stringent assessment to identify them? Because they are the ones who are meant to develop our future citizens. They must be rewarded with the highest possible salary of all professionals — with attractive perks and incentives — because they are the cream of the cream of society.

Only when a high benchmark is set for teacher selection, a high benchmark is automatically set for the country. Unless education is focused on human development, a country will not develop.

The Importance of Human Endeavour — Wishes Don't Fly, They Need Wings

Wishes don't fly, birds fly. No sooner had I realised this truth for the umpteenth time during my run this morning than I received a full load of warm bird droppings on my head and shoulders. I looked up. Right above my head, a seagull was perched on a branch of a tall gum tree. I threw my hands up, whinging, 'Why?' The bird did not move or answer; it kept looking towards the river, seemingly oblivious to the consequences of its very natural act.

As I could not find a tap or water fountain nearby, I decided to move on, without messing with Nature's surprise gift. Wiping it with my handkerchief would not only have rendered the handkerchief unusable for the rest of my run but would also smear my gift all over my scalp, which would not have been a very good feeling. I hoped it would dry up soon, and it did. To the east, the sun suddenly appeared from behind the dark clouds on the horizon and shone brightly, albeit briefly before the mischievous clouds hid it again. I had no other option but to forgive the innocent bird. After all, it had only answered the call of nature, as we all do; it was not a deliberate, punishable act. In some cultures, it is believed the recipients of such gifts are lucky and due to receive Nature's bounties. Well, I had not made any such wish to receive this gift, none at all; it had happened unexpectedly and suddenly!

After running a couple of hundred metres or so, I saw a few morning walkers and a couple of cyclists standing around — albeit complying with social distancing requirements — and looking intently towards a group of canoers in the river. It seemed they had all stopped to watch a pod of dolphins playing in the river. I too stopped briefly, at a safe distance from the others, and watched the dolphins playing for a few moments. I also took a picture, hoping my phone camera would capture the magic moment when a dolphin would spring gleefully out of the water; however, that did not happen.

Thinking about it, I had not wished to receive either of the two gifts this morning, but things do happen every now and then, whether we wish for them or not. Nature is not a slave to our wishes, a reminder of a popular proverb: *If wishes were horses, beggars would ride.*

Since I can remember, I may have made zillions of wishes, which have never been answered. I may have lost count of my wishes to wake up in a more humane and considerate world, much more peaceful and happier than it seems to be now, where people are kinder and more empathetic to one another and to other life species; where religion is not used, abused and misused for personal material gain and for unleashing atrocities on less privileged people. My wishes for friendship between traditional foes — countries, communities and individuals — and for a general improvement in the lives of marginalised and less privileged people seem to have fallen on deaf ears. My wishes have been altruistic. Oh, I am sorry! Is it too early to conclude this assertion? Have I forgotten about COVID-19?

(It is another thing that most of my predictions have come true but this is solely based on my ability to think outside the box and consider all possibilities, using a sharp eye that can decipher patterns and my sixth sense.)

I have not wished much for myself, which may sound unbelievable, perhaps arrogant. I do not have any such hedonistic wish list. I am thankful for being privileged, for being who I am and for what I have. If wishing well for one's family can be considered hedonistic, then I may have made many hedonistic wishes. I distinctly recall how, a decade ago, I had desperately wished that my mother would recover from her terminal illness before she passed on suddenly at a relatively young age of sixty-three. Wishes don't fly! Actions fly but only if the Higher Design allows them to fly. Laws of Nature prevail. Where they are violated, Nature punishes mercilessly.

To test the mechanism and effectiveness of wishes, and immunise myself from the *fear* of death (and not death itself, as death is inevitable for each one of us), there have been numerous times when I have just wished that I would die suddenly in my sleep or of a massive heart attack or in a road crash, without having to become old, fragile or sick. My wishes have not been answered, at least not yet. Being a frequent traveller, there have been numerous occasions when my plane took an unusually long period of time to land or there was severe turbulence and I prepared myself mentally for the worst — without any grudge, remorse or regret — and became ready to depart, while I saw my fellow passengers tightly holding on to their armrests, looking pale and nervous, some praying and some crying.

A few years ago, someone asked me, 'If Lord Ram suddenly appeared before you, what would you ask for?' I replied, 'I would not ask for anything material, I would request Him to let me accompany Him.'

Some people may ask, 'Would you not like to grow old and play with your grandchildren and see them grow?' My answer is, 'It is not entirely in my hands. They are not born yet, they will arrive in their own time. What is the point of discussing things that are not in our control?'

Some readers may be wondering if I am a normal person. Stereotypical thinking requires one to fear death and not talk about it in the sense I am talking. Who wants to die, let alone wish to die? Thinking about it, it is generally our fear of death and the unknown (after death) that pushes many people to figuratively do all kinds of figurative gymnastics and acrobatics to defy death and live as long as possible. And why should one not try to live long? For many people, living life is a matter of pleasure, a gift and an opportunity for satisfying all five senses through hedonistic enjoyment of material pleasures.

I have been fortunate enough to have lived a little more than fifty-five years and contributed positively to the world for more than thirty-five years of my life by now and done everything that a fortunate person is expected to do. I am physically and mentally healthy, living the core message of my 2017 book, *My Life Does Not Have* to Be Unhappy. On a daily basis, I engage myself in the three activities of meditation, oxygenation (aerobic exercises) and living to an altruistic purpose in life that are essential for living a more fulfilled and meaningful life. Unless Nature has other designs, I would not like to be become old and fragile and sick, or remain bedridden or be bound to a wheelchair, or turn out to be a leech on my family or the taxpayer, in general, and leach out their resources that can otherwise have better uses.

To avoid any misinterpretation, it is important to clarify that, yes, on numerous occasions, I have wished that I die but that does not mean I'll take my own life. Committing suicide is one of the greatest cowardly crimes that one can commit against one's parents, particularly one's mother, as well as against humanity as a whole. Our life is a gift to us from our mother, who has conceived, carried us for months and delivered us, risking her own life in the process and compromising on her comforts for many years — before, during and after our birth. She has nurtured us so that we can live. Our father too has worked hard to help us survive and grow. Thereafter, the whole world takes care of us and, as such, we are accountable to the world community. It is our duty and moral responsibility to look after our physical, mental and spiritual wellbeing. The world community — our parents, elders, teachers, researchers, doctors and governments — has heavily invested in each one of us, whether we realise this fact consciously or not.

Coming back to the topic of wishes, and without getting distracted further, a logical and important question arises: 'Why have my wishes not been answered?'

The answer can be any or all of the following:
- Perhaps, I may have been wishing in the wrong places or at the wrong times.
- Perhaps, the Granter may be too preoccupied with doing other more important tasks, such as:
  - keeping the sun burning, just like an engine driver of the past, chucking coal in the furnace to keep the rail engine running;
  - traffic policing the planets so that they don't collide and cause

a catastrophic end to the entire cosmos — another big bang; and/or

- keeping our beautiful Earth spinning about its axis, as a top, and making it go around the sun so that each one of us equally enjoys the day (to work) and the night (to sleep) and various seasons, without monotony.

- Possibly, I am too insignificant for the Granter.
- Perhaps, as a horrible possibility, the Granter does not exist at all.

My colleague, Payam Sadeghi, also a philosopher in his own right apart from being an able engineer, says:

Perhaps, God does not exist. Even if He exists, either He is too powerless to change anything on the Earth or too preoccupied with watching soccer all the time, munching chips. Is it not rather strange that He (God) just can't see or doesn't care that children and innocent individuals die in war or due to hunger and disease? Can't He see that most people in the world are poor and uneducated, and constantly being exploited — used, abused and misused — by a small percentage of privileged individuals? Does He really care? Can't He see how militarily big and wealthier countries bully and exploit smaller countries, thereby deciding the fate of common people in those unfortunate countries? What is God for if He can't act to stop bad things happening on Earth?

Well, these thoughts raise many more questions than can ever be answered with a logical and rational mind without, of course, using some form of belief to defend God (Nature, the Granter, the Maker) and justify His inaction or inertness. Some people may use the theories of destiny and karma for our suffering, which goes into the controversial domain of reincarnation. Some people may say God is testing us. But why, what have we done? Definitely, God can't be sadistic, one who derives pleasure from our miseries. Surely, we have not understood the truth well enough, not yet.

If God starts listening to our 'petty' hedonistic wishes, imagine the time it will take Him to fulfil our hundreds of wishes on a daily basis. Considering that we are about 8 billion people living on the planet, and growing, it is unfair we distract Him from what He is already doing for us in terms of the stability of our cosmos and our ecosystem.

God or no God, things do happen, as and when they are meant to happen — as a direct result of human endeavour — or naturally, as surprises and unexpected gifts to us from Nature, such as the two gifts I received this morning. After all, our Earth was created about 4.3 billion years ago and has survived all these years. The sun will last for another 5 billion years, it has already exhausted nearly half of its capacity. The human population has increased nearly eight times in the last 400 years and we are currently nearly 8 billion people on the planet.

Things keep happening irrespective of our wishes. The collective actions of those 8 billion people on our planet, together with the actions of all other life species (including our ecosystem) and, most importantly, our individual actions, decide our now and tomorrow, notwithstanding the roles played by the sun, the moon and the stars.

Wishes don't fly, birds fly. Flies, moths and insects too fly. Even ants fly. Humans were not meant to fly, Nature did not give them wings. Humans needed machines and mechanical wings to fulfil their timeless wish to fly. It took a sustained human endeavour for us to fly; many dreamers lost their lives in the process before the wish was fulfilled. Yet where are we now? Most planes are grounded in this global COVID-19 lockdown. Perhaps, the growing size of a large hole in our ozone layer had wished they be grounded so that the human race could survive, at least for now and some more time, which goes on to teach that wishes must be made exercising due wisdom, with extreme care and foresight. Well, that is another thing …

To conclude, wishes don't fly on their own, they need wings. Our actions and efforts are their wings. Unless our actions — honest, sincere, focused and sustained — back our wishes, they won't be fulfilled. Actions matter. Efforts count.

My only wish is that, at the end of the day, I close my eyes without guilt that I did not try enough and do my best. Nonetheless, due to my insignificance in the Higher Design, I am neither ashamed of anything nor fearful.

This section of this chapter has a much wider global significance, beyond the lives of simple individuals, their small worlds and their basic needs. It aims to remove many common fears and remind us of our insignificance in the scheme of things and the Higher Design. If you are one of those fortunate individuals whose prayers and wishes have been fulfilled and that too without making much effort, count your blessings and be thankful, as most people in this world are not as fortunate. Good people suffer through no fault of their own and lose everything in a moment. How much of our life is really in our control?

The lives of more than 90 percent of the world population are dependent more or less on the whims and wishes of the remaining 10 percent. It is that overwhelming majority that fits into this proverb, the remaining 20 percent are just outliers. The wishes of that majority don't generally come true. For them, *wishes don't fly, actions fly*, but even that does not always happen, as COVID-19 has just proved.

Beware of Capitalism to Prevent Human Exploitation

As the world is moving gradually into a phase of lifting the lockdown, it becomes a brazen case of 'survival of the fittest'. To keep a country running and kick-start the economy, calculated risks are taken, which, in this context, mean a potential loss of human lives. Paradoxically, humans are willing to pay the price, partly due to their compulsion to earn their daily bread and partly because they have been feeling caged in the last few weeks and, therefore, want to break free. There is always a price to be paid for both survival and freedom, one way or another.

As the human population today is four times what it was 100 years ago, humans are perhaps seen as being too numerous and, therefore, relatively expendable. The matters of the economy have, as a direct result of the phenomenal growth in human numbers, overtaken human lives in terms of their importance and priority.

In capitalism, humans are seen as nothing more than labourers, workers, building blocks, numbers and commodities that are used by a few to achieve greater wealth and comfort and, more importantly, greater control and power over other humans, which they call progress and happiness.

Capitalism is cold and emotionless. It is heartless and lacks empathy. It sees humans as sheer commodities. Once a commodity becomes weak or slow or high maintenance for any reason, it is seen as dead wood. Capitalism thrives on getting rid of dead wood to maximise profits. The phrase that underlines the evolution of life on Earth, 'survival of the fittest', applies shamelessly to capitalism. Countries and governments that promote capitalism exploit opportunities, such as the current situation, to their maximum by allowing their dead wood to perish.

The capitalistic mantra is simple: 'if you are old, diseased or weak, and of no use to anyone, it is better you disappear so that your pension and the cost of your health care, to prolong your life, is saved'. But, equally, an argument can be that prolonging life could be in the best interests of capitalism in terms of healthcare cost. It may not be in the interests of governments that pay public healthcare costs, but it is very good for capitalism as it creates a market that can be exploited com-mercially.

The Cambridge dictionary defines 'capitalism' as: 'an economic, political, and social system in which property, business, and industry are privately owned, directed towards making the greatest possible profits for successful organisations and people'.

Human greed will undoubtedly take a great toll on human survival itself. As we are unlikely to learn from the current opportunity, our future generations will definitely pay a big price for our impatience and mindless consumption. Unfortunately, our myopic eyes cannot foresee the magnitude of that price. We lack vision. Capitalism fuels consumption. A century of progress that never was! Our world was like a house of cards, a bubble, a growing building with poor foundations, it could not sustain even over a period of few weeks. Our population grew four times in the last century but our priorities were misplaced. It was a case of too much, too soon, too fast. What did we achieve? Young people were induced into living from one pay check to another pay check, without saving for the rainy day. Borrowing became a norm; mortgage an accepted way of life. We were used as consumers, as pawns, as a herd. Who benefited? All crashed. Our global artificial glamourous structure came crumbling down in a matter of a few weeks. What did we do in the last 100 years other than creating, sowing and harvesting the seeds of fear and hatred, and manufacturing and using deadly weapons? Why did we not invest in brotherhood, peace and human health?

Death — A Reminder to Respect Life and Live it Full and With Purpose

Death is an intrinsic part of life but humans generally fear death. A nagging fear against death, deep into our psychology, invariably dilutes the quality of our life itself and, as a consequence, we don't live full and fearless before breathing our last. The purpose of this section is to lead the reader from the 'fear of death' to the 'death of fear' in your mind.

The inevitability of our death and the reality of our mortality and the transitory nature of our lives are the reasons why we should live life to the full, fearless and beautifully, and act as good humans. But why is death generally feared, given that it is inevitable for anyone who is born? Why is even talking about it such a taboo for many of us considering it is the most certain thing in our life? A reason may be that deep inside us — despite our religious beliefs about reincarnation, heaven and help, and so on — we don't really believe that anything outside our physical existence exists in this universe. But who knows? Is that important to know? Perhaps not!

The truth is that one who exists must certainly die. As birth marks the beginning of life, death marks its end. Existence and life are, therefore, intertwined with death. Death is a logical destination of existence. If one did not exist, one would not die. One who is born must die one day. But can one know when? Life has a finite period. For varied reasons, some tend to live relatively longer than others. But no one can escape death at the end of one's life. For believers in reincarnation, death may also mark the beginning of another life cycle, just as an old, worn-out shirt is thrown away and a new shirt is worn.

It is our fear of death that drives our general thought process — what and how much we eat, exercise, travel, work and so on. We do everything to prolong our life span so as to defer the moment of reckoning when we pass into the unknown — oblivion, the abyss or ether or simply nothing. Because we fear death to such an extent that we keep running away from it, even talking about it becomes taboo for many of us. Some people can't even sleep for fear of death.

Paradoxically, many of us also tend to fool ourselves into believing that we will never die. It is that self-hypnosis that makes us run after material wealth and power. If only we would really understand that all the wealth and power that we have or which we have been running after will not accompany us after we stop breathing and heart stops beating altogether, we could possibly make a more judicious, ethical and moral use of our finite life span before the death of our physical existence.

Many wise and realised souls have advised us to 'die before our death'. They did not want us to commit suicide though. They just wanted to make us understand, and not just know, that our death is inevitable and does not allow us to carry our material wealth with us beyond the last door. Knowing and understanding are two different things. We know many things but how many of us really understand them, even up to our final moment?

The wise souls wanted us to realise the reality of our transitory physical existence, which is characterised generally by pain and suffering. Buddha's Four Noble Truths and Eightfold Path are all about this suffering of ours. Until this truth really sinks in, we live in the mortal fear of death. Only after we embrace the possibility of our death, we overcome that fear and start living fully and fearlessly, with a sense of detachment of course. It is the realisation that we are just mortals which can help us to become good humans and work selflessly for one and all, and not only for ourselves or some, without bias or prejudice or discrimination. The acceptance of our mortality makes many of us live a moral and ethical life, without much greed or lust for power or material wealth.

Definitions of the term 'death'

Before we move on, let us try to understand the meaning of the term 'death'. It is generally defined as the 'permanent cessation of all vital functions; the end of life'. Merriam-Webster also provides the following synonyms for 'death', which can be helpful in developing an understanding of the subject: curtains, decease, demise, dissolution, doom, end, exit, expiration, expiry, fate, grave, great divide, passage, passing, quietus, sleep.

In an article titled 'Defining death', the Australian Museum defines death in three main ways — legal, cultural and clinical. Some excerpts of the article are reproduced below:

- In Australian law, death is generally defined as either irreversible cessation of circulation of blood in the body of the person or irreversible cessation of all function of the brain of the person.
- For the Roman Catholic Church, death is the complete and final separation of the soul from the body ... Followers of religions like Zen Buddhism and Shintoism believe that the mind and body are integrated and have trouble accepting the brain death criteria to determine death. Some Orthodox Jews, Native Americans, Muslims and fundamentalist Christians

believe that as long as a heart is beating — even artificially — you are still alive.

- To be legally brain dead, all function of both the upper and lower brain must cease … Brain death … occurs after a stroke, or an impact that causes the brain to swell and push against the skull, preventing blood from flowing to the brain … [it] is quite different from reversible coma … death of only the upper brain (cerebral hemispheres) will not have consciousness, memory, knowledge or thought, but the living lower brain (brain stem) allows the heart to pump, the lungs to breathe and the body to function …

Our existence

Our holistic existence comprises two domains — physical and spiritual.

- Our physical existence —our body — is a three-phase system of solids, fluids and air/gases, like soils, which reduces to ashes (upon cremation) or dust (upon burial). Soils exist as a three-phase system — solids, water and air. Water and air fill the pores (voids) within the soil particles (solids), partially or fully.
- Our spiritual existence — in the form of our soul or spirit and as reflected by our mind in the form of our thoughts and emotions, including feelings, such as love, empathy, care and compassion, as well as their opposites — is believed to be associated with our energy field, which is invisible. It is this energy field that separates a living body from a dead body.

As per various religious beliefs, the term 'death' is generally used in the context of one's physical existence but not spiritual existence. There is a set of religious beliefs about the journey of a soul (or spirit) after the death of its host body. All these religious beliefs are debatable on any given day. What happens to our soul — our spirit, our energy — upon the death of our body, no one knows for sure! From atheistic and agnostic perspectives, therefore, an important question arises: 'What happens to the soul? Does it die too when the body dies?'

If religious beliefs are not able to provide a logical answer to this question, can science answer it? An attempt is made in the following paragraphs to answer this question.

Understanding death through science

The following laws of science may provide useful guidance for attaining some understanding as to what could possibly be happening to us after our physical death. Although the arguments can't be considered to be definitive, a reader will still be able to find some solace on reaching a logical conclusion, albeit a dead end, beyond which, of course, one's imagination will be the sole lighthouse or a beacon in this never-ending internal journey that has teased the human race from time immemorial.

The Law of Conservation of Mass (also known as the principle of mass conservation) is simply, 'Matter is neither created nor destroyed'. As per the law, although mass can neither be created nor destroyed, it may be rearranged in space or the entities associated with it may be changed in form. An understanding of this vital aspect of the law is very important in the context of understanding 'death'. 'Mass conservation' was initially demonstrated (in chemical reactions) by a Russian scientist and polymath, Mikhail Vasilyevich Lomonosov (1711–1765), who also made important contributions to Russian literature and education, as a writer, poet, historian and grammarian. In 1785, it was rediscovered by a French chemist and nobleman, Antoine-Laurent de Lavoisier (1743–1794), popularly acknowledged as the 'father of modern chemistry'. He also significantly influenced the history of chemistry and history of biology.

The Law of Conservation of Energy (also known as the First Law of Thermodynamics), as discovered in 1842 by Julius Robert Mayer, simply states: 'Energy is neither created nor destroyed'.

German-born physicist Albert Einstein (1879–1955) deduced there is no fixed point of reference in the universe and, as such, everything is moving relative to everything else, which gave birth to his Special Theory of Relativity in 1905, in which the term 'special' means it applies only to special cases — frames of reference in constant, un-changing motion. The Special Theory of Relativity determines that: (a) the laws of physics are the same for all non-accelerating observers; and (b) the speed of light in a vacuum is unchanging (299,338 kilometres a second) and independent of the motion of all observers.

Through his famous equation, $E = mc^2$, Einstein proposed 'mass' and 'energy' are different manifestations of the same thing and, therefore, interconvertible. In the equation, the two laws — Conservation of mass and Conservation of Energy — are merged into a single Law of Conservation of Mass-Energy, which simply means: 'The total amount of mass and energy in the universe is constant'. The equation explains the release of a huge amount of energy in a nuclear explosion.

In light of these laws of science, it is established that mass and energy can neither be created nor destroyed. It is also understand that mass and energy are interconvertible. So, which part of us dies upon our perceived death — our mass (body) or our energy (soul)? Perhaps none; seemingly both just change form after one's physical death.

As per a phenomenon called time dilation, time does not pass at the same rate for everyone; a fast-moving observer measures time passing more slowly than a (relatively) stationary observer would. Also, a fast-moving object appears to be shorter along the direction of motion, relative to a slow-moving one. This effect is very subtle until the object travels close to the speed of light. Due to the increase in mass, as an object travels fast, Einstein said that matter cannot travel faster than light. The mass increases with velocity until the mass becomes infinite when it reaches the speed of light. An infinite mass would require infinite energy to move, which is impossible.

In 1915, Einstein published his Theory of General Relativity, which applies to frames that are accelerating with regard to each other. He proposed that space and time were interwoven into a single continuum known as space-time. According to him, events that occur at the same time for one observer could occur at different times for another. He also realised that massive objects caused a distortion in space-time, felt as gravity, which can be visualised by imagining a large body placed in the centre of a trampoline pushing down into the fabric, creating a depression. Any object moving at its edge would be pulled in due to the gravity and spiral inwards towards the body.

Interestingly, gravity keeps taking a toll on the human body as it ages till the last moment of one's physical existence. Finally, as everything else on the Earth, we humans return to Mother Earth.

As Einstein's theory helps to provide a useful way forward in one's general acceptance of and respect for death as part of one's life, it would be reasonable, therefore, to know a little bit more about Einstein and who influenced him.

David Hume influenced Einstein
Although not strictly fitting into the context of this chapter, the following paragraphs are considered important in the context of this book in so far as the human mind is concerned, as reflected by noted philosophers, especially David Hume (1711–1776), the Scottish philosopher from the Age of Enlightenment, who is understood to have greatly influenced many thinkers, including Einstein. His famous work, *A Treatise of Human Nature* (1739–40), is known to have influenced Einstein's thinking about space and time.

Based on an article by Karl Tate, dated 05 March 2015, *Einstein's Theory of Relativity Explained (Infographic)*, acknowledging Hume, Einstein wrote: 'It is very well possible that without these philosophical studies, I would not have arrived at the solution'.

In an essay in aeon (https://aeon.co/essays/what-albert-einstein-owes-to-david-humes-notion-of-time), titled, *No absolute time*, Matias Slavov wrote: 'Two centuries before Einstein, Hume recognised that universal time, independent of an observer's viewpoint, doesn't exist'. The essay talks about a letter from Einstein to Moritz Schlick, philosopher and physicist, in 1915, in which he expressed his gratitude to Hume: 'Hume, whose Treatise of Human Nature I had studied avidly and with admiration shortly before discovering the theory of relativity. It is very possible that without these philosophical studies I would not have arrived at the solution.'

Hume, who was an empiricist, sceptic and naturalist, believed scientific concepts must be based on experience and evidence, and not just reason alone. He maintained that time did not exist separately from the motion of objects. Developing a naturalistic science of man that looked into the psychological basis of human nature, Hume argued against the existence of innate ideas. He proposed that all human knowledge comes solely from experience and argued that inductive reasoning and belief in causality result from mental habit, which cannot be justified rationally. He said humans never actually 'perceive' that one event causes another, but only experience the 'constant conjunction' of events, which means that, for drawing any causal inferences from one's past experience, it is necessary to presuppose that the future will resemble the past. Hume said such a presupposition cannot itself be grounded in prior experience.

As a sentimentalist, Hume maintained that ethics are based on emotions or sentiments rather than abstract moral principle. He opposed philosophical rationalism, maintaining that 'passions rather than reason' govern general human behaviour, which is boldly reflected in his famous proclamation: 'Reason is and ought only to be the slave of the passions'.

Hume denied that humans have an actual conception of the self, proposing that humans experience only a bundle of sensations, and that the self is nothing more than this bundle of causally connected perceptions.

Hume's views on philosophy of religion were controversial during his time. In his various writings concerning religion, Hume puts forth a systematic, sceptical critique of the philosophical foundations of various theological systems, which may lead one into thinking that one of his most basic philosophical objectives was to discredit the doctrines and dogmas of traditional theistic belief, thereby portraying him as more of an atheist.

In summary, David Hume influenced utilitarianism, logical positivism, the philosophy of science, early analytic philosophy, cognitive science and theology. Hume's general thinking aligned him with other noted philosophers, such as Immanuel Kant, John Locke, George Berkeley, Francis Bacon and Thomas Hobbes, who maintained similar thoughts.

As per Stanford Encyclopaedia of Philosophy (https://plato.stanford.edu/entries/kant-hume-morality/), German philosopher Immanuel Kant (1724–1804), also from the Age of Enlightenment, also credited Dave Hume for inspiration, acknowledging that 'Hume had awakened him from his dogmatic slumbers'.

As per his doctrine of transcendental idealism, Kant argued that space and time, and causation are mere sensibilities, as 'things-in-themselves' but their nature is unknowable. He maintained space, time and causality, which are the necessary ways in which phenomena are related to one another, do not have an existence separate from phenomena or outside of us. He proposed these forms of interrelatedness originate in our mental faculties and are, thus, mind-dependent.

He argues that one perceives objects not as they are in themselves, but only as they appear to one in accordance with one's sensibility. The doctrine, thus, limits the ability of one's perception to one's sensibility. He denies that one can have the ability to perceive things as they truly are independent of how one may experience them through one's cognitive faculties. He believed the human mind shapes and structures experience. In one of his major works, the *Critique of Pure Reason* (1781; second edition 1787), he proposed worldly objects can be intuited a priori (beforehand), and that intuition is independent from objective reality.

Kant attempted to explain the relationship between reason and human experience. He believed that reason is also the source of morality, and that aesthetics arise from a faculty of disinterested judgement. He proposed that perpetual peace could be secured through universal democracy and international cooperation, believing this would be the eventual outcome of universal history, although not rationally planned.

To conclude, in the death of my grandparents, mother, teachers and friends, I have learnt a thing or two about life and death. I believe one should go when one is healthy and kicking.

These Words

This poem, as well as the four other poems in this book, was written in the months of April and May 2020, during the COVID-19 lockdown days. They reflect my feelings and views on life, as the world had suddenly turned on its head and life had become whimsical. Those days, I worked from home and derived inspiration and companionship from Urdu *ghazals* (a form of ode or an amatory poem, with origins in seventh-century Arabic poetry) written by some of India's notable poets, and sung by Jagjit Singh in his deep, melodious voice. Jagjit Singh (1941–2011) was an Indian *ghazal* singer, composer and musician. He has been acknowledged as the Ghazal King or King of Ghazals. He was like a mighty river. On his passing, the river just stopped but did not cease to exist. He lives on.

This poem emphasises the immortality of words and human thoughts, feelings and emotions, irrespective of the intrinsic subjectiveness of their importance in the eyes of readers. It also gives an expression to my love for the Urdu language. While acknowledging the sweetness and completeness of the Urdu language, I acknowledge the role of a number of notable Urdu poets and *ghazal* singers who have influenced me. I express my deep gratitude to them and to all other Urdu poets and singers, whom I call angels. I've chosen to not write the English translation of the *ghazal* in verse form, mainly to respect the *ghazal* and prevent any inadvertent distortions in its essence. Nevertheless, the words reflect my innate feelings of the time.

*****

What belonged to me once, now belongs to you too; my words and some thoughts now belong to you too.

These words depict some of the most special moments of my life; they enshrine some of my most innate feelings and thoughts.

These thoughts entail prostration and emotions too, questions and conversations too, prophecies and humanity too; these words reflect not only my worship but my (perceived) infinity too, my helplessness and desperation too, my plea and spirituality too.

My request to you, if you feel disinterested in my words or thoughts, don't disrespect or dishonour them, these words contain the intensity of my feelings.

If these words and thoughts don't carry any importance for you, just leave them alone; these words and thoughts are quite important for those for whom you don't care; so, they are dear to me, and those who are not born yet.

Only these words and thoughts are left behind when we depart from this world; no one carries one's status, throne and crown, prestige or position from this world when one departs from here.

This world is just a thought where all big and small dreams live and thrive; day and night, we all remain occupied with mundane things but only to perish in the end.

I have fallen in love with a language, which is called Urdu; it has something that others may not have. I concede Urdu may not be my mother tongue but, without doubt, it is as sweet and complete as my mother tongue.

I am grateful to those angels who introduced me to Urdu; the depth of (Mirza) Ghalib thoughts through the velvety and golden voice of Jagjit (Singh) introduced me to Talat (Mahmood and Aziz), Mehdi (Hassan) and Pankaj (Udhas) and then I also met Majaz (Lakhnawi, 1911–1955), Maqdhoom (Mohiuddin, 1908–1969), Sahir (Ludhianvi, 1921–1980), Wasim (Barelvi) and (Javed) Akhtar.

*****

Yeh Alfaz

Jo thhae mere' apne' kabi, woh ab aap ke' be ho gaye';
Mere kuchh alfaz aur chundh khaylat ab aap ke be ho gaye'.

Yeh lafz meri zindaghi ke kucchh lamhe' hai azeem-o-khaas;
In lamhun mein meri zindaghi ke' hai kuchh khaas khaylat-o-ehsaas.

In alfaz mein hai bandaghi be and kufr be, bebassi be aur majboori be,
iltija be aur roohaniyat be;
In khayalatun mein hai sajda be hai aur jazbaat be, swalaat be hai aur
guftgu be, risalat be hai aur insaaniyat be.

Iltija hai tumse', lage' agar nahi dilchasp tumhe' yeh lafz mere ya khayalat;
Na karna beizzat inko ya bekadr kabi tum, hai in lafzun mein meri jid-
dhat-o-jazbaat.
Agar tumhari nazar mein ahmiyat nahi hai in alfaz-o-khayalat ke, bas
rahene' do;

Yeh lafz-o-khyalat bahut aham hai unke' liye jinkee parwah nahi tumhe'
lekin azeez muje hai jo, aur unkee be jo paida nahi huea hai woh.

Reh jaate' hai sirf yeh lafz aur khayalat hamare' jaane ke' baad;
Na leta hai koi apnee haisiyat, takht-o-taj, shan-e-showkat ya rutba iss
jehan se marne' ke' baad.

Duniya hai bas ek khayal, chhotee' bade' sabi khwab rehte' hai jahan;
Rehte' hai din raat musroof iss duniya mein saare, aakhir hote' hai hum
sab fanaa.

Hua hai ishq muje' uss zuban se, naam hai jiska Urdu; iss mein hai jo
orun mein kahan;

Maana ki maadr-e-zuban nahi hai meri Urdu, magar beshak hai yeh zuban sheereen and mukammal jaise' meri madr-e-zuban.

Hun mein shukar-guzaar un sab pharishtun ka jinhone' mulakaat karvayee meri Urdu se;
Ghalib kee bulandi ne Jagjit kee la-fanna makhmalee awaaz mein maere taruf karaya Talat, Mehdi aur Udhas se, phir mile' Majaz aur Maqhdoom, saath mein Sahir, Wasim aur Akhtar be' mile'.

Chapter 8

OUR OPPORTUNITIES

This chapter provides a philosophical commentary on the timely opportunities provided to humankind by the COVID-19 pandemic. It attempts to define the 'real' human growth and virtues of healthy social distancing. It also tries to have a peep into the kind of world that may possibly await us on the other side of the pandemic

This chapter ends with a poem, *Don't Feel Lonely*.

Real Progress for Human Sustainability

Humans will be deemed to have made progress and evolved only after they transcend all human-made walls between them and treat one another as humans from one large family of Great Humanity. No human is born with a label of any kind; humans affix various labels on themselves, which invariably create distrust, disharmony and discord between them, all due to mutual fear and apprehension. History works against them. Their mutual fears and apprehensions are driven by their past events. They must not allow their past to ruin their present and future.

With most things in life, learning takes a long time and so does unlearning. The longer it takes to learn, the longer it takes to unlearn. Habits become our second nature, almost instinctive. But we are good at making adjustments and adapting to new rules set by humans or Nature.

When in uncharted waters, as we all currently are, it is prudent to not only follow our inner voice and gut feelings but, more importantly, also our global collective wisdom, where available. There is no wisdom in foolishly experiencing to learn what others have already experienced and suffered as a consequence.

At times, the price of moving ahead is not being able to retract your steps and return, as all doors get closed behind you, one after the other. Then, it becomes a long and lonely journey where you are your own company, confidant, master, slave, friend and foe. In darkness, when lucky, lonely beacons on the horizon or lonely stars in the sky may guide you. On bright sunny days, mirages may deceive you.

This phase of human history provides excellent opportunity to each one of us to relearn, exploiting our full brain capacity. We must verify the authenticity of any information or message that comes our way on social media. Let us stop being led as a herd.

One must become humbled 'naturally' and not by force. That happens only when one's arrogance and ego are broken away permanently after one becomes realised. An internally broken and realised person is unlikely to be arrogant again. In Kashmiri, there is a word for 'broken' —*footmut*. Unless our prayers come from the within (from our heart and conscience) and not from our head — intellect, wisdom or ego — they are useless and ineffective.

Before us, we have the example of Trotkacharya (Adi Sankara's fourth disciple) who headed the northern mutth of India after Sankara, after being appointed by Sankara himself. He was not perfect in Sanskrit grammar or knowledgeable, but he had a great, loving heart which he selflessly devoted in the service of his illustrious master. His peers would call him *mood* (a dimwit), as he would not participate in any discourse with them.

Sankara finally said to the Brahmins, 'Your perfection in grammar (during the recitation of Sanskrit shalokas) will not save you in the end. *Baj Govindam, mood matee* (recite the Lord's name from heart, you fool)'.

Our real growth will happen only when we are absolutely humbled, fallen on our knees, with our heads hanging low and looking for help, not from God but from our fellow humans, without being bothered about their religion, caste, ethnicity, wealth, colour or gender. At that point, we will see every human as a human, without label, as a child of Nature — a child of God.

COVID-19 will undoubtedly break us down internally and crush our arrogance and ego to attain that point of truth and realisation. Our suffering will continue till we do not realise the humanness of our fellow humans, especially of the poor and the unprivileged.

Our internal breaking (of our ego) is absolutely necessary for our spiritual growth. One can't be connected to roots, which is necessary for growth, unless there are internal cracks, which happen only when one is broken — without ego, softened, humbled, like soil (and not a rock). Breaking is necessary, absolutely necessary, otherwise growth will never happen. Plants may grow on rocks but they too need cracks in rocks to extend their roots deep into it. Cracks and internal breaking are necessary. Resistance to breaking is impossible as the growing process occurs. Realisation of one's insignificance is necessary. So rocks must break to allow any kind of growth over them.

Unless we are deeply broken from within ourselves and awakened to reality, our prayers and meditation will just overflow without having any effect. Our cracks allow our prayers to come from deep within us. Only after that will our meditation help us to remain awakened and connected with the truth.

It is time we face the reality. It is time we face life. It is time we face ourselves and accept who we are and how we really look. It is time we stop dyeing our hair and painting our face. It is not the time to remain hidden behind illusion and run away from our physical reality and conscience. It is time we develop respect for our ageing and older people.

The Great Pause

This phase of human history, aptly termed 'The Great Pause' by some intellectuals, presents each one of us with an excellent once-in-a-life-time opportunity to reflect on ourselves and the world we live in. We have been presented with a timely opportunity to assess how we have been living, which could best be described as mere *existence* for many of us, rather than *living deliberately*, as we rush through our lives with a mindlessly fast-paced lifestyle. Now we have the time to reflect and decide why and how we must live our lives *deliberately*.

The current phase is meant for self-correction and becoming good humans. If not now, then when? It may be our last opportunity to turn things around, not only for us individually but also collectively for the entire human race and our beautiful planet. At a time when the world has paused for a while and no one is rushing ahead of us, which may have otherwise caused us anxiety due to our intrinsically competitive nature, envy or jealousy, we must avail this time to try and set things right within ourselves.

We have a chance to learn good habits and unlearn bad habits. We must stop being indolent and stop trashing useful information and wisdom that come our way. We must stop beating the cooks (a metaphor for teachers) who feed us, we must stop biting the hands that feed us. We must stop being self-indulgent in the short-term, cheap, mundane pleasures of life, which have proved a sheer waste of time in the past.

Our mobile phones have been our biggest distraction in recent times. It is a great facility in so many ways but equally our biggest enemy in many other ways. It has the potential to dilute the quality of our lives if we misuse it, which we generally do. There should a time and place for it — how and when we use it. We must verify the authenticity of any information or message that comes our way on social media. Social media is useful but can become dangerously toxic if misused. We must set a time and duration for using it and desist from forwarding messages and videos that potentially pollute our mind with toxic hatred against fellow humans. Why should we waste our invaluable time in negative activities?

During this Great Pause, we must focus on our self-improvement rather than wasting our time and energy in negative criticism of other people or indulging in political campaigns (knowingly or unknowingly) against other communities and nations. Instead, we must try and develop creative hobbies — from a range of creative and performance arts, such as singing, music, writing, reading, bird-watching, walking, running, baking, painting, pottery and acting — to keep us engaged and mentally healthy.

Most importantly, we must learn to live life *deliberately*. What does that mean? Sadly, many of us may not know what that really means.

Living deliberately means doing everything — sleeping, entertaining, educating, reading, exercising, eating, romancing, contemplating, cooking, baking and so on — with purpose and thoughtfulness, while remaining mindful of ourselves and the environment around us. Living deliberately means not just skimming through things cursorily or doing things half-heartedly, with a distracted mind. For example:

- Let us learn how to enjoy the food we eat, respect it and not rush through this most important chore of our daily life. While eating our lunch or dinner, let us not watch the television or be distracted by our mobile phone at the same time. Lunch or dinner time, as the case may be, is meant for a family to sit down together and interact positively, while partaking of Nature's gift and human toil with gratitude. We must never take our food for granted. Who knows, we may reach a time in our life when we may have many dollars in the bank but not a grain to eat or a drop of water to drink!

- When we watch the television, let us enjoy the show that we are watching with keen interest and joy, and try to use it as an educational tool. It is a bad idea — for both our mind and eyes — to switch constantly between the television and mobile phone screens.

- When we use our mobile phone, let us put it to good and productive use. Misusing a mobile phone is misusing a great facility. We may lose this great facility one day, as per the law of Nature, if we continue misusing it.

- When we go out for a walk, let us observe the environment around us deliberately; greet our fellow walkers with a smile and interact with them, if possible; watch the sky and listen to birds. Our ears don't have to be plugged during our walk, let us keep them open for our own safety and to remain connected with the environment.

- When we do some reading, as part of our formal study or for our leisure, let us not just skim through what we are reading. Let us try and understand what has been written and why. Let us introspect and ask questions, where possible. Reading is learning, let us not disrespect it.

- When we play, let us put our heart into the sport that we play and play the best we can.

- When we go to sleep, let us switch off all other distractions to sleep well, preferably at the same time every night and for at least seven hours.

- When we laugh, let us laugh whole-heartedly, uninhibited.

- When we get upset or angry at anything, there is no harm in swearing, uninhibited, but never at strangers or in any outdoor setting. Bottling up anger is bad for our mental and physical health. Swearing and expressions of anger are just human. If our basic nature is characterised by short-temperedness and anger, it would be a good idea to regularly punch a punching bag and let go of our emotions on a daily basis.

- When we are romancing, let us romance with all our heart, without mobile phone distractions.

- When we are cooking, let us cook with all our heart and produce healthy and delicious food.

In short, living deliberately means being with a person, a thing or an activity 100 percent at any given point of time, and not just half-heartedly or cursorily.

Live in the moment. Be it, feel it, live it fully.

COVID-19 has presented each one of us with an excellent opportunity to revisit our relationships and deeply gel with our families and friends. Perhaps Nature may have discovered our environment — physical, mental, spiritual and environmental — had alarmingly heated up, because we were just rushing blindly through our lives; we wanted everything yesterday. At that rate, we would have burnt ourselves dead. So, Nature may have decided to put the *full* brakes on our lives and forced us to recede and contemplate where we were going and, instead, decide where actually we should be heading and how to live life deliberately.

In the broader context and in our greater interest, this Great Pause may have been necessary, not only for us but more for our children and their future generations. We had polluted our environment to extremely dangerous levels, now we are paying a heavy price for our mindless actions and negligent inaction. This price was logically necessary so that our future generations could breathe in a cleaner environment and thrive in a much healthier world than the world we inherited or helped to create.

Let us, therefore, take this time to sit down and reconnect internally, and not superficially, with ourselves and our families and friends. Let us contemplate deeply to reflect and start living life deliberately. Reconnection with ourselves and our conscience is necessary to be able to connect with the wider world. Life is a boon, an opportunity, a promise, a precious gift. Let us not waste it. COVID-19 may have thankfully given us this last opportunity to rediscover life and start living happily, beautifully, deliberately, with accountability and responsibility. Thanks to COVID-19 for waking us up to rediscover life and prompting us to live its core objectives deliberately.

COVID-19: A Timely Reminder from Nature?

Our world is being rocked by unbelievably unsettling times. It is like being on a ship in the middle of an ocean that has suddenly been hit by a massive storm, or sitting in an aircraft that has run into extremely rough weather.

Undoubtedly and logically, perhaps due to our unpreparedness, it must be an extremely humbling experience for each one of us, extremely frustrating too for most of us due to our helplessness. For example, the Australian government will not allow us to travel out of Australia and the Indian government will not allow us to enter India, both borders are closed. One by one, countries have closed their borders. So how do we visit our families? Our helplessness can be likened to the helplessness of a caged bird that has suddenly lost freedom and the ability to fly at will, as if its wings have been clipped.

The world seems to have turned on its head. Is it a nightmare? No, not really; it is real!

COVID-19 is impartial, it does not discriminate. It does not care who you are — rich or poor, powerful or weak, man or woman, black or white, pretty or ordinary. Like all other elements of Nature, it does not see your religion, caste or nationality.

Wealth and power have suddenly become practically redundant, perhaps as a strong reminder from Nature that it reigns supreme. Perhaps, humans have outgrown their relevance on the Earth, our egos grown too big for our heads. Nature has finally slapped us humans, loud and heavy. The human ego has been hammered. Many a lion mews like a cat now. Hopefully, with this humbling experience, human cockiness — at least of the powerful and the wealthy — may become a thing of the past. If an arrogant individual remains cocky despite knowing what has befallen humanity, such an individual must either be a robot or a supreme being with skin as thick as the tyre of a mining dump truck, without a mind.

It is commonly said, *Every cloud has a silver lining.* However, practically, not every cloud is seen to have a silver lining. Such a thing may happen only when a certain set of environmental conditions are met, especially with the sun and the cloud aligned with the line of sight. It is my hope that:

- COVID-19 has a silver lining.
- We avail ourselves of the present time as an opportunity to find and befriend ourselves.
- Most of us humans survive and come out wiser.
- This experience unifies the world.
- The survivors understand and recognise the oneness of the human race and the importance of human unity and peaceful coherence.
- Humans understand and recognise there is just One God — One Omnipotent, Omniscient Nature, with various shades and temperaments — that witnesses all and treats all without bias or discrimination. As a result, I hope it brings about much needed religious harmony.
- Our perspective towards life changes and we are reminded about uncertainties in life and the transitory nature of life itself.
- We are taught to live in the moment and to not take life, its comforts and bounties, for granted.
- World leaders with big egos are forced to speak to one another and work collaboratively to save the human race.
- We learn the importance of hygiene in our daily lives.
- We get rid of our personal bad habits of touching our face, including nail biting, picking our nose and touching our eyes.

Well, all these are only hopes. What is going to happen, no one knows. Human nature is very complex; it invents conditions and situations that potentially bring misery and suffering.

The world won't be the same for those who survive this storm. People's psychology and behaviours won't be the same. Economies won't be the same. Human priorities won't be the same. COVID-19 is shaking up everything as we speak — our lifestyle, behaviours, social life, economy, jobs, travel, shopping, personal habits and what not. Things taken for granted earlier have suddenly become extremely important, proving every dog indeed has its day. Toilet rolls have become a luxury, people fight for them now, some even cry. The world will never be the same.

While we need to do everything possible to stop COVID-19 from spreading, we must stay as calm as possible and keep ourselves healthy and entertained at home. Panic will worsen the situation, as our judgement and social behaviour will be impaired. COVID-19 is not a ball. Let us not try to catch it and pass it on to others. We must keep ourselves away from it.

If COVID-19 does not make us socially responsible and caring humans, what will? If it does not make us humble and peace-loving humans, what will?

COVID-19 has proven what the Saibaba of Shirdi had said, *Subka Malik Ek*, which means 'We all have one and the same Maker'. He also urged people to keep *Shradha* and *Saburi*, which mean faith and patience, come what may. His advice is quite apt and valid for the current, dark times. We must bide the present time with patience, keeping faith in whoever we believe in, socialise responsibly and look after our personal hygiene as well as the upkeep of our mental and spiritual health.

While remaining indoors, within the safety of our homes, we can enjoy ourselves by listening to good music and singing along as much as possible. We can also read books and play indoor games. Yoga and meditation will be highly beneficial. We must desist from watching toxic television programs that feed on sensationalising events by scaring and exploiting people's psychology, only to raise their Television Rating Point (TRP) rating. In short, we must use our time judiciously and fruitfully.

We are fortunate to have inherited a vast treasure of beautiful songs, with inspiring, uplifting music, which can prove highly beneficial for our health and help to see us through the present depressing times. We must keep ourselves engaged with positive thoughts and creative work. Undoubtedly, the present times present us all with an excellent opportunity to find and befriend ourselves, which can be considered as the silver lining of this dark, ominous cloud hovering over our heads.

Patience, prudence, pragmatism and prayers — the 4Ps — are the need of the hour. Unbelievably interesting times are upon us, delivering a previously unimaginable, incomprehensible and indecipherable message from Nature. For how long will this nightmare last, no one knows. I hope the nightmare ends soon.

In any case, after COVID-19 departs, the world will never be the same. In the meantime, let us do everything possible to help ourselves and the people around us to survive. Let us also take this opportunity to find ourselves; some of us may have got lost in the dazzle of materialism before COVID-19 arrived. Can COVID-19 be, therefore, a timely message from Govind (one of the Lord's names in Hinduism)?

After COVID-19: A Rosebush on the Other Side?

The Other Side of the current phase — hopefully, lurking over the horizon and possibly beginning in a few months or, perhaps, even a year from now — will undoubtedly not be a sharp turnaround and return to the 'old' normal, but a hazy, long and bumpy transition to a 'new' normal, characterised by numerous turnings and tossing, with unnerving crests and troughs on the way. After a testing phase of alternating hope and despair, which may be two to three years long, the new normal will not be the same as the old normal. Many permanent changes will happen to our lives and how we think and live, many of which may indeed be happening as we speak, some good and some quite different, just like a beautiful rosebush, adorned with vicious thorns underneath if you look closely.

Those of us who manage to reach the other side will possibly find:

- Negative talk and petty whinges of the present, a result of our materially pampered lifestyle of late, would have faded to a seemingly distant past. Instead, more serious discussions related to deliberate and responsible living would have taken their place.
- Global issues, like global warming, gaining more attention and being discussed more vigorously than before.
- The definition of wealth and a wealthy person would have changed and possibly been rolled back by a few decades or even a century.
- Austerity would have become the new norm. Thriftiness, with a frugal mindset, would have become common lifestyle features.
- Community lifestyle would have returned. People would have realised the benefits of having a healthy family, true friends and caring neighbours.
- People would travel around with extreme care and caution, not only internationally, but locally too.
- The automobile and aviation industries would have taken a serious dent and possibly would be struggling to survive. It would be a similar case with the hotel and hospitality industries.
- Air travel, especially international air travel, would have become a rare luxury and fallen beyond the reach of many people. Even local travel would have become expensive.
- As people would have discovered ways of working from home and the ease of online learning, everyday road traffic would have considerably reduced, causing much less air pollution and mental stress.
- Memories of the blue sky — mostly due to minimal vehicular emissions on roads — would remain fresh for at least a decade or so.

- People would have woken up to the need to reduce the global population by consciously undertaking voluntary population control measures.
- Human greed and the tendency to make bad investments would have lessened. Investments in real estate would have fallen.
- People would have gotten used to a more hygienic lifestyle.
- People would have become humbled, and learnt to live in the moment and respect Nature.
- Spiritual and religious polarisations may have occurred. Many people would have differentiated the God concept from Nature and possibly become atheists.
- Many traditional and popular places of religious worship and pilgrimage, which had been profiting until now practically as commercial businesses, would have lost their attraction to a considerable extent. Many people would have lost faith in them.
- Many religious leaders and popular gurus offering short-cuts to spirituality would have lost their credibility and attraction for failing to do anything meaningful during the pandemic. How long could they have thrived anyway on just talk and promises? They will have been exposed.
- Governments would have become more dictatorial and adept at doing things, and people would have gotten used to following their orders obediently, without question. This is not such a bad thing as long as their focus is on the welfare of humans, without any bias or discrimination based on religious, caste or ethnic divisions. They would have learnt how to get the job done. They would have mastered the art of negotiating and navigating through the silly resistance of individual people and political parties, which virtually paralysed many democratically elected governments in the past.
- Countries would have learnt the need to be totally self-reliant. The current crisis has forced countries, and even individual

states within them, to unilaterally take their own decisions. How governments have reacted and responded will go down deep into the memory of stakeholders, which may impact on international trade, international travel and the international education industry.

- The current crisis may have forced many countries to become more inward-looking and invest their resources in the (re) development of their own construction and manufacturing sectors, without relying too much on overseas partners. On the surface, this may appear as selfish but that is how it may logically turn out to be.

In short, on the Other Side, the world may look more like the world of the 1950s, which not many of us have seen!

Many of us have been waiting for it to happen for quite some time. It had to happen, as our globe seemed to be heating up too fast. Humans had to pay a big price for their own survival and sustainability. Thanks to coronavirus, we would otherwise have been heading towards our total annihilation given the arsenal we have proudly accumulated globally. We were consuming and living mechanically and mindlessly. As a significant cost, and an unfortunate one, some humans had to die so that the remaining humans could come to their senses and become more responsible towards one another, as well as take care of the environment and the ecosystem. On the Other Side, humans would have learnt to live deliberately and responsibly, in harmony with Nature.

COVID-19 will undoubtedly break us down internally. It will crush our arrogance and ego and force us to realise the truth. Our suffering will continue so long as we do not realise the humanness of our fellow humans, especially of the poor and the unprivileged.

It is time we faced up to the reality. It is time we faced life. It is time we faced ourselves and accept who we are and how we really look. It is time we admitted we have made mistakes in the past and commit ourselves to make the necessary amends. It is not the time to remain hidden behind illusion and run away from our physical reality and conscience. It is time we developed respect for experience and older people, and history.

What has happened had to happen; there were valid reasons for it happening. We humans have been the prime reason why it has happened, how we bred, lived and worked, and our mindless consumption. Now, there is no point in crying over the spilt milk, no point in being angry or rueful. Most importantly, there is no point in finger-pointing at particular countries or blaming particular communities. A militarily fought World War III or internal strife within countries is the last things we can afford at this point in time when our very existence hinges in the balance. Similarly, what happens in the future is not all within our individual control. In the meantime, therefore, it is prudent we live one day at a time as best as we can, within the confines and safety of our homes, follow all government instructions and medical advice, and take all possible care of ourselves, our families and friends, neighbours and the community at large, using all possible legal means.

We will survive, for sure. There will be light at the end of the tunnel. There will be a rosebush on the Other Side, far away, over the horizon. Hope ... hope sustains life!

Virtues of healthy social distancing

We endeavour to keep up our appearances and exhibit our best behaviour in formal settings but our mask mysteriously disappears in informal settings. Why? The answer is 'because we are humans'. It is intrinsic to the human character to act deceptively and use camouflage to maximise our gains. No wonder many people who fall in love also tend to fall out of love after some time. The search for an ideal and perfect human is, therefore, like chasing a mirage: both just don't exist.

We all stink but those among us who use the best perfumes and know how to groom themselves cleverly — to mask and camouflage themselves — appear to be relatively more presentable than the rest. We are all similar in our eating, sleeping and breeding habits. Our body ages the same way; our hair turns grey and we become bald. We start growing hair in strange places on our body where we hate to see it. We develop cavities in our teeth and our gums weaken with age. Finally, when we lose our teeth, we use dentures. Our eyes weaken, prompting us to wear glasses. Our ears weaken too, as we grow older, prompting us to use hearing devices. But how many richer, older people accept ageing and stop their endeavours to prevent showing their true age? The answer is 'not many'. Hair dye, dentures, wigs and cosmetics become their saviours.

From outside, to an inexperienced eye, the lives of celebrities, godmen and the influential may look fabulous and charming but they alone know what it takes to keep up their public image and made-up appearance. Appearances are deceptive. Ask their immediate family members and, if successful, you will discover many other shades of their overall person- ality that remain mostly invisible to the common eye. How do we then decide which shade depicts them correctly? All shades are realistically valid, those that are visible to the public eye and those that are seen only by those who are closest to them. It all depends on how close you wish to see them. The closer you move towards them, the more disappointed you are bound to get. Expectations bring misery and suffering.

American writer Mark Twain (1835–1910) wisely reminds us, 'Distance lends enchantment to the view', which means things look better than they actually are when they are seen from a distance. From a distance, the grass looks lush green but only when one sees it up close can one spot bare patches in it. It is for this reason of potential disenchantment and to prevent oneself from disillusionment, many wise people have advised us against getting too close to our friends and relatives and all those whom we love dearly.

A Kashmiri proverb that emphasises the importance of healthy distance in relationships goes: *Dhoori dhoori saet chhu murtch ti maethhaan*, which means *even black pepper sweetens from distance*. In his famous book *The Prophet*, philosopher Kahlil Gibran (1883–1931) also advocates for a respectable distance:

You were born together, and together you shall be forevermore.
You shall be together when the white wings of death scatter your days.
Ay, you shall be together even in the silent memory of God.
But let there be spaces in your togetherness,
And let the winds of the heavens dance between you.

Love one another, but make not a bond of love:
Let it rather be a moving sea between the shores of your souls.
Fill each other's cup but drink not from one cup.
Give one another of your bread but eat not from the same loaf.
Sing and dance together and be joyous, but let each one of you be alone,
Even as the strings of the lute are alone though they quiver with the same music.

Give your hearts, but not into each other's keeping.
For only the hand of Life can contain your hearts.
And stand together yet not too near together:
For the pillars of the temple stand apart,
And the oak tree and the cypress grow not in each other's shadow.

The above advice was aimed for partners in the context of the institution of marriage; nevertheless, it is also applicable to most other social relationships, including social friendships and peer relationships between colleagues at work.

Indian poet Wasim Barelvi (1940–) says: *Jo dekne' mein bahut he kareeb lagta hai, usi ke' baare' mein sonchho toh fasla nikle*, which means, *once we focus only on the person closest to us, we spot the distance (differences)*.

To save disappointment, therefore, it is wise to keep a healthy distance from other people and not to get too close to them due to likely misalignment between our expectations of them and their behaviour or performance and their expectation of us.

Don't Feel Lonely — a poem conceived in the COVID-19 lockdown

Sun gives you light, air, food, warmth and all you need to thrive;
Moon soothes many a tormented soul, keeps many a dream alive.

Stars twinkle, make one wonder, charm many a young and old;
I am with you, as are the sun and the moon and stars manifold.

Alone are churches, temples, mosques and the pyramids;
Alone are towers, the Burj, the Eiffel, the Qutb and the Willis.

Alone are rivers, the Amazon, the Mississippi, the Nile and the Ganges;
Alone are mountains, the Alps, the Himalayas, the Pamir and the Andes.

Alone are planets, Jupiter, Venus, Mars and Saturn;
Alone are oceans, the Atlantic, the Indian, the Pacific and the Southern.

The world travels with you wherever you go, you are never alone;
Why feel lonely, I am with you, as are stars and the sun and the moon.

You are never alone, nor are stars or the moon or the sun;
I am with you, now and forever, close your eyes and look within.

In this noise, we are all together, from one silence to another one;
You are with me, I am not alone, nor are stars or the moon or the sun.

From nothing it all started, back to nothing it will all return;
The sun, the moon and stars, and all things you see here shall return.

Till the sun shines, be a sun or a moon or a star wherever you go;
Till the earth moves, be a tree or run like a river in any way you can do.

Chapter 9

REFLECTIONS

This chapter includes my reflections on life and various aspects of life, between November 2019 and July 2020, in short paragraphs. These include my reflections on deliberate living, caution against perfectionism and idealism, importance of wisdom and positive thoughts, distortional human growth, good governance and good leadership, definition of true democracy, happiness, fear and arrogance, freedom, education, darker shade of love, war, nature, Kashmir, importance of learning from history, power of pen and need to get rid of gun.

This chapter ends on a positive note that we humans shall prevail over the current COVID-19 pandemic and all forces that challenge our survival, now and in the future.

Wisdom makes the difference

I may make mistakes in identifying between different shades of grey but I am not so dumb that I can't differentiate between black and white. Even a colour-blind person can do that.

I wish intelligent people were able to differentiate between wise and unwise, right and wrong, just and unjust acts, and moral and immoral intent. But that is only a wish! In the real world, intelligence is used both ways — for and against humanity — by most humans who are driven by a materialistic mind or corrupted by power.

Intelligence is never the same as wisdom. While intelligence is myopic, short term and generally hedonic, wisdom comes with a long-term vision and altruism.

***

A noble mind needs just one good reason not to do something that may potentially cause pain in other humans (or animals). A corrupt mind comes up with a thousand reasons to defend such wrong actions. Power corrupts. It awakens and feeds the internal corrupt human.

***

I need your genuine sincerity and not your flowery greetings, hollow promises and cosmetic respect.

***

Humans are intrinsically good. But some get corrupted by power — social, religious, corporate, wealth and political.

Life and living

All lives matter, not only white or black lives, from all races, religions, castes and backgrounds.

***

Veganism or vegetarianism is not only respecting animal lives but also upholding human dignity and respecting humans who are not vegans or vegetarians, and not hurting or humiliating them — by words or actions — or claiming any higher moral or ethical pedestal.

***

We are like candles that shine gloriously till wind blows them out or the wick runs down.

***

Rose bushes hurt the hands that prune them. Mothers die during childbirth. Soldiers and firefighters lose their lives in the call of their duty. Doctors contract deadly infections while serving sick people. Candles must burn to give light. That is life. Doing good acts come at a cost.

***

To know life, we must live life in all its shades. To know humans, we must know ourselves well.

***

Our life is just a story, which finally becomes history. Truth does not become history, we become history.

***

You realise your true existence only after you realise you are smaller than the smallest speck of dust that there is. Your real growth starts only after that realisation.

***

The size of your world defines your significance. Your pride and ego keep shrinking as your world keeps growing.

***

Live today as if tomorrow never exists. A well-lived day is a well-lived lifetime. Tomorrow, if you are fortunate enough to see it, will be a result of what the entirety of humanity does today and the mood of Mother Nature, both of which are beyond your understanding and control. Most importantly, don't allow your yesterday to cast a dark shadow on your today. Let it go.

***

Human life must always take precedence over anything else. The economy is due to healthy humans and not necessarily the other way around. Humans have survived and thrived when there was no concept of the economy as we understand this term now.

***

For sustainable peace, women must have equal representation in all aspects of life, including governance.

***

We see what is within us, beauty lies in the eyes of the beholder. We see what we want to see. It takes one to know one. Good and bad, noble and evil are subjective. What may appear noble to one, may appear evil to another. None of us is perfect, yet we become judges. What goes around comes around. We reap what we sow.

***

Why can't we learn to think, love and live like children? Children know how to live. Innocence, instinctive learning and relative purity of mind are their greatest assets. They think and live uninhibited. They don't live in silos. Things change when adults pollute their mind.

***

Activity is the essence of human nature. Whether in a waking mode or a sleeping mode, the human mind hardly ceases its movements. Dreams and thoughts keep filling it. The human body and mind remain restless and fidgety. Meditation is a way to put both to rest every now and then.

***

Another day, another opportunity to live and let live, another opportunity to love and be loved, another opportunity to forgive and be forgiven, another opportunity to make a positive impact in this world, another opportunity to know and befriend ourselves.
Let us do our best today.

Don't rush, live

There is a vast difference between living, existing and rushing. Unfortunately, these days, most humans confuse the last two terms with the first term — 'living'. Living deliberately is something that most humans must learn to do to enjoy this unique gift of life and live through its every moment.

Multi-tasking has taken away the joy of doing things. These days, most people seem to be just rushing. No wonder mindfulness is being preached to slow down and enjoy the ever passing moments of life, and be conscious and aware of oneself and one's surroundings.

***

The mobile phone has significantly reduced the quality of life for most humans. With divided attention, one is never present one hundred percent anywhere, in any situation, at any point of time, be it resting, walking, entertaining, romancing, working or even sleeping. Even when on a date, young people generally communicate through their phones, using their fingers, instead of looking into each other's eyes, holding hands or talking.

What is the purpose of making things faster — whether it is cars, trains or internet connectivity — as we will always be falling short? Most of us are currently using 4G and some 5G. Soon, we'll be talking about 10G and it will keep going.

***

During the COVID-19 lockdown days, I grew a beard, which turned out to be predominantly greyish white, contrasting with a predominantly brown moustache. My father, a clean-shaven man with black dyed hair in his late seventies, was visibly unhappy to see my bearded appearance during a videoconference and asked me to shave it off.

I replied, 'Life is unpredictable and coronavirus is temperamental. I too could die anytime like those thousands of people who die every day around the world. Before dying, however, I want to know how I actually look. My beard makes me realise that I may have lived a full life. So, I have no regrets. I have been fortunate to have lived and grown to see myself with a white beard. You too should be happy for me, not many people live to see themselves in grey and white. I suggest you stop dyeing your hair and grow a beard like me.'

My father was not impressed and continued to insist his son should shave his white beard. My father also admitted that his younger look made him feel young at heart too.

***

You reflect and ask if it was worth it? You live in the past. Your expectations make you sad. Life takes its own course, beyond our control. Moments — good, bad and the ugly — define it. How we live them, and don't carry them with us, defines our present.

***

Among the greatest challenges faced by us humans is the challenge to be able to voluntarily switch off our smartphone(s), computer (tablet) and television, then sit down and enjoy our own company. Doing nothing for a while, even for thirty minutes at one single time in a day, has increasingly become very difficult for most of us and rather impossible for many.

Many of us have developed a high dependency on smartphones. We have not even spared our infants and toddlers, many of whom don't eat without playing with a smartphone.

Verily we have enslaved ourselves to our smartphones.

Our life is a bubble

Many big and mighty came and left their legacies and stories here. But they too departed. Their pride and power departed too. They were all bubbles. Bigger bubbles had bigger pride and spectacular endings.

***

Is there anything that is constant and does not move or change? Perhaps nothing! Change is constantly happening, in every moment, even in the elusiveness of this moment!

***

Is it possible to measure the infinite with the finite? Can a variable be measured by another variable if the boundary conditions are not constant? If something is elusively ever changing in character and form, and can't be understood or captured, can it be deemed real? If it appears different to different minds, is it real or an illusion? If its relevance and existence change with the state of one's mind and one's belief, is it real? If it becomes visible to one and invisible to most, is it real?

***

The human mind is limited and finite, and the finite can't decipher or hold the infinite. The air inside a balloon can know the outside atmosphere only when the balloon bursts and both merge, and once that happens, knowledge and knowing become irrelevant, as the knower and the known become one. Being is what it is all about. Let us learn to be.

***

For an individual, there is no bigger certainty or truth except death. Rest is an individual's imagination or belief. Realistically, no one knows what happens after death. Most religious people fool themselves with thoughts of hell and heaven, which no one has seen and perhaps don't exist except in our mind.

***

Every moment, everything is working or in motion — our sun, earth and moon; sea levels and tides; clouds; our blood, heart, lungs, liver, kidneys and intestines; and our brain impulses and thoughts. We are all working and moving every moment, even during our sleep. Nothing is constant or idling. This world will also pass on. We'll all pass on and our bodies will go back into the dirt which nourishes us through food. We'll all get recycled.

***

In the continuum of life, there are no first and last chapters. Periods in life can, however, be compartmentalised into chapters. Life redeems itself, supports itself and redefines itself. It sustains itself both at perceivable macro levels and at invisible microscopic levels. Intelligent life is marvellous at cellular level.

***

Little by little we die, as our environment dies. Our greed keeps outstretching our needs and thinning our resources. We consume our planet greedily. We confuse consumption with progress and happiness. Economic growth, and not human development, drives our policies.

***

Our world is a big circus. We all play our designated parts in it. The ring master gets his job done. Spectators clap and enjoy seeing what they pay to see. After the show, all return to their sheds to sleep, only to work in another show the next day.

***

Very often, we deliberately fool ourselves. We bury our head in sand

and close our eyes for fear of looking into the eyes of the reality that looks right into our eyes and our soul. We fear handling the truth. As it happens, the ground slips away right under our feet and we keep getting buried, ever deeper.

Myth of perfectionism and idealism

Nature is all pervading, it contains everything and everything contains it. Nature is omnipresent, omniscient and omnipotent. It nurtures and nourishes all life on earth. All life and its means of sustenance are due to Nature. It is also the greatest teacher that provides all knowledge.

But Nature is not perfect; it does not always remain the same, either geographically or chronologically, although its routine remains more or less unchanged. Its changing moods are reflected by weather patterns and climatic changes.

One day it will be warm and sunny, with glorious sunshine and a soothing breeze, lulling one into an ecstatic nap and reveries. Suddenly, the next day, it will be entirely opposite of the day earlier. Sometimes, its moods change a few times during the course of a day. And then how can one forget its periods of wrath and extreme moods — scorching sun, freezing cold, blizzards, cyclones, floods, forest fires, volcanic eruptions, tsunamis and earthquakes.

So, if Nature is not perfect or ideal, how can humans be expected to be perfect or ideal? Aren't they a creation and part of the same, imperfect Nature? Aren't they nourished by the same, imperfect Nature?

The creation of the idea of human perfection or idealism has been a deliberate mischief by clever humans of the past to set themselves apart from others who are not so clever. Those clever ancestors of ours had capabilities to mould themselves — attain sophistication — and raise bars, which only they could reach, leaving most other humans feeling inferior.

What else could be the reason that an overwhelming portion of the human race in the world is, and has always been, unprivileged and underprivileged, and working for and following a disproportionately small portion of the human population?

The ideas of perfectionism and idealism have generated immense unhappiness in the world. People have been made to look for and chase mirages.

If only humans realised this truth, no one would feel inferior to anyone else — big or small, wealthy or privileged, white or black. People would feel comfortable in their natural skin and respect themselves as they are. There would be mutual acceptance and respect within the human community, there would be peace and harmony. Intrinsic human dignity would be upheld.

***

Unless you know yourself, how can you know others? If you are not perfect, it does not make any sense you call others imperfect. Introspect and know yourself, don't judge others. Imperfect yardsticks produce imperfect measurements. Imperfect people make imperfect judgements.

***

There are no 'wise' communities. There are wise individuals within communities — all communities. The difference is that in some communities, such wise individuals are allowed to lead the community and the entire community progresses, whereas in other communities, they are gagged by the masses and the entire community regresses.

***

The world is currently caught in a fight between 'realism' and 'idealism'.

In the 'real' world, might is right. The gig fish eats the smaller fish, by hook or by crook. It is a human jungle, capitalistic and materialistic. Humans are cruel to not only animals but other humans too. In the real world, strife is a norm — perpetual — dangling from one extreme to the other. This world is real but unsustainable due to human imprudence, greed, arrogance and misadventure. Its crash is inevitable.

In the 'ideal' world, every human is considered equal. Humanity takes precedence and priority over everything else. Environmental sustainability of the planet is emphasised. All life forms are looked after. This is a more sustainable world.

Time alone will tell which world will eventually win. I hope the latter. The solution may be in following 'realistic idealism'.

***

Idealism must conform to realism otherwise it becomes a punishment for those who practise it. It must adapt to the real world, the actual circumstances and the changing times. Pragmatism, and not idealism in a strict sense, is more prudent for achieving practical solutions. All humans are the same and equal — don't divide them.

***

We must be a little kind on others and not get carried away and put ourselves on a high moral pedestal in judging others or ourselves. All humans are the same and equal. Each one of us is equally capable of doing all those things — the good, the bad or the ugly. All it takes is the right situation or the right circumstances for us too to do them. After all, we all share the same genetic code. Our DNA is 99.9 percent the same as the person next to us.

***

To achieve a sustainable peace in the world, it is important that we stop further divisions among us humans and, in fact, strive to remove the divisions — little by little — one at a time — that are already there or are being created. Each of those divisions is a foundation for perpetual discord.

***

It is true that all those tags we apply to others and ourselves make our life journey interesting and less monotonous, but it is also true those tags become the reasons for our mutual bias and discrimination. On any day, I would like chose a monotonous life rather than an unsettled life riddled with discord and strife. The thrill may look exciting but it also kills, and it invariably does, sooner or later, us or the other person.

Accept and respect humans as humans alone

Every human is as complete as the cosmos. No human is less than the other. It looks bizarre to see mortals prostrating before other mortals.

***

Acceptance of humans only as humans, and without any label, is the sign of one's spiritual growth and emancipation and, therefore, one's true progress.

***

Only when we see ourselves in other humans, without seeing their race or caste or religion, we become true humans and soldiers of peace. It starts with us individually. Let us initiate the process, one step at a time, and not wait for the other person to take the initiative. Let us start doing what we determine is right.

***

Regardless of how some ignorant individuals act foolishly, adding fuel to the fire and deepening pre-existing racial and religious divides — by grotesquely celebrating the death and suffering of individuals from the other side — I continue to believe in the inherent goodness of humans and maintain that humans on the whole are intrinsically good. The world continues to thrive by overcoming negativity within itself; otherwise, it would have folded up long ago after being consumed by hate, anger and violence.

Sometimes, when our teeth bite our tongue, we don't knock out our teeth, we remind ourselves to chew carefully and gently. Let us show fortitude in the current challenging times, given the brevity of human life. Only then, verily, will we be able to achieve sustainable peace and progress in our world. Let sense prevail. Let wisdom and foresightedness prevail. Let truth prevail!

***

It seems Einstein was right, yet again, in his prophecy about the possible use of sticks (spears) and stones in World War IV when asked how World War III will be fought. The Chinese and Indian soldiers, perhaps in a pre-drill for World War IV, have demonstrated how deadly even sticks and stones can be.

Peace be to the fallen soldiers on either side. Humans deserve respect, every human life is precious. Let wisdom prevail on either side and tempers cool down fast. Hope the border tension de-escalates. War does not help anyone, humanity loses. But humans are humans — proud, egoistic, unpredictable and emotional.

***

It will take humans, especially from the male gender, a thousand years, or possibly more, to make up and compensate for all their past and current wrongs against humans of the female gender.

***

It does not matter how badly they treat you, you treat them well, as you treat the members of your family. Each one of us is a part of one global family.

***

People who deliberately show disrespect to others may sense a (false) win. But little do they know they may have lost a bit of their soul and humanness in doing so.

***

Speak with others and treat them as you would like your children, colleagues and service providers to do with you. Respect others and be respected. Your children and others learn from you. Be humble, empathetic and courteous.

***

Our etiquette, courteousness, language and respect for other people define us and our values. We may differ in our views and opinions from other people; our behaviour towards them — in person or behind their back as well as on social media — portrays our character and how good we are.

Distortional development of the human world

The human world is witnessing a distortional development, which may potentially twist and tear it apart. In terms of technology and artificial intelligence, it is alarmingly accelerating into the future. However, in aspects of basic inter-human relationships, it is shockingly turning out to be regressive.

***

It is baffling to see humans turning against their own kind even during the current dark times when the entire human race is under threat from an invisible bug and battling to survive. Are humans, therefore, the most dangerous species on the earth? Yes and no, both. Some, who strive day and night to save human lives, such as the medical researchers and health workers, could be termed as angels. Others, who undermine them and their efforts, need God's intervention to fill their hearts with empathy, love and care.

***

Unless and until humans don't learn to accept and respect humans in all colours, looks and shapes (as Nature has created them) and from all ethnicities and religions (based on where they were born), there will be strife, social disorder, unhappiness and suffering in the world.

***

Only those who strive to uphold and respect the freedom of others understand the true essence of freedom. Those who genuinely respect and love their own parents and children must know how important it is to uphold the respect and dignity of parents and children of other people.

***

The truth, they say, is bitter. But it does not have to be bitter and not always. Also, it depends on which side of truth you are on — sufferers or aggressors or oppressors? It may become bitter for only those who may have brought unnecessary mental and physical sufferings to others in the first place. Otherwise, nothing should be sweeter or more beautiful than truth. Truth alone triumphs (Satyamev Jayte)!

***

In the current season of 'lies', one who lies cleverly and convincingly prevails in a discussion and wins an argument. It is becoming increasingly more and more difficult to assess the veracity of claims and counterclaims of people who wield power and influence. Technology works both ways — for and against us. It is abused and misused by most of us.

Lies won't benefit anyone — you or your perceived or real adversaries. Sooner or later, everyone will potentially lose and irreparably suffer due to the consequences of lies spoken or spread by you. Lies cause damage and cost lives.

***

A serious socio-political problem plaguing the world is that some people (thankfully, not all) have moved so far to the right that to them everyone else looks to be on the left. Actually, it is their problem to adjust themselves and their skewed perception. They must return to the middle to be able to see and focus on the real issues of the world and not get caught up in more illusory matters.

***

The Homo-Sapiens may be 200,000 or 300,000 years old and we may be living in the twenty-first century, yet our survival instincts, greed, and conniving and aggressive ways are no less than those of our cave-dwelling ancestors. As a matter of fact, we are better hunter and gatherers now and a much more dangerous species than what we would have been in the past. Our acting skills have evolved with time. We lie with much greater ease and finesse. The range of our weapons and armoury has considerably increased. It is very difficult, if not impossible, to set our friends from our enemies.

***

Standing in the middle makes one appear as a 'leftist' to the 'rightists' and as a 'rightist' to the 'leftists'. It is like being between a rock and a hard place. It is a constant struggle to save oneself from the double-edged sword of Damocles that dangles constantly over one's head. Anyone can pounce on you without warning — from the left or from the right.

Walking in the middle is walking on a dangerously thin edge, which is alarmingly becoming thinner with time. To survive, the middle-path walkers must be deeply rooted humanists, otherwise they will be blown away by the polarised wind.

***

Community harmony is most important for the health and progress of a nation — any nation on our beautiful planet. It is inappropriate and irresponsible to blame ethnicity, religion or national background for the crimes and bad behaviour of an individual or a few individuals.

Can we blame their religious backgrounds for all rapists, murderers, corrupt individuals, robbers and thieves, scammers, bootleggers, fake religious gurus and impostors, blackmailers and other criminals?

Stereotyping communities for the faults and wrongdoings of a few individuals undermines communal harmony and potentially leads to strife and community discord. Stereotyping can potentially undermine the harmony among communities that cohere in a multicultural, multi-ethnic and multi-faith country. For peace and progress of the country, all peace-loving humans must watch out for such elements who try to brainwash and incite the innocent and ignorant amongst us.

***

Little by little we die, as our environment dies. Our greed keeps outstretching our needs and thinning our resources. We consume our planet greedily. We confuse consumption with progress and happiness. Economic growth, and not human development, drives our policies.

***

Any economic growth or infrastructural development that take place or are allowed to happen without first ensuring the health and sustainability of the environment (air, water, flora, fauna, wetlands, forests and ecosystems) and the health of people (mental, moral, ethical and physical) are useless and completely meaningless. Such economic growth and infrastructural development are counterproductive.

***

Many a time, the human in us does the same or similar things that we accuse others of doing and, as such, our claims for moral superiority invariably crumble down. It is another thing that we never admit our own failings, indulgences and trespasses. The mirror looks deep into our soul but we find reasons for shying away from it.

***

The (near-spherical) shape of the earth is such that each one of us is always (geometrically) situated at or near its centre (in a two-dimensional projection) wherever we are located on its surface. Many (egotistical) fools among us believe they are literally the centre of the world and it is all about them and them alone, in terms of their importance. That thought has the potential to make them arrogant, anxious and insecure. Spiritually, however, it is not incorrect to say 'you are the centre of your own (internal) universe'. These differing perspectives — at different levels of reality — are interesting.

***

In this new age of denial, authenticity is readily challenged and all depends upon who you are. Might has become truly right, as never before. On the one hand, thanks to technology, it has become fairly easy to record facts and present proof. But, on the other hand, thanks to the very same technology, things can easily be doctored and distorted. Therefore, everything that is presented is seen as dubious and becomes a matter of doubt, debate and discussion. As they say, one who lives by the sword dies by the sword. We have no one to blame but ourselves. Thankfully, this will also pass.

***

We never realise what is going to hit us when we are intoxicated with power, wealth and fame. Our vanity, jealousy and the very impermanence of the material things that we accumulate through our lives invariably get the better of most of us. Ashes to ashes in the end, only a story is left behind.

Real human growth and progress

Humility, empathy and fearlessness mark the ultimate growth of a human.

***

Empathy and care drive this world. So do fear and greed. The direction of the world depends upon which ones prevail.

***

Our suffering must purge us of the poison inside us — hate, anger, greed, revenge and retribution. It must emancipate us.

***

On the other side, we will be judged only as humans, without labels of any kind. History will also judge us solely as humans. Those of us who realise this truth and manage to grow out of their labels as fearless humans — without bias, hate or prejudice — serve the real purpose of life and humanity.

***

The progress and growth of a country are reflected in the general behaviour of its people.

***

No matter how much wealth you have, if you don't feel secure or are fearless, you have got nothing.

***

Realised and fortunate are those souls who voluntarily open that last door and step out willingly at the end of the journey rather than those who are kicked or pushed out against their will. Life is an opportunity to achieve that spiritual and mental preparedness for voluntarily opening that last door and stepping out willingly.

***

Our greatest asset is our body; it must be kept safe and healthy. Our greatest wealth is our integrity, it must be maintained — once lost, it is lost forever. Our growth and progress are reflected by our fearlessness, compassion and empathy.

***

Communication should ideally be respectful and constructive even when sharp differences in opinion exist between two or many people. Practically, however, our emotions and our stereotypical notions and opinions about one another get the better of our etiquette, mannerisms and protocol.

A heated and disrespectful exchange does not help us or our viewpoints. A civil conversation between two individuals — without making any personal jibes — reflects the culture of an educated community. Knowing 'good', understanding 'good' and being 'good' are three different things. All are useless unless you actually do good deeds.

***

All humans are soul mates. Our life energy (soul/spirit) is believed to be from the same one Supreme Energy (Divinity), which merges back into it. Our ethnicities may be deemed different but only superficially. Science says we all came from the same ancestors in Africa. We should not allow the ignorant among us to divide and exploit us. Let the inherent goodness in us prevail. Let the inherent good human in us rise and triumph over our internal demons.

***

It is baffling to see that, in this day and age, when the human race should transcend and rise above human-made socio-religious-political divisions — to address their real human issues — a deliberate attempt is made by a small group of humans around the world to keep such divisions alive, to grab and use power, by using a sickening 'divide and rule' policy.

***

Thanks to the ongoing efforts of humans, one is able to decipher and understand the laws of Nature — through a scientific approach — and be able to fly tens of thousands of miles in a matter of a few hours, comfortably, while sitting, eating and entertaining oneself. This was practically extremely difficult, if not impossible, not that long ago. The impossible becomes possible with technology, thanks to humans and their ever inquisitive, tireless scientific endeavours.

***

Time tests us, our friends and our friendships. On many occasions, most of us fail to come up to our expectations from our friends and their expectations from us. The depth and strength of our commitment to our friends and friendship make the difference. Our character defines our commitment.

***

Commitment is everything. It defines you. If you can't honour your word and commitment, you can't be expected to honour anything.

Good governance and a real leader

The head of government of a country must be a poor people's champion, as they are the only ones who really need to be helped and looked after well. The unprivileged and underprivileged, poorer sections of the community always need a good leader and effective governance. In any country, the educated and privileged well-to-do upper class of the community knows how gain enough resources — financial and otherwise — and look after themselves regardless of who rules the country.

***

How sinful it is to blame poor people for their poverty when it must be the educated and privileged who must be blamed, as it is because of us and people like us that poor people have been deliberately kept poor so that we can continue to exploit them, compelling them to serve us, not out of love or respect for us.

Time to get rid of the gun

It looks bizarre that while half of the world strives to save and comfort human lives, the other half keeps undermining their efforts by constantly using the existing means and developing new means of destruction of human lives. Guns must be permanently banned across the globe, at least for all civilians and even police. Why would police need them if the public is unarmed? One does not need to shoot unarmed criminals. Only the soldiers standing at the country's borders could be allowed to keep and use them.

***

A gun is the most dangerous and undesirable thing developed by a human, against a human or an animal. It is a curse on humans. In hindsight, one would wish that guns had never been created.

***

The right to own a firearm is no right, it is a blatant abuse and gross violation of basic human rights, to live and cohere peacefully.

Power of a pen

The real power lies with teachers and educationists, at all levels from the nursery to university. They wield the true power — the power of the pen, the power of education. If all of them, unanimously, across the globe, demand their respective governments to confiscate and destroy all existing guns from all civilians in their countries and back their demand resolutely with an indefinite strike, this miracle may possibly happen.

Teachers and educationists must realise that their noble efforts will produce better and more effective and quicker results if peace is allowed to prevail by disarming all civilians. Unless guns are snatched away, a teacher's work will be like spot fixing, without improving the entire human race.

***

May educationists realise and use their true strength and power to change the world for the better!

***

The safety of a rider lies with the horse that he rides. The horse can kill the rider in a number of ways but it chooses against it. Is he afraid of the rider? Strength is meant for saving lives, and not taking them. Power is for providing protection and not removing it.

***

Let us not say, do or write anything that we may deeply regret later. All actions have consequences, some could be unacceptable.

Numerous ways to realise abstract realities

Abstract realities can be understood and described in numerous ways, with no one way more correct than the other or wrong. Strangely, seekers of truth and followers of abstract realities argue with one another in defence of their personal understanding of the subject matter.

***

Are dreams real? Are thoughts real? These questions are among many questions about the truth that have teased the human mind from time immemorial. They may never help to know the truth unless the human mind surrenders and stops trying to understand it.

***

Parents, like God, are known by many names — formal and nicknames — by their own parents, siblings, friends, colleagues and strangers, and later by their partners, children and grandchildren. How disappointing to see individuals related to them differently fight one another!

Relevance of forms

Forms (idols) have an important use in the beginning, just like a primer. Try teaching alphabets to a blind child, with no hands. Even Braille becomes useless to him. Try explaining an 'apple' to a blind child without toes or fingers or a sense of smell. Thus, eyes (and forms) have their own important use in the beginning.

As we grow, we meditate with our eyes closed and the forms lose their relevance. Forms must become redundant as we grow otherwise they become our fetters. The same is the case with religions and places of worship. There is no harm in practising a religion or visiting a religious place as long as one is not too attached to them or considers them the sole source of truth and the final word of God. There are numerous realities, not only one.

Faith keeps one going

Faith keeps one going. It starts with faith in one's parents and grows to include faith in one's siblings and other family members, community elders, teachers, friends, doctors, law and order, and government. Finally, as one ages and becomes older, it shrinks to faith mainly in oneself and, perhaps, one's God.

***

Removing faith and/or confidence from a person is much more humiliating and painful than removing that person's life altogether. Not many humans like to live a degraded life, as slaves or vegetables, without self-respect or dignity. All humans have dignity and deserve respect.

***

A country, a community, a race or a religion can't be termed as being good or bad, they are all far above such descriptions. Individuals and their actions can be termed as good, or not so good, or ugly. If a person is good, humane and noble, it is because that person is intrinsically good. Similar is the case with people whose actions can't be called good or noble by any definition whatsoever.

***

One may call God with 100 different names or define God in 100 different ways, does it matter? Atheists deny the existence of God altogether, does that also really matter? Nothing really matters. The name does not change the reality or the truth. Even I am called by five different names, do I change? What is in a name?

Sikhism represents benevolence and humanism

To me, based on a consistently demonstrated practice and proven general characteristics, Sikhism means Selfless Service (to one and all, without exception or expectation); Supreme Self-Sacrifice (to save the weak and the defenceless, without exception or expectation); Spirituality (to connect with the One Universal Energy); and Sikhi (strive and seek the knowledge that leads to the Universal Truth).

Sikhism is, thus, all about being a saintly soldier on the Earth, in this life. It seems to capture the essence of Lord Krishna's important message to humans in the Bhagwad Gita. Thinking deeply, it also seems to capture the essence of Gautam Buddha's important message to humans, to alleviate one's suffering in this life: Realise the Four Noble Truths and follow the Eightfold Path.

Imperfect humans can't make perfect judgements

Our imperfection must be factored into the depth and quality of our judgement of others. Our judgement of others can't be taken seriously unless we are perfect humans, like a mechanical robot, with German precision, containing all knowledge about everything.

✱✱✱

All humans are imperfect and to err is only human; only the degree of imperfection varies between people. One's education, experience and age may help one in achieving some improvement but not very much. So, one must not judge others too harshly unless one is absolutely perfect.

***

Unless you have known yourself, how can you know the other person? Unless your yardstick is perfect, how can you measure others? Introspect, don't judge others. An imperfect yardstick will make imperfect measurements. An imperfect person can never make perfect judgements.

***

Be careful in drawing conclusions and passing judgement on people, situations and incidents. Assess carefully the veracity of the information and the credibility of the source or the person passing that information to you. Discard the information if the person is dodgy or untrustworthy. Accept the information only if you can trust the person with your life or the life of your children, and also if the person does not have any personal axe to grind.

***

Petty matters that normally dominate human life are reduced to insignificance as one rises and gains a wider perspective. From above, Earth usually looks beautiful and many things make sense. Ugliness and disorder fill us up and make us ugly as we fall.

***

Many social media users now speak like experts on other religions, thanks to a sustained campaign over the last number of years. They would be much better off in understanding their own religion and knowing who they are. Many of them have no clue about their own religion. They give most unscientific and funny answers when asked why they say or do certain things.

***

We are increasingly getting obsessed with religion, some even to the point of paranoia. As if we were the ultimate experts on all religions, we freely pass judgement on this religion or that religion, surprisingly, without having any understanding of our own religion. What do we know? Zilch!

***

Your unfounded and tall claims of your innocence and good intent, and constant denial of allegations of your infringements and trespasses do not lend any credibility to your lies. You must walk the walk to earn some much-needed credibility, with trust, faith and goodwill to prove your integrity.

***

You don't miss any opportunity to degrade and undermine me, and falsify my history. How can you expect and demand that I remain blinded to your trespasses and still be friends with you? You consider me as your possession and I mistook you as my friend. For you, I am just a commodity, a rich resource. I complete your existence but you don't complete mine.

***

How can you talk about building a bridge to reach out and embrace me when you are not only undermining the foundations of the bridge but also carrying a torch to burn it? What is your intention of embracing me with that dagger hidden under your cloak? Who are you?

***

When we get tunnel-vision or are blinded by 'our' truth, all 'other' truths that we disregard — deliberately or inadvertently — sooner or later combine and devour us. Our paranoia and obsession with 'our' truth lead to our ultimate downfall. No one's truth is greatest; all truths are valid and real in equal measure. Truth is not big or small.

Positive thoughts bear positive fruit

Be positive, always, in every situation, no matter what. Positive thoughts are positive seeds that invariably bear positive results and sweet fruit in many cases. Positive thoughts instil mental stability and precede confident actions, with happy and fulfilling outcomes.

***

Things are not complicated; one's limited thinking and a skewed perception renders them complex. So long as things are assessed with a lazy mind and perceived with a narrow and superficial vision, one can't easily appreciate the bigger picture or fathom the levels of hidden realities. But as soon as one's thinking deepens and perception widens, the levels of complexity disappear.

***

When things are not in your hands, it is prudent to let them go off your mind too. You can do only so much. Learn to be surprised, keep your expectations low, if not none. What belongs to you will come to you. Don't be hard on yourself, you are not God. Learn to accept your limitations.

Nature does not listen to the petty wishes of humans

Nature reigns supreme. Its laws don't bend for anyone. It does not matter how powerful, wealthy, wise, handsome, pretty, clever or arrogant we are, each one of us will at some point in time bite the dust. The truth is that point in time is unknown; it can be the next moment, the next hour, the next day.

***

Till we are stiff, hard and strong, Nature will keeping pounding us until we are not broken down and pulped. Gravity will keep pulling us down to Mother Earth till we merge into it. Nature does not like stiffness and hardness. Rocks weather out, degrade and break down slowly into soil. Metals corrode and rust, and finally become dirt. Big and tall trees wither, fall and decay when their roots weaken.

***

What looks new and bright today will become history tomorrow. Youth surrenders to age. What looks strong and invincible today will weaken and die as per the law of Nature. Mighty roaring rivers finally merge and disappear into quiet oceans. Thundering clouds disappear. The softness and sustainability of water reflects its strength and versatility. It remains humbly close to earth, adapting and changing its form as per the conditions. It nurtures and nourishes life but it can also destroy.

***

Nature delivers critical messages to humans in advance of difficult times, as a warning, clearly or convolutedly, through its own kind or directly. An old English saying, 'Coming events cast their shadows before', captures this statement, as noted in Thomas Campbell's poem, 'Lochiel's Warning'. Notably, many such messages are generally under-stood only after the event. Why? There could be several reasons.

Following a simple deductive analysis, a reason could be that the sensitivity and the capacity of receivers to decipher the complexity of a message are not sufficient. Or, perhaps, one's overthinking and a degree of intrinsic complexity in one's thinking process can blind one to notice simple things that look one straight in the eye. As a silver lining though, this also works as a blessing for most people, for it must not be very easy for those who can decipher such messages well in advance to handle them in light of their consequences and then live to see the event unfolding. As they say, 'ignorance is bliss'; certainly, yes, but only to an extent.

***

Nature does not become less of Nature when it unleashes destructive natural calamities on the Earth, such as earthquakes, cyclones, tsunamis, floods and drought as extreme weather periods and even disease. Nature comes in all shades: good, bad and ugly. Similarly, humans are born with three basic characteristics — Satogun (truth), Rajogun (royality) and Tamogun (toxicity) — with none higher than the others. Each one of us has satva, rajas and tamas. But we are char-acterised by the character that we feed the most through our thoughts and action.

***

If ignorance is bliss, knowledge is pain. Owls watch silently like the wise. Ants remain busy with their nests. Jackals and other scavengers feast on leftovers. Wolves prowl around but lions don't bother, they just rule.

***

Don't lose hope for miracles and good things to happen even if they appear to be improbable. How many things happen exactly as per our expectations? Nature follows its laws, whereas humans don't. Be patient and wait for Nature to act. Things will happen.

Happiness

Happiness is seeing Sakha —our nine-year-old Siberian husky — excitedly standing on his hind legs with uninhibited joy on being served his dinner in the evening.

***

In Sakha, we see numerous shades of our own moods, behaviours and general character, and those of our parents and grandparents. This is why I no longer use the term 'dog' or 'bitch' in describing humans whose intents, behaviours and actions disgust me.

***

Dogs are far better than many humans. They are omnivores but they can't be only vegans or vegetarians.

Fear and arrogance

Arrogance is a sign of weakness. Strong people don't feel the need to show their strength, they know they are strong.

***

Fear leads to hate, hate leads to anger, anger leads to aggression. We become paranoid with people we are afraid of.

***

Hate and fear blind our mind, bury our soul and dwarf the humanity in us. Hate consumes us from within like nothing else.

***

Spreading deliberate fear and alarm among people — to mislead them and gather their support — as part of deliberate warmongering has historically always brought significant death and destruction to the world. Recent world history is witness to this.

Decisive moments in the transitory state of life

Let us take some moments every day and sit quietly by ourselves — without phones or the television or any other distraction — and try to look where we are heading to and then contemplate and try to imagine what may possibly be waiting for us at the end of the path that we have been treading unknowingly or on purpose.

***

He slowed down behind a car that started turning into the left street. A moment later, he noticed another car that was on his right moving fast ahead and changing into his lane. That car crossed the traffic light just in time but he had to wait for a few minutes at the traffic light, which eventually cost him many more precious minutes. In life also, similar things happen. People who are at the right time and at the right place strike it better than those who are not that lucky.

True democracy

Democracy is not total annihilation, stifling or crippling of the oppo-sition; democracy is working proactively to uphold and nurture the socio-political conditions in the country where all people, including the opposition, fearlessly speak up and are able to challenge the ideas and actions of the government.

***

Democracy means listening to the opposition without setting pre-conditions — or following preconceived solutions, schemes or plans — in order to find acceptable and practical solutions for the entire community, without disadvantaging the significant section of the community that is represented by the opposition.

***

Systematic annihilation and absence of opposition in a so-called dem-ocratic system leads to anarchy, which is worse than a dictatorship. It undermines the political system itself, leading to chaos and confusion, and even tyranny in extreme situations.

***

Systemic gagging of opposition — through threat or coercion or blackmail — is the most undemocratic political act and, in essence, an act of treachery against your country.

***

Being a democrat does not give one the right to harass, criticise or victimise those who don't agree with you.

***

A pro-democratic activist who physically threatens a pro-socialist activist is actually an anti-human activist.

***

Democracy and humanism complete each other. They go hand in hand and one is incomplete without the other. It is a similar case with communism or socialism. Both systems are founded on inherent care for humans, with respect, and upholding their dignity and improving their lives.

***

Democracy without opposition is hollow. It is like a structure without a foundation.

***

A vibrant democracy is one that has a vibrant opposition. A healthy democracy is one where the government and the opposition listen to each other, without any mutual disrespect. A progressive and practical democracy is one where the two sides roll up their sleeves to work together to identify and implement viable solutions for improving the lives of all people supporting both sides.

Democracy is not only scoring victories over your opposition at the ballot box or in parliament; it is about listening respectfully to each other and taking on board each other's views and concerns on matters of national interest and taking a practical course acceptable to both sides, with the sole aim of serving people, all people, from both sides.

***

A nation that sees, treats and looks after its people equally — regardless of their gender, looks, colour, caste, ethnicity, religion, wealth or poverty — can be considered to be one stable, progressive and sustainable nation. If not, a nation can potentially collapse along its cracks.

***

A country becomes a nation due to its people and not just by occupying a piece of land. Only when people cohere happily and peacefully, and show mutual respect and acceptance, can a country be deemed sustainable and progressive.

***

On the one hand, an ideal democracy, as intended by the Greek origina-tors of the term 'democracy', requires you to receive the support of most people, which is practically very difficult if not impossible. On the other hand, in practice, you can claim 'victory' if just 50.1 percent of people who voted selected you. That term 'victory' depicts only the 'result' of a warlike situation, which befits the way elections are 'fought'.

The election result, however, does not give you the right to claim the entire community has voted for you just because 49.9 percent of voters did not vote for you. It is not morally and ethically right to claim you have the support of all those who may not have voted for you in the first place.

The existing majority-vote system promotes half-democracy, as potentially nearly half of the voters may feel disenfranchised. Such a system needs a realistic change. The answer may be somewhere between the two extremes.

***

Democracy is not majoritarianism or populism. In a democracy, all people — irrespective of their socioeconomic background, ethnicity, religion and caste — must be represented and their basic human rights taken care of. Democracy must be inclusive and not driven by the fear factor.

***

In healthy democracies, politicians don't dare to make fools of people as people retain long memories and never forgive; there is no second chance. In compromised democracies, however, devious politicians are usually repeat offenders and people can repeatedly get distracted and fooled.

***

As a child, I used to be wary of the street bully — there were a few everywhere I lived — and the school bully — again, there were a few, along with their sidekicks and henchmen. There used to be a few college bullies also one had to save oneself from. Then, for a couple of decades, I thought such bullies did not exist in the adult world. I thought people grew up with age. I was wrong.

Bullies come in many shapes and forms and are at all levels of human existence, operating everywhere: in the neighbourhood, community, on social media and in politics. The problem is when bullies become politicians and have the potential to cause serious and irreparable harm to the world.

In democratic systems, these bullies flourish easily and become potentially much more dangerous. Although they actually function as dictators, they wear the deceptive cloak of a democrat and easily exploit the known and proven weaknesses of democracy that are based on the majority-vote system.

Freedom

There is difference between freedom and entrapment.

There is difference in freedom and slavery.

There is difference in being free and being subjugated.

There is difference in fighting for freedom and being seen as revolting.

There is difference between a freedom fighter and a rebel, depending on which side you are on.

There is difference between the terms 'martyred' and 'killed', depending on which side you are on.

A freedom fighter can be called a rebel, or even a terrorist, by the occupying country.

History is temporarily written by the mighty and freedom is defined by the mighty. But power is whimsical and aggressors withdraw after a while when their might abandons them. Every dog has his day.

***

Borders and boundaries trap me, regions and religions trap me, left and right traps me, up and down traps me, laws and regulations trap me, do's and don'ts trap me, good and bad traps me, right and wrong traps me. My body traps me. I want to be home, free.

***

I had many friends who would fly with me, some very high and over long distances. But, one by one, as time turned on its head, they feared being judged by those who did not agree with me or those who would feel threatened by me.

One by one, my friends — even close ones — left me and started flying with the wind. I continued flying, but alone and against the wind of time. I fly high, to dizzying heights, as I am free from any baggage or obligations. My friends have indeed left me free.

***

An individual who takes away the freedom of other people deserves to be bereft of freedom. Only when we understand the essence of our freedom, we respect the freedom of others.

Bullies are always bullied by other bullies. Thinking about it, a prisoner and a jailer both remain imprisoned in the same jail, one keeping an eye constantly on the other. Likewise, when we take our dog for a walk, with a leash around his neck, the dog also takes us for a walk, with the same leash around our wrist and hand, both remain tied to the same leash.
We become trapped as soon as we trap others. Our freedom lies in setting all others free.

***

Patriotism and nationalism are two different words, with some shade of similarity but with different objectives and intentions. Sadly, many people use them wrongly and are confused by their meaning.

One may call oneself a nationalist but may not necessarily be a true patriot. Patriotism is born out of love for one's country. It is more altruistic, noble, inclusive and proven generally by one's self-sacrifice for one's country. It is not for asserting power. When a soldier knowingly sacrifices their life while defending the country, their act can be called patriotism.

***

In 2020, no nation can claim to be absolutely independent. As such, all nations are interdependent in medicine, food, economy, strategy, science and technology, education and so on.

Freedom is an individual mindset, more about one's psychology than reality. Freedom means having the ability to think freely. It is another thing if one can act freely, as not many can. There are consequences to every action we undertake.

***

No one can you set you free except you yourself.

My Kashmir

I feel suffocated, I can't cry loud. My Kashmir has been snatched away from me and I am gagged. I can't fight to reclaim my Kashmir, I am outnumbered. I have also become weak and tired. If I make noise and cry out, I will be slapped and kicked and stripped further. If I were a woman, I could say that I have been married against my will to a physically much larger and powerful man, who seduced me and outraged my modesty on the promise of gifts, which never existed. In my forced marriage, I have never been loved, I have been raped.

***

While culture binds, religion divides people. Culture is much stronger than religion. To prevail over culture, therefore, religion piggybacks on it and confuses people between the two before taking over.
It is because of the toxicity of religion that people from the same culture fight one another.

***

The staple food of Kashmiri Pandits in Kashmir until four decades ago was white, starchy, boiled rice and one or a few types of green leafy vegetables, with long red chillies. Over the course of the year, dozens of seasonal green leafy vegetables were available for consumption. During winter months, they would also eat rice with lotus root, as a delicacy — in various forms, on its own or in combination with a number of other vegetables and, especially, with local fish — from freshwater lakes and rivers, and a variety of home sun-dried vegetables and dried fish.

At times, during winter, they would also eat Siberian migratory birds if available in the market. Chicken was not consumed in most households for spiritual reasons. Lamb would be consumed but in moderation. Thus, their staple food resembled Chinese food in so many ways.

***

Kashmiris are one of the most tenacious and resilient ethnic people in the world. We have weathered a very complex and difficult history. We are born from the sacred soil of Kashmir, which was a seat of learning and had a university two thousand years ago. We have produced great Buddhist and Hindu scholars and equally world conquerors. We are excellent hosts too, very warm and hospitable. Our roots are from Eastern Europe, west Asia, Kyrgyzstan, Kazakhstan, Tajikistan, Tibet and China.

***

The cries of those fallen Chinar leaves in Kashmir during autumn, when we walked over them — inadvertently or deliberately — mirrored those little cries of our own little hearts. Our soul recorded those little cries, reminiscent of our little pains.

The leaves look so beautiful when they sit on the branches where they are born and where they live. Even in their death after their fall, they preserve their beauty. Some make a new home within the leaves of our books. Such is life.

***

When people call me a Kashmiri — Koshur — I feel alive again, my soul awakens every single time. When people speak with me in the

Kashmiri language, I love it, I feel at ease and at home. My heart feels young again and the child in me is joyful.

History and learning

Acceptance of the existence of an issue is the first step to working out its solution. Wilful denial and blissful ignorance both contribute to the continuation of the issue.

***

There are three types of students: (1) the 'traditional' type, who remains grateful for being led by hand and mentored to walk by their teacher before they learn to run; (2) the 'mean' type, who learns to stand and walk from their teacher and, when they start running, they tend to show off that they know better than their teacher and even show the audacity to challenge and mentor their teacher; and (3) the 'pragmatic' type, who moves on quietly, with or without learning, without making any fuss whatsoever.

Of the above, the 'traditional' type is the most fortunate, as they maximise their learning and continue to learn long after they have completed their studentship. The reason is, instead of showing off and challenging their teacher, they record everything the teacher says or does and, in their own time, happen to decipher things that they may not have understood earlier. They are naturally gifted with rare virtues, such as patience, stoicism and fortitude.

***

History teaches us two things. One, that 'nothing remains constant'. What rises also falls. Strength gives in to weakness and falls, and the weak rise and become strong. Finally, everything passes — youth, good looks, strength, power and authority. All merge back with Mother Earth from which we all came and which sustains us through our life. Two, that 'nothing succeeds like success'. When our efforts pay off, we take the credit, pat our back, stand proud and sound boisterous. But when we fail, despite making equal or more effort, we blame others and Lady Luck.

Foundations

Foundations must be protected and looked after well, both of a structure or a nation. When they are eroded or undermined, by humankind or Nature, the fall is imminent, of a structure or a nation, as the case may be.

***

What defines a nation? What defines a human? What is the relation between the two? Who owns a nation? Who owns a human? They own each other, but do they? Don't they both belong to the whole world too?

Education

The purpose of education, in this day and age, is generally seen as creating employability and for living a good life, which is justifiable in many cases, especially in most communities in developing countries. However, holistically, its purpose is truly fulfilled only when educated people consciously cease to do things that are wrong by any measure (ethically, legally and morally) and medically proven to be bad for one's health, such as smoking and drinking and mindlessly killing animals for consumption.

Unless education transforms one into a conscientious, moral, ethical, empathetic, compassionate and caring human being, it has not played its true role with a person.

***

Adult education — of people above fifty-five, both literate and illiterate, men and women — is possibly the quickest mode for achieving gender parity, equality and equity, especially in developing countries.

Older people need as much education as younger people, or perhaps more. Gender bias issues can't be easily addressed if the cultural environment and the general thought process between home and school have a time lag of decades or centuries in many instances.

A darker shade of love

Our obsession with someone or paranoia for or against some act or belief indirectly mark the importance of that person, act or belief in our lives — as a darker shade of our love for that person, act or belief.

***

Loving and hating can't happen at the same time. Building and burning bridges can't happen at the same time. Healing and killing can't happen at the same time. How can you expect a warm hug when you carry a retributory dagger in the cloak you wear?

How can you build and cross bridges when you are bent upon undermining their foundations? How can you call yourself a responsible citizen when you nurture and spread hate and fear against your fellow humans? How can you call yourself spiritual when you proactively act against it? How can you hope to bring peace to yourself and the world when you use force and fear to achieve it?

***

A birdcage imprisons a bird but protects it from predators. Many criminals prefer jail to death at the hands of their enemies or public. In life, numerous situations, facilities and relationships work both ways — for and against us. Our protection becomes our prison.

***

Some people choose the deadliest form of revenge. They nourish and show care, sometimes with gestures of love, to prolong the pain and suffering of their victim. Through periodical, sudden and unprovoked stabs — sometimes gently and sometimes with violent anger — they make their victim bleed slowly, without attracting any reaction.

Leaders

Oppression, suppression, violence, rape, religious exploitation and war continue to make headlines in 2020 despite significant progress made in science and technology by humans. It is not clear, in terms of human suffering, if today's world is any different than what it was a thousand or two thousand years ago.

The human race is facing a number of real threats and issues — climate change and environmental degradation, poverty and hunger, illiteracy and exploitation, disease and so on — but sincere leadership in the world is missing.

***

If you don't know your flock or herd well enough, don't even think of leading it. A good shepherd is one who proactively cares for his flock/herd and is always humane. He bonds with them spiritually. He walks with them physically, in rain and sun, and never abandons them.

***

Leaders don't create their followers, people create their leaders. Smart individuals, who know street politics and have the ability to sense the emotions of the public and gauge their thoughts — and then act to mould themselves in that image — tend to become successful leaders. Yes, it is also true that, once chosen, a leader undoubtedly directly or indirectly nurtures their followers through their thoughts and deeds. In a nutshell, therefore, in democracies, people always get what they wish for and deserve.

***

Objectives and intentions define actions and programs. They come with consequences. Programs and actions having potentially unacceptable consequences must be dumped. We are accountable and responsible for our actions; we take the credit and are also liable for what we do.

***

I don't like to use the binoculars of 'good' and 'bad' to look at leaders; I use the binoculars of 'wisdom' and 'vision' to identify caring, compassionate and empathetic leaders.

The precarious geopolitical scenario

The human race faces not one but several challenges around the world. Coronavirus is just one of them. The world armies are constantly arming themselves with more and more sophisticated and deadlier weapons while our global environment is reacting to our misdeeds. Hunger and poverty loom as ever. Infighting among humans for all kinds of stupid reasons, mostly created deliberately, keeps disturbing life in general. Trust is low, and so is happiness. We might be at the top of the food chain but we certainly don't top the wisdom chain.

***

The current geopolitical situation looks quite delicate, economically and militarily. One miscalculation can spiral out beyond control, sending us hundreds of years back. We must not make the world situation any more precarious and dangerous than what it already is. For geopolitical reasons, therefore, it is not wise to fall into a controversial debate on whether the virus is natural or lab-made; it is prudent that one sticks only to the facts.

***

We may divide humans based on nationality, wealth, religion, ethnicity, caste, colour and what not, our enemy, coronavirus, does not differentiate between us. It sees us all as ONE. So do our sun and moon, and the oceans, rivers, trees and mountains.

***

We are ONE people. Let us all fight our common enemy together.

This virus is impartial. It does not discriminate. It does not care who you are — rich or poor, powerful or weak, man or woman, black or white, pretty or ordinary. Like all other elements of Nature, it does not see your religion, caste or nationality.

***

Given that humans are responsible for the spread of the virus, we are expected to learn a vital lesson and find ways to stop it too. That expectation is based on the proviso that humankind's positive side will logically prevail over our negative and ugly sides. As with Nature, whom we reflect and are a part of, each one of us exhibits all these three shades of good, bad and ugly to a greater or lesser extent on a daily basis but, generally, most of us let our positive side prevail.

***

About 100 years ago, we suffered much more — many times over. We must collectively fight this virus instead of pointing fingers at one another. We have done it in the past and we'll do it once again. We shall prevail.

***

Let us stick together. This virus has proved, yet again, we humans are all alike, our anatomy is the same and Nature is ONE. It does not discriminate or differentiate. Only when we act and stick together can we keep such viruses away from the human race.

***

Hold on to your positivity and don't lose faith in yourself. In the current storm, one can be easily distracted. All news that comes to you is not helpful and all social media posts that you receive are not true or reliable. Filter out the toxic forwards, keep your mind healthy.

***

Many anxious, tired humans wonder, 'Will coronavirus ever go away?' The answer is: 'Yes, like everything else, it will also go away, but in its own time.' Extreme care and patience are the need of the hour to let it slide away, slowly but surely. Human impatience and the conscious push to return to the old normal is unwise, it will prolong human misery. The second wave will be more painful and deadlier, as seen around the world.

A human baby normally takes nine months to come out of its mother's womb. Any impatient or hasty attempt by the mother to speed up the process and return to the old, or new, normal proves futile and could actually be counterproductive and potentially disastrous for her and her baby, and their family. Patience and care are warranted.

***

A general wisdom is 'don't wait for things to happen, you happen to things'. But in some tricky situations, that may be construed as imprudence or belligerence. In such situations, one must wait patiently for the dust to settle before deciding what to do. Patience always matters no matter what.

War

Wars are fought at various levels — starting from bedrooms and the brains of political leaders, flowing on to their offices, later gravitating down to bureaucrats and army generals — but fought actually on the ground by foot soldiers having no luxury to think.

Foot soldiers — unlike political leaders — have no personal agenda or animosity against the soldiers they fight against. They just follow orders and fight. Fighting is their work — their duty — and they are paid for it. On the ground, soldiers fight to kill enemy soldiers — who are also humans, with families back home, dressed similar to them and paid to do their duty while defending their own.

Soldiers have no luxury of living in the past or in the future. That one moment on the battlefield, which defines the sum total of their life and life's learning, is all they have. That one moment tests them as a human being, a colleague, a friend and a citizen. That one moment — and how they live it — decides if they live or die. That one moment is a moment of their action, a moment of their spirituality, a moment displaying their human values, a moment of their life and a moment of their death. That one moment defines their spirituality in action — both Miri and Piri in one moment, as defined by the sixth Sikh guru, Guru Hargobind Singh jee. That one moment makes them sacred warriors.

***

The next four months are expected to be delicate for the world — due to the pandemic, the South China Sea conflict, the Ladakh stand-off and the US presidential election.

We shall prevail

These are extremely tough times — testing our faith, trust, confidence and all that we have known and learnt, but we must not give up, not just yet when the fight has just begun. We shall prevail.

These dark times will go away as they came, as do solar eclipses. History sides with the unrelenting and unyielding human spirit, endeavour and resolve to overcome and achieve; that is how we have survived similar, or perhaps worse, times in the past. We shall prevail.

We grew and advanced, we reproduced, we did all the required physical rigour, we produced and provided for our children. It has always been the human endeavour that has seen us survive Nature's repeated onslaughts. We shall prevail.

We cut through the mountains, we bridged the seas. We mined the oceans, we reached to the stars. We dived deep into the earth, we produced electricity. We learnt to travel fast. We made bridges, roads and railways. We managed to fly against all odds. We shall prevail.

We made medicines for numerous diseases that would kill hundreds and thousands of us at one go in the past. We learnt agriculture and produced plenty of food. Where we could not do, we created machines that could do, we made appliances and gadgets. We shall prevail.

God may have created the universe but we humans developed the earth and looked after ourselves. All together, we comprise Nature's invincible energy. There is nothing that we can't do. We shall help ourselves as we always have. We can and we shall prevail.

Let us have faith in ourselves and our undying human spirit, resolve and endeavour. We humans are not helpless, we are resolute. We, collectively, make the driving force that has shaped our lives. We shall prevail, now and always.

REFERENCES

Chapter 1

https://dictionary.cambridge.org/dictionary/english/

Chapter 3

ABC News, 31 August 2020. *India's migrant workers would 'rather starve' than face humiliation of return to cities after coronavirus lockdown*, https://www.abc.net.au/news/2020-08-31/plight-of-indias-migrant-workers-during-covid-19-lockdown/12574886

ABC News, 8 July 2020. *President Jair Bolsonaro has COVID-19, but don't expect Brazil's coronavirus response to change*, https://www.abc.net.au/news/2020-07-08/brazil-president-jair-bolsonaro-tests-positive-for-coronavirus/12432718

ABC News, 4 May 2002. *Coronavirus has fuelled racism against Asian-Australians, but why isn't official data showing it?*, https://www.abc.net.au/news/2020-05-05/coronavirus-racist-attacks-asian-australians-missing-data/12211630?nw=0

ABC News, 9 April 2002. *As coronavirus sparks anti-Chinese racism, xenophobia rises in China itself*, https://www.abc.net.au/news/2020-04-09/coronavirus-intensifies-anti-foreigner-sentiment-in-china/12128224

Al Jazeera, 4 June 2020. *Pregnant elephant's death in India triggers 'hate campaign'*, https://www.Al Jazeera.com/news/2020/06/pregnant-elephant-death-india-triggers-hate-campaign-200604101245365.html

Al Jazeera, 15 May 2020. Indian media accused of Islamophobia for its coronavirus coverage, https://www.Al Jazeera.com/news/2020/04/indian-media-accused-islamophobia-coronavirus-coverage-200417064109353.html

Al Jazeera, 13 April 2020. *Indian doctors face censorship, attacks as they fight coronavirus*, https://www.Al Jazeera.com/news/2020/04/indian-doctors-face-censorship-attacks-fight-coronavirus-200410063124519.html

Al Jazeera, 27 March 2020. *'Stigmatised': India's coronavirus 'heroes' come under attack*, https://www.Al Jazeera.com/news/2020/03/india-coronavirus-heroes-attack-200327070916157.html

AS, 27 May 2020, *Coronavirus India news summary: cases and deaths - 26 May*, https://en.as.com/en/2020/05/26/latest_news/1590449839_184033.html

BBC, 14 June 2020, Coronavirus: *India to use 500 train carriages as wards in Delhi*, https://www.bbc.com/news/world-asia-india-53039868

BBC, 4 June 2020. *India outrage after pregnant elephant dies eating 'firecracker fruit'*, https://www.bbc.com/news/world-asia-india-52918603

BBC, 31 May 2020. *India coronavirus: Why is India reopening amid a spike in cases?*, https://www.bbc.com/news/world-asia-india-52808113

BBC, 3 April 2020. *Coronavirus: Islamophobia concerns after India mosque outbreak*, https://www.bbc.com/news/world-asia-india-52147260

BBC, 3 April 2020. Coronavirus: India doctors 'spat at and attacked', https://www.bbc.com/news/world-asia-india-52151141

CNN, 8 July 2020. *Trump administration begins formal withdrawal from World Health Organization*, https://edition.cnn.com/2020/07/07/politics/us-withdrawing-world-health-organization/index.html

CNN, 7 July 2020. *Brazil's Jair Bolsonaro tests positive for Covid-19 after months of dismissing the seriousness of the virus*, https://edition.cnn.com/2020/07/07/americas/brazil-bolsonaro-positive-coronavirus-intl/index.html

Deccan Herald, 25 June 2020. Coronavirus Lockdown: Indian Railways suspends regular train services till August 12, https://www.deccanherald.com/national/coronavirus-lockdown-indian-railways-suspends-regular-train-services-till-august-12-853721.html

Firstpost, 15 July 2020. *Rajasthan Political Crisis Updates: BJP to hold meeting of party MLAs; ex-CM Vasundhara Raje likely to attend, say reports*, https://www.firstpost.com/politics/rajasthan-political-crisis-updates-bjp-to-hold-meeting-of-party-mlas-ex-cm-vasundhara-raje-likely-to-attend-say-reports-8595371.html#live-blog-20200714151630

Firstpost, 01 April 2020. *Tablighi Jamaat congregation was held despite ban on events with more than 50 participants*, https://www.firstpost.com/india/tablighi-jamaat-congregation-was-held-despite-ban-on-events-with-more-than-50-participants-8212021.html

Foreign Policy, 16 June 2020. *India's Islamophobia Creeps Into Nepal*, https://foreignpolicy.com/2020/06/16/india-islamophobia-hindu-nationalism-nepal/

India Today, 30 June 2020. *Telangana: Animal body condemns killing, hanging of monkey*, https://www.indiatoday.in/india/story/telangana-animal-cruelty-monkey-tirtured-abused-hanged-death-tree-khammam-district-fiapo-condemns-1695561-2020-06-30

India Today, 22 March 2020. *Coronavirus: Indian Railways suspends all passenger trains till March 31*, https://www.indiatoday.in/india/story/coronavirus-all-passenger-trains-to-stop-plying-till-march-31-1658409-2020-03-22

India Today, 20 March 2020. *MP govt crisis: Kamal Nath announces resignation, Congress falls and BJP rejoices*, https://www.indiatoday.in/india/story/madhya-pradesh-govt-crisis-floor-test-kamal-nath-congress-bjp-1657768-2020-03-20

John F. Kennedy Presidential Library and Museum, https://www.jfklibrary.org/learn/education/teachers/curricular-resources/elementary-school-curricular-resources/ask-not-what-your-country-can-do-for-you, retrieved on 10 July 2020

National Geographic, 27 May 2020. *'They treat us like stray dogs': Migrant workers flee India's cities*, https://www.nationalgeographic.com/history/2020/05/they-treat-us-like-stray-dogs-migrant-workers-flee-india-cities/

NDTV, 30 June 2020. *India Accounts For 45.8 Million Of World's "Missing Females": UN Report*, https://www.ndtv.com/india-news/india-accounts-for-45-8-million-of-worlds-missing-females-un-report-2254485?amp=1&akamai-rum=off

NDTV, 25 June 2020. *Delhi: Man, 57, Stabbed To Death After Argument Over Feeding Stray Dogs*, https://www.ndtv.com/india-news/delhi-man-57-stabbed-to-death-after-argument-over-feeding-stray-dogs-2251757?amp=1&akamai-rum=off

NewsBytes, 7 July 2020. *Vikas Dubey murdered politician in 2001, 25 cops turned hostile*, https://www.newsbytesapp.com/timeline/india/63070/296279/when-policemen-turned-hostile-to-protect-vikas-dubey

POLITICO, 15 April 2020. *15 times Trump praised China as coronavirus was spreading across the globe*, https://www.politico.com/news/2020/04/15/trump-china-coronavirus-188736

Railway Technology, 23 June 2020. *How the railway industry went the extra mile during Covid-19*, https://www.railway-technology.com/features/covid-19-railways/

Reuters, 4 March 2018. *Trump praises Chinese president extending tenure 'for life'*, https://www.reuters.com/article/us-trump-china/trump-praises-chinese-president-extending-tenure-for-life-idUSKCN1GG015

SBS Punjabi News, 30 June 2020. *'Go back to your f**king country, you brought coronavirus here': Indian student racially abused, assaulted in Adelaide*, https://www.sbs.com.au/language/english/audio/go-back-to-your-f-king-country-you-brought-coronavirus-here-indian-student-ra-cially-abused-assaulted-in-adelaide

SBS News, 8 May 2020. *UN says coronavirus has sparked a 'tsunami of hate and xenophobia'*, https://www.sbs.com.au/news/un-says-coronavirus-has-sparked-a-tsunami-of-hate-and-xenophobia

SOS Children's Villages, *Poverty In India: Facts And Figures On The Daily Struggle For Survival*, https://www.soschildrensvillages.ca/news/poverty-in-india-602#:~:text=Search-,Poverty%20in%20India%3A%20Facts%20and%20Figures%20on%20the%20Daily%20Struggle,they%20are%20considered%20extremely%20poor. , retrieved on 11 July 2020

South China Morning Post, 30 May. *You Chinese virus spreader': after coronavirus, Australia has an anti-Asian racism outbreak to deal with*, https://www.scmp.com/week-asia/people/article/3086768/you-chinese-virus-spreader-after-coronavirus-australia-has-anti

The Economic Times, 7 July 2020. *US military to stand with India in conflict with China, indicates White House official*, https://economictimes.indiatimes.com/news/defence/us-military-to-stand-with-india-in-conflict-with-china-indicates-white-house-official/articleshow/76828634.cms

The Economic Times, 16 April 2020. *India sending hydroxychloroquine to 55 coronavirus-hit countries*, https://economictimes.indiatimes.com/news/politics-and-nation/india-sending-hydroxychloroquine-to-55-coronavirus-hit-countries/articleshow/75186938.cms

The Guardian, 10 July 2020. *US imposes sanctions on senior Chinese officials over Uighur abuses*, https://www.theguardian.com/world/2020/jul/10/us-imposes-sanctions-on-senior-chinese-officials-over-uighur-abuses

The Guardian, 10 July 2020. *Indian police kill gangster suspected of murdering officers day after arrest*, https://www.theguardian.com/world/2020/jul/10/indian-police-kill-man-suspected-of-murdering-officers

The Guardian, 11 June 2020. https://www.theguardian.com/world/2020/jun/11/indian-man-upsets-wife-by-bequeathing-land-to-two-elephants

The Guardian, 17 April 2020. *Belarus crowdfunds to fight coronavirus as leader denies it exists*, https://www.theguardian.com/world/2020/apr/17/belarus-crowdfunds-to-fight-coronavirus-as-leader-denies-it-exists

The Guardian, 29 March 2020. *'There are no viruses here': Belarus president plays ice hockey amid Covid-19 pandemic* — video, https://www.theguardian.com/sport/video/2020/mar/29/there-are-no-viruses-here-belarus-president-plays-ice-hockey-amid-covid-19-pandemic-video

The Hindu, 14 July 2020. *Rajasthan political crisis updates*, https://www.thehindu.com/news/national/rajasthan-political-crisis-day-2-july-14-2020/article32074665.ece

The Hindu, 04 June 2020, *Pregnant elephant dies after eating cracker-filled fruit*, https://www.thehindu.com/news/national/kerala/pregnant-elephant-dies-after-eating-cracker-filled-fruit/article31746611.ece

The Hour, 27 March 2020. *No lockdown here: Belarus' strongman rejects coronavirus risks. He suggests saunas and vodka*, https://www.thehour.com/news/article/No-lockdown-here-Belarus-strongman-rejects-15162113.php

The Organisation for World Peace, 21 June 2020. *Islamophobia In India Threatens Religious Cohesion In Nepal*, https://theowp.org/islamophobia-in-india-threatens-religious-cohesion-in-nepal/

The Shovel, 2 July 2020. *America to stop measuring gun-related deaths in an effort to eradicate gun crime*, https://www.theshovel.com.au/2020/06/26/america-to-stop-measuring-gun-related-deaths-in-an-effort-to-eradicate-gun-crime/?utm_source=newsletter&utm_medium=email&utm_campaign=america_to_stop_measuring_gun_related_deaths_in_an_effort_to_eradicate_gun_crime&utm_term=2020-07-02

The Sydney Morning Herald, 7 June 2020. *Almost 400 anti-China attacks since pandemic began*, https://www.smh.com.au/politics/federal/almost-400-anti-china-attacks-since-pandemic-began-20200607-p550a8.html

The Tribune, 18 June 2020. *Jammu Covid-19 victim's nephews die at cremation site; duo dehydrated in PPE kits, claim kin*, https://www.tribuneindia.com/news/j-k/jammu-covid-19-victims-nephews-die-at-cremation-site-duo-dehydrated-in-ppe-kits-claim-kin-100954

Trading Economics. *India Unemployment Rate*, https://tradingeconomics.com/india/unemployment-rate, retrieved on 10 July 2020.

Washington Post, 2 May 2020. *Coronavirus is spreading rapidly in Belarus, but its leader still denies there is a problem*, https://www.washingtonpost.com/world/europe/coronavirus-is-spreading-rapidly-in-belarus-but-its-leader-still-denies-theres-a-problem/2020/05/01/a2532ba0-8964-11ea-80df-d24b35a568ae_story.html

Migrant crisis

ABC News, 19 May 2020. *India enforced the world's biggest lockdown. But critics say it's taken a heavy toll*, https://amp.abc.net.au/article/12246746

Channel 7 News, 1 June 2020. *Migrants walk 2000 km in scorching heat to get home, then one dies from snakebite*, https://7news.com.au/lifestyle/health-wellbeing/migrants-walk-2000km-in-scorching-heat-to-get-home-then-one-dies-from-snakebite-c-1071737.amp

National Geographic, 27 May 2020, *'They treat us like stray dogs': Migrant workers flee India's cities*, https://api.nationalgeographic.com/distribution/public/amp/history/2020/05/they-treat-us-like-stray-dogs-migrant-workers-flee-india-cities

SCMP, 17 May 2020. *Analysis | Coronavirus lockdown: if India treats its migrant workers like dirt, blame it on caste*, https://amp.scmp.com/week-asia/politics/article/3084650/coronavirus-lockdown-if-india-treats-its-migrant-workers-dirt

The Guardian, 4 May 2020. *Destitute migrant worker in India forced to pay train fares home*, https://amp.theguardian.com/world/2020/may/04/coronavirus-destitute-migrant-workers-india-forced-pay-train-fares-home

The Japan Times, 21 April 2020. *India's migrant workers fall through cracks in coronavirus lockdown*, https://www.japantimes.co.jp/news/2020/04/21/asia-pacific/india-migrant-workers-coronavirus/

Thomson Reuters Foundation, 2 June 2020. *Nearly 200 migrant workers killed on India's roads during coronavirus lockdown*, https://news.trust.org/item/20200602142210-9afn1/

Islamophobia

ABC News, 25 April 2020. *Indian Muslims face stigma, blame for surge in infections*, https://abcnews.go.com/amp/Health/wireStory/islamophobia-large-cluster-affects-indias-virus-fight-70344026

Aljazeera, 15 May 2020. *Indian media accused of Islamophobia for its coronavirus coverage*, https://www.aljazeera.com/news/2020/04/indian-media-accused-islamophobia-coronavirus-coverage-200417064109353.html

Anadolu Agency, 28 April 2020, *Ruling Indian party lawmaker: Do not buy from Muslims*, https://www.aa.com.tr/en/asia-pacific/ruling-indian-party-lawmaker-do-not-buy-from-muslims/1821744

Deccan Herald, 24 April 2020. *Hate against Indian Muslims: Widening Gulf?*, https://www.deccanherald.com/amp/opinion/hate-against-indian-muslims-widening-gulf-829180.html

Financial Times, 3 May 2020. *India cracks down on Muslims under cover of coronavirus*, https://www.ft.com/content/34ad9282-74d7-4a85-a629-a9655339c366

Karvaan India, 4 May 2020. *India cracks down on Muslims under cover of coronavirus – Financial times*, https://www.karvaanindia.com/2020/05/04/india-cracks-down-on-muslims-under-cover-of-coronavirus-financial-times/

The Conversation, 20 May 2020. *India's treatment of Muslims and migrants puts lives at risk during COVID-19*, https://theconversation.com/amp/indias-treatment-of-muslims-and-migrants-puts-lives-at-risk-during-covid-19-136940

The Diplomat, 04 May 2020. *Hate Goes Viral in India*, https://thediplomat.com/2020/05/hate-goes-viral-in-india/

Nine News Australia, 16 March 2020. *Coronavirus: People in US line up to buy weapons fearing civil unrest*, https://m.youtube.com/watch?v=WN1T-MimVOz0

The Japan times, 20 April 2020. *In Modi's India, coronavirus fallout inflames divisions between Muslims and Hindus*, https://www.japantimes.co.jp/news/2020/04/20/asia-pacific/narendra-modi-india-coronavirus-muslims-hindus/

The Jerusalem post, 8 May 2020. *Coronavirus: Indian politician warns against buying produce from Muslims*, https://m.jpost.com/international/coronavirus-indian-politician-warns-against-buying-vegetables-from-muslims-626968/amp

The News Arab, 13 May 2020. *India clamps down on Muslims under cover of coronavirus*, https://english.alaraby.co.uk/english/amp/indepth/2020/5/13/india-clamps-down-on-muslims-under-cover-of-coronavirus

The New York Times, 12 April 2020. *In India, Coronavirus Fans Religious Hatred* https://www.nytimes.com/2020/04/12/world/asia/india-coronavirus-muslims-bigotry.amp.html

The Sydney Morning Herald, 22 May 2020. *US pulls out of Open Skies treaty, Trump's latest treaty withdrawal*, https://amp.smh.com.au/world/north-america/us-pulls-out-of-open-skies-treaty-trump-s-latest-treaty-withdrawal-20200522-p54vd8.html

The Washington Post, 23 April 2020. *As the world looks for coronavirus scapegoats, Muslims are blamed in India*, https://www.washingtonpost.

com/world/asia_pacific/as-world-looks-for-coronavirus-scapegoats-india-pins-blame-on-muslims/2020/04/22/3cb43430-7f3f-11ea-84c2-0792d8591911_story.html?outputType=amp

Chapter 4

ABC News, 17 May 2020. *India's coronavirus lockdown: The good, the bad and the ugly of Narendra Modi's COVID-19 measures*, https://amp.abc.net.au/article/12241654

Al Jazeera, 2 July 2020. *Photo of toddler sitting on his grandfather's body angers Kashmir*, https://www.Al Jazeera.com/amp/news/2020/07/pro-tests-kashmir-civilian-killed-indian-military-200701173440775.html

Al Jazeera, 1 July 2020. *Report highlights high death toll in Indian-administered Kashmir*, https://www.Al Jazeera.com/amp/news/2020/07/report-high-lights-high-death-toll-indian-administered-kashmir-200701190426771.html

Al Jazeera, 28 June 2020, *Kashmir Muslims fear demographic shift as thousands get residency*, https://www.Al Jazeera.com/news/2020/06/kashmir-muslims-fear-demographic-shift-thousands-resi-dency-200627103940283.html

BBC News, 11 May 2020. *India Coronavirus: Pregnant student Safoora Zargar at risk in jail*, https://www.bbc.com/news/amp/world-asia-india-52608589

Deccan Chronicle, 7 December 2016. *'Retrofit: What is the cost of a human life in India?'*, https://www.deccanchronicle.com/amp/opinion/op-ed/071216/retrofit-what-is-the-cost-of-a-human-life-in-india.html

Hindustan Times, 8 June 2020. *'Kashmiri Pandit sarpanch killed by terrorists in Anantnag, parties condemn attack'*, https://www.hindustantimes.com/india-news/kashmiri-pandit-sarpanch-killed-by-terrorists-in-anant-nag-parties-condemn-attack/story-KaeSpT9BYDYtn0wFHrCSdM.html

Hindustan Times, 9 June 2020. *'We won't leave Kashmir', says family of slain Pandit sarpanch'*, https://m.hindustantimes.com/india-news/we-won-t-leave-kashmir-says-family-of-slain-pandit-sarpanch/story-0kDX-1akVDdIXo61JrAiUoO_amp.html

Huffpost, 10 June 2020, *What Was His Fault?': Family And Neighbours Mourn Kashmiri Pandit Sarpanch Killed By Suspected Militants*, by Kaiser Andrabi, https://www.huffingtonpost.in/amp/entry/village-chief-shot-dead-kashmir-anantnag_in_5ee07925c5b6b9cbc769a26d/

India Today, 16 June 2020. *'27 terrorists of JeM, LeT, Hizb killed in past 17 days in Kashmir: J&K DGP'*, https://www.indiatoday.in/india/story/27-jem-let-hizb-terrorists-killed-in-past-17-days-kashmir-jk-dgp-1689395-2020-06-16

News Intervention, 10 June 2020. *'Ajay Pandita's sacrifice will not go in vain, other Pandit families will relocate in Kashmir Valley'*, by Dr Simrit Kahlon, https://www.newsintervention.com/ajay-panditas-sacrifice-will-not-go-in-vain-other-pandit-families-will-relocate-in-kashmir-valley/

The Conversation, 7 May 2020. *India uses coronavirus pandemic to exploit human rights in Kashmir*, Kashmir, https://theconversation.com/amp/india-uses-coronavirus-pandemic-to-exploit-human-rights-in-kashmir-137682

OpIndia, 9 June 2020. Kashmir: *'LeT's new proxy group TRF takes responsibility for the assassination of Sarpanch Ajay Pandita, says no 'political stooges' will be spared'*, https://www.opindia.com/2020/06/pakistan-sponsored-terrorists-trf-lashkar-responsibility-sarpanch-assassination/

Outlook, 8 May 2020. *'What''s the truth behind TRF in Kashmir?'*, https://www.outlookindia.com/newsscroll/whats-the-truth-behind-trf-in-kashmir/1828587

Outlook, 12 June 2020. *'My father was brave, I too have to be brave: Niyanta Pandita'*, https://www.outlookindia.com/newsscroll/amp/my-father-was-brave-i-too-have-to-be-brave-niyanta-pandita/1863912

The Economic Times, 31 January 2019. *'Supreme Court directs Sahara chief Subrata Roy to appear before it on February 28'*, https://economictimes.indiatimes.com/news/politics-and-nation/supreme-court-directs-sahara-chief-subrata-roy-to-appear-before-it-on-february-28/articleshow/67773422.cms?from=mdr

The Economic Times, 29 April 2020. 'The Resistance Front: New name of terror groups in Kashmir', https://economictimes.indiatimes.com/news/defence/the-resistance-front-new-name-of-terror-groups-in-kashmir/articleshow/75440416.cms?from=mdr

The Guardian, 17 June 2020. 'Himalayan flashpoint could spiral out of control as India and China face off', https://www.theguardian.com/world/2020/jun/16/himalayan-flashpoint-could-spiral-out-of-control-as-india-and-china-face-off

The Hindu, 9 June 2020. 'Kashmiri Pandits' organisations condemn killing of sarpanch in Anantnag', https://www.thehindu.com/news/national/kashmir-pandits-organisations-condemn-killing-of-sarpanch-in-anantnag/article31784041.ece/amp/

The Hindu, 9 June 2020. 'Kashmiri Pandit sarpanch killing a targeted one by Hizb, says DGP', https://www.thehindu.com/news/national/pandit-sarpanch-killing-a-targeted-one-by-hizb-says-dgp/article31788607.ece/amp/

The Kashmir Walla, 10 June 2020. "We're in disbelief": Ajay Pandita's killing reminds of Kashmir's vulnerable grassroots politics', https://thekashmirwalla.com/2020/06/were-in-disbelief-ajay-panditas-killing-reminds-kashmirs-vulnerable-grassroots-politics/

The Print, 2 December 2019. 'Why Kashmiri Pandits may never return to the Valley - The only meaningful 'return' can be had through truth and reconciliation, by Shivam Vij, https://theprint.in/opinion/why-kashmiri-pandits-may-never-return-to-the-valley/329103/?amp

The Tribune, 15 June 2020, 'J&K administration announces Rs 20 lakh relief for sarpanch Ajay Pandita's family', https://www.tribuneindia.com/news/j-k/jk-govt-announces-rs-20-lakh-relief-fund-sarpanch-ajay-panditas-family-97774

The Quint, 19 January 2020. 'How, 30 Yrs Ago, Kashmiri Pandits Became Refugees in Their Country', by Aliza Noor, https://www.thequint.com/amp/story/news%2Findia%2Fexodus-of-kashmiri-pandits-january-1990-refugees-in-their-country-valley-pain-separation-trauma-jammu-delhi-camps

The Washington Post, 30 April 2020. *India is using the pandemic to intensify its crackdown in Kashmir*, https://www.washingtonpost.com/opinions/2020/04/30/india-is-using-pandemic-intensify-its-crackdown-kashmir/?outputType=amp

Chapter 5

ABC News, 6 July 2020. *Suspicions cyber sabotage behind fire at Iran nuclear facility, but Israel says it's 'not necessarily' involved*, https://www.abc.net.au/news/2020-07-06/iran-nuclear-site-fire-causes-significant-damage,-official-says/12424586

ABC News, 5 July 2020. *Coronavirus update: WHO reports record daily high in global infection rates as pubs, hairdressers reopen in England*, https://www.abc.net.au/news/2020-07-05/coronavirus-update-australia-covid19-england-pubs-india-spain/12423322

ABC News, 4 July 2020. *China issues warning to India, as tensions flare with Philippines over South China Sea*, https://amp.abc.net.au/article/12422354

ABC News, 1 July 2020. *Australia to spend $270b building larger military to prepare for 'poorer, more dangerous' world and rise of China*, https://www.abc.net.au/news/2020-06-30/australia-unveils-10-year-defence-strategy/12408232

ABC News, 27 June 2020. US coronavirus cases reach biggest single-day increase of pandemic, https://www.abc.net.au/news/2020-06-27/us-coronavirus-cases-reach-biggest-single-day-increase/12399820

ABC News, 23 August 2019. *Australia and Vietnam agree on efforts to restrict Chinese expansion in the South China Sea*, https://www.abc.net.au/news/2019-08-23/australia-vietnam-unite-in-efforts-in-the-south-china-sea/11443648

Al Jazeera, 1 July 2020. *Pakistani PM says 'no doubt' India was behind deadly attack*, https://www.Al Jazeera.com/amp/news/2020/07/pakistani-pm-doubt-india-deadly-attack-200701042713276.html

Al Jazeera, 24 June 2020. *India, Pakistan to expel embassy staff in tit-for-tat spy dispute*, https://www.Al Jazeera.com/news/2020/06/india-pakistan-expel-embassy-staff-tit-tat-spy-dispute-200623175955276.html

Al Jazeera, 12 June 2020. *Missiles used to attack Saudi Arabia of 'Iranian origin': UN*, https://www.Al Jazeera.com/news/2020/06/missiles-at-tack-saudi-arabia-iranian-origin-200612035300642.html

Al Jazeera, 1 June 2020, *India expels Pakistan embassy officials for 'espionage'*, https://www.Al Jazeera.com/news/2020/05/india-expels-paki-stan-embassy-officials-espionage-200531175238362.html

BBC, 15 July 2020. *Huawei 5G kit must be removed from UK by 2027*, https://www.bbc.com/news/technology-53403793

BBC, 1 July 2020. *Coronavirus: US buys nearly all of Gilead's COVID-19 drug Remdesivir*, https://www.bbc.com/news/amp/world-us-canada-53254487

BBC, 27 June 2020. *Coronavirus: US has 'serious problem'*, says Fauci, https://www.bbc.com/news/world-us-canada-53200834

Bloomberg, 23 June 2020, *Saudi Arabian Cities Come Under Attack From Yemeni Rebels*, https://www.bloomberg.com/news/articles/2020-06-23/saudi-intercepts-ballistic-missile-headed-to-riyadh-from-yemen

Brookings, 11 June 2020. *Up Front — Interpreting the India-Nepal border dispute*, https://www.brookings.edu/blog/up-front/2020/06/11/interpret-ing-the-india-nepal-border-dispute/

Brookings, 24 April 2020, Order from chaos, *COVID-19 will prolong conflict in the Middle East*, https://www.brookings.edu/blog/order-from-chaos/2020/04/24/covid-19-will-prolong-conflict-in-the-middle-east/

Business Insider Australia, 25 June 2020, *Australia's economy looks to be in surprisingly decent shape, according to the IMF, as it navigates a worsening global recession*, https://www.businessinsider.com.au/australian-econo-my-forecast-imf-covid19-2020-6

Business Standard, 5 July 2020, *Coronavirus LIVE: India reports biggest spike of 24,850 new cases in 24 hrs*, https://www.business-standard.com/article/current-affairs/coronavirus-live-updates-india-cases-650-000-delhi-maharashtra-tamil-nadu-corona-cases-world-covid-tracker-vac-cine-latest-news-120070400103_1.html

Channel 9 News, 29 June 2020. *Coronavirus: Dr Anthony Fauci warns Congress new US cases could rise to 100,000 a day*, https://amp.9news.com.au/article/441a1bd2-fa73-4d64-9615-c55dd8538d93

CNBC, 2 July 2020. *U.S.-China relations are headed for the 'darkest chapter yet,' says Eurasia Group*, https://www.cnbc.com/2020/07/02/us-china-re-lations-headed-for-the-darkest-chapter-yet-eurasia-group.html

CNN, 4 June 2020. *India and Australia sign pacts to strengthen military ties as tensions simmer in South China Sea*, https://amp.cnn.com/cnn/2020/06/04/asia/india-australia-military-agreements-intl-hnk/index.html

DW News, 15 July 2020. *Trump ends Hong Kong's special status with US, sanctions China*, https://www.dw.com/en/trump-ends-hong-kongs-spe-cial-status-with-us-sanctions-china/a-54180209

Foreign Policy News, 29 May 2020. *Trump Cuts U.S. Ties With World Health Organization Amid Pandemic*, https://foreignpolicy.com/2020/05/29/trump-pulls-out-of-who-coronavirus-pandemic-glob-al-health-covid-china-beijing-influence-international-institutions-glob-al-health/

Hindustan Times, 12 December 2017. *Length of Indo-Nepal border could change after re-demarcation: Officials*, https://www.hindustantimes.com/india-news/length-of-indo-nepal-border-could-change-after-re-demar-cation-officials/story-LQ0YBKuGU4WroCKaYLl78H.html

History: Cold War History. *The Cold war is Over*, https://www.history.com/topics/cold-war/cold-war-history , retrieved on 5 July 2020

International Monetary Fund, June 2020. *World Economic Outlook Reports, World Economic Outlook Update, June 2020 — A Crisis Like No Other, An Uncertain Recovery*, https://www.imf.org/en/Publications/WEO/Issues/2020/06/24/WEOUpdateJune2020

Janes Defence News, 24 June 2020, *Houthis claim cruise missile attack on Saudi Arabia*, https://www.janes.com/defence-news/news-detail/houthis-claim-cruise-missile-attack-on-saudi-arabia

News.com.au, 7 July 2020. *Coronavirus Australia live: Reports of over 190 new Victoria cases*, https://www.news.com.au/world/coronavirus/australia/coronavirus-australia-live-all-res-idents-in-melbourne-banned-from-nsw/live-cover-age/284785987152496de2b907a4420e90df

The Canberra Times, 3 July 2020. *China warns Australia over Hong Kong visas*, https://www.canberratimes.com.au/story/6817420/china-warns-australia-over-hong-kong-visas/?cs=14231#gsc.tab=0

The Diplomat, 13 June 2020. *Hong Kong Protest Marks Anniversary of Violent Police Clash*, https://thediplomat.com/2020/06/hong-kong-protest-marks-anniversary-of-violent-police-clash/

The Guardian, 7 July 2020. *Hong Kong: first person charged under new security law*, https://www.theguardian.com/world/2020/jul/06/hong-kong-first-person-charged-under-new-security-law

The Guardian, 3 July 2020. *Fire or explosion damages building at Iran nuclear site*, https://www.theguardian.com/world/2020/jul/02/fire-or-explosion-damages-building-at-iran-nuclear-site

The Hindu, 3 June 2020. India open to including Australia in Malabar naval exercise, https://www.thehindu.com/news/national/india-open-to-including-australia-in-malabar-naval-exercise/article31740876.ece

The Japan Times, 4 July 2020, *Two U.S. aircraft carriers enter South China Sea as China conducts its own military exercises*, https://www.japantimes.co.jp/news/2020/07/04/asia-pacific/two-us-aircraft-carriers-south-china-sea-china/

The New York Times, 21 April 2020. *U.S. Warships Enter Disputed Waters of South China Sea as Tensions with China Escalate*, https://www.nytimes.com/2020/04/21/world/asia/coronavirus-south-china-sea-warships.html

Wall Street Journal, 3 July 2020. *U.S. Sends Two Aircraft Carriers to South China Sea for Exercises as China Holds Drills Nearby*, https://www.wsj.com/articles/u-s-sends-two-aircraft-carriers-to-south-china-sea-for-exercises-as-china-holds-drills-nearby-11593816043

Yahoo News, 7 July 2020. *China censors Hong Kong internet, US tech giants resist*, https://au.news.yahoo.com/china-censors-hong-kong-internet-us-tech-giants-035413439--spt.html

Zee News, 21 June 2020. *Protests in Nepal against government's failure to stop Chinese interference, COVID-19 and corruption*, https://zeenews.india.com/india/protests-in-nepal-against-governments-failure-to-stop-chinese-interference-corruption-2291229.html

Chapter 6

ABC News, 4 July 2020. *China issues warning to India, as tensions flare with Philippines over South China Sea*, https://amp.abc.net.au/article/12422354

Al Jazeera, 31 August 2020. *Tension as India, China accuse each other of border violations*, https://www.aljazeera.com/news/2020/08/china-provocative-movements-border-thwarted-india-200831061515700.html

Al Jazeera, 6 July 2020. *China 'pulling back troops' after deadly border clash: India*, https://www.Al Jazeera.com/amp/news/2020/07/china-pulling-troops-deadly-border-clash-india-200706091813810.html

Al Jazeera, 3 July 2020. *Modi takes veiled dig at China on visit to disputed border area*, https://www.Al Jazeera.com/amp/news/2020/07/india-modi-visits-ladakh-region-troops-clashed-china-200703055736037.html

Al Jazeera, 2 July 2020. *India PM Modi shuts Weibo account amid border tensions with China*, https://www.Al Jazeera.com/amp/news/2020/07/india-pm-modi-shuts-weibo-account-border-tensions-china-200702071223144.html

Al Jazeera, 30 June 2020. *India bans 59 mostly Chinese apps amid border dispute*, https://www.Al Jazeera.com/news/2020/06/india-bans-59-chinese-apps-border-dispute-200629180545547.html

Al Jazeera, 30 June 2020. *China says concerned over India banning dozens of Chinese apps*, https://www.Al Jazeera.com/amp/news/2020/06/tiktok-denies-sharing-indian-user-data-chinese-government-200630045148586.html

Al Jazeera, 24 June 2020. *Indian jets fly over Galwan as China again blames India for clash*, https://www.Al Jazeera.com/amp/news/2020/06/indian-jets-fly-galwan-china-blames-india-clash-200624105950727.html

Al Jazeera, 22 June 2020. *Five things to know about the India-China border standoff*, https://www.Al Jazeera.com/amp/news/2020/06/india-china-border-standoff-200621111215771.html

BBC, 31 August 2020. *India accuses China of 'provocative military movements' at border*, https://www.bbc.com/news/world-asia-india-53971397

BBC, 25 June 2020. *Galwan Valley: Satellite images 'show China structures' on India border*, https://www.bbc.com/news/amp/world-asia-53174887

Business Standard, 5 July 2020, *Coronavirus LIVE: India reports biggest spike of 24,850 new cases in 24 hrs*, https://www.business-standard.com/article/current-affairs/coronavirus-live-updates-india-cases-650-000-delhi-maharashtra-tamil-nadu-corona-cases-world-covid-tracker-vaccine-latest-news-120070400103_1.html

Channel 9 News, 29 June 2020. *Coronavirus: Dr Anthony Fauci warns Congress new US cases could rise to 100,000 a day*, https://amp.9news.com.au/article/441a1bd2-fa73-4d64-9615-c55dd8538d93

Chanel 9 News, 29 June 2020. *Satellite images show build-up on disputed India-China border*, https://amp.9news.com.au/article/06b02fae-7341-4558-a184-a8813ae68bd0

CNBC, 2 July 2020. *U.S.-China relations are headed for the 'darkest chapter yet,' says Eurasia Group*, https://www.cnbc.com/2020/07/02/us-china-relations-headed-for-the-darkest-chapter-yet-eurasia-group.html

Gulf News, 20 June 2020. *Indian PM Narendra Modi's statement on 'no Chinese incursion' stirs a controversy*, https://gulfnews.com/world/asia/india/indian-pm-narendra-modis-statement-on-no-chinese-incursion-stirs-a-controversy-1.72154571

Hindustan Times, 4 July 2020. *Indian Air Force geared up for combat role in China border area*, https://www.hindustantimes.com/india-news/indian-air-force-geared-up-for-combat-role-in-china-border-area/story-bo1QFkr5MLip0u7Amf0GBI.html

Hindustan Times, 17 June 2020. *A timeline: India-China's deadliest border clash since 1975 explained*, https://www.hindustantimes.com/india-news/a-timeline-india-china-s-deadliest-border-clash-since-1975-explained/story-9Ct6lHQKkRuXM5w2K5xmwO.html

History: Cold War History. *The Cold war is Over*, https://www.history.com/topics/cold-war/cold-war-history , retrieved on 5 July 2020

India Today, 30 August 2020. *Indian Navy deploys warship in South China Sea 2 months after Galwan clash*, https://www.indiatoday.in/india/story/indian-navy-deploys-warship-in-south-china-sea-2-months-after-galwan-clash-1716779-2020-08-30

India Times, 20 August 2016. *The Story Of The Sumdorong Chu Standoff - When India Avoided War With China Through Sheer Diplomacy*, https://www.indiatimes.com/news/the-story-of-the-sumdorong-chu-standoff-when-india-avoided-war-with-china-through-sheer-diplomacy-260266.html, retrieved on 28 June 2010

India Today, 8 July 2020. *IAF carries out night time patrol in eastern Ladakh; to maintain high-level of readiness: Sources*, https://www.india-today.in/india/story/iaf-carries-out-night-time-patrol-in-eastern-lada-kh-to-maintain-high-level-of-readiness-sources-1698146-2020-07-08

India Today, 3 July 2020. *PM Narendra Modi in Ladakh: 5 things to note as troops look into Chinese eye*, https://www.indiatoday.in/news-analysis/story/narendra-modi-in-ladakh-things-to-note-1696527-2020-07-03

India Today, 30 June 2020. *China occupies hills near Pangong Tso, obstructs patrols. Locals say they are living in fear*, https://www.indiatoday.in/india/story/china-occupies-hills-near-pangong-tso-obstructs-patrols-locals-say-they-are-living-in-fear-1695320-2020-06-30

India Today, 30 June 2020. *China was surprised in Doklam, never thought India would challenge it: China expert Yun Sun*, https://www.indiatoday.in/india/story/china-was-surprised-in-doklam-never-thought-india-would-challenge-it-china-scholar-yun-sun-1695672-2020-06-30

India TV, 17 June 2020. *India-China LAC Standoff: 1975 Tulung LA to Galwan clashes, times when China crossed the RED line*, https://www.indiatvnews.com/news/india/india-china-border-faceoff-lac-ladakh-stand-off-tulung-la-galwan-vally-clashes-doklam-sumdorong-chu-626863

NDTV, 30 August 2020. *Indian Navy Sent Warship To South China Sea After Ladakh Clash: Report*, https://www.ndtv.com/india-news/indian-na-vy-sent-warship-to-south-china-sea-after-ladakh-clash-report-2287648

NDTV, 8 July 2020. *"Construction Of Strategic Roads, Bridges To Be Expedited": Rajnath Singh*, https://www.ndtv.com/india-news/rajnath-singh-says-construction-of-strategic-roads-bridges-to-be-expedited-2258866?amp=1&akamai-rum=off

NDTV, 25 June 2020. *UK PM Boris Johnson Says China-India Standoff "Very Serious, Worrying"*, https://www.ndtv.com/india-news/uk-pm-boris-johnson-says-china-india-standoff-very-serious-worrying-2251969?amp=1&akamai-rum=off

The Canberra Times, 3 July 2020. *China warns Australia over Hong Kong visas*, https://www.canberratimes.com.au/story/6817420/china-warns-australia-over-hong-kong-visas/?cs=14231#gsc.tab=0

The Economic Times, 13 June 2020. *A history of Sino-Indian feuds: Times when China had to back down*, https://economictimes.indiatimes.com/news/defence/a-history-of-sino-indian-feuds-times-when-china-had-to-back-down/articleshow/76357150.cms?from=mdr

The Hindu, 14 June 2020. *Forgotten in fog of war, the last firing on the India-China border*, https://www.thehindu.com/news/national/forgotten-in-fog-of-war-the-last-firing-on-the-india-china-border/article31827344.ece

The Indian Express, 18 June 2020, *Line of Actual Control: Where it is located, and where India and China differ*, https://indianexpress.com/article/explained/line-of-actual-control-where-it-is-located-and-where-india-and-china-differ-6436436/

The Indian Express, 16 June 2020. *Explained: The strategic road to DBO*, https://indianexpress.com/article/explained/lac-stand-off-india-china-darbuk-shyok-daulat-beg-oldie-dsdbo-road-6452997/

The Print, 31 August 2020, *After missile sites, China now builds heliports along LAC in Ladakh and near Doklam*, https://theprint.in/defence/after-missile-sites-china-now-builds-heliports-along-lac-in-ladakh-and-near-doklam/492534/

War on the Rocks, 8 June 2020, *Tension High, Altitude Higher: Logistical and Physiological Constraints on the Indo-Chinese Border*, https://waron-therocks.com/2020/06/tension-high-altitude-higher-logistical-and-phys-iological-constraints-on-the-indo-chinese-border/

Chapter 7

Australian Museum, 'Defining death', 20 November 2018, https://australianmuseum.net.au/about/history/exhibitions/death-the-last-taboo/defining-death/

www.ingramcontent.com/pod-product-compliance
Lightning Source LLC
Chambersburg PA
CBHW022347280326
41935CB00007B/109